H   red Mental Health Care

About the Authors

Nosheen Akhtar, MScOT, currently works for the Ontario government as a Senior Program/Policy Analyst within the Ministry of the Solicitor General with the goal of affecting system-level change. She works in the Employee Wellness Unit where she provides expertise on psychological health programming for corrections staff and their managers, e.g., resource development, information dissemination, and program evaluation.

Cheryl Forchuk, PhD, is the Beryl and Richard Ivey Research Chair in Aging, Mental Health, Rehabilitation and Recovery at the Parkwood Research Institute in London, ON, Canada. She is a Distinguished University Professor at the Arthur Labatt Family School of Nursing (Western University) with a cross appointment to the Department of Psychiatry, Schulich School of Medicine and Dentistry (Western University). Dr. Forchuk has published on many topics including transitional discharge, therapeutic relationships, technology in mental health care, poverty, housing, and homelessness.

Katherine McKay, MD, is an Assistant Clinical Professor (adjunct) in the Department of Psychiatry and Behavioural Neurosciences at McMaster University, Canada. She is an inpatient psychiatrist on the Sans Souci Program for Transition and Recovery serving people with severe and persistent mental illness in rural Ontario, Canada, at Waypoint Centre for Mental Health Care. Dr. McKay's research interest has focused largely on marginalized communities as well as education in the field of mental health.

Sandra Fisman, MD, is a Professor at the Schulich School of Medicine and Dentistry, Departments of Psychiatry, Paediatrics and Family Medicine, Chair of the Department of Psychiatry at Western University and Chief of the London Hospitals Mental Health Services, Canada. As a child and adolescent psychiatrist, she gave "birth" to several new programs which continue to be an important part of the service system, both in terms of models of care and sustainability.

Abraham (Rami) Rudnick, MD, PhD, is a certified psychiatrist and psychiatric rehabilitation practitioner and a PhD-trained philosopher. He is a Professor in the Department of Psychiatry and the School of Occupational Therapy at Dalhousie University in Canada, and the Clinical Director of the Nova Scotia Operational Stress Injury Clinic. One of his main areas of expertise is person-centered care for people with mental health challenges and, as a key part of that, psychiatric/ psychosocial rehabilitation on which he has published many papers, chapters, and books, and presented and taught across the world, as well as led and provided consultation for service development and quality improvement initiatives. He has received Canadian and international awards for his work.

Handbook of Person-Centered Mental Health Care

Nosheen Akhtar, Cheryl Forchuk,
Katherine McKay, Sandra Fisman,
& Abraham Rudnick

Library of Congress of Congress Cataloging in Publication information for the print version of this book is available via the Library of Congress Marc Database under the Library of Congress Control Number 2020939237

Library and Archives Canada Cataloguing in Publication

Title: Handbook of person-centered mental health care / Nosheen Akhtar, Cheryl Forchuk, Katherine McKay, Sandra Fisman, & Abraham Rudnick.

Names: Akhtar, Nosheen, author. | Forchuk, Cheryl, author. | McKay, Katherine, author. | Fisman, Sandra, author. | Rudnick, Abraham, author.

Description: Includes bibliographical references and index.

Identifiers: Canadiana (print) 20200255533 | Canadiana (ebook) 20200255584 | ISBN 9780889375680 (softcover) | ISBN 9781616765682 (PDF) | ISBN 9781613345689 (EPUB)

Subjects: LCSH: Mental health services. | LCSH: Client-centered psychotherapy.

Classification: LCC RA790 .A44 2020 | DDC 362.2—dc23

Cover image: © matdesign24 – iStock.com

PUBLISHING OFFICES

USA: Hogrefe Publishing Corporation, 361 Newbury Street, 5th Floor, Boston, MA 02115
            Phone (857) 880-2002; E-mail customerservice@hogrefe.com

EUROPE: Hogrefe Publishing GmbH, Merkelstr. 3, 37085 Göttingen, Germany
            Phone +49 551 99950-0, Fax +49 551 99950-111; E-mail publishing@hogrefe.com

SALES & DISTRIBUTION

USA: Hogrefe Publishing, Customer Services Department,
            30 Amberwood Parkway, Ashland, OH 44805
            Phone (800) 228-3749, Fax (419) 281-6883; E-mail customerservice@hogrefe.com

UK: Hogrefe Publishing, c/o Marston Book Services Ltd., 160 Eastern Ave.,
            Milton Park, Abingdon, OX14 4SB
            Phone +44 1235 465577, Fax +44 1235 465556; E-mail direct.orders@marston.co.uk

EUROPE: Hogrefe Publishing, Merkelstr. 3, 37085 Göttingen, Germany
            Phone +49 551 99950-0, Fax +49 551 99950-111; E-mail publishing@hogrefe.com

OTHER OFFICES

CANADA: Hogrefe Publishing, 82 Laird Drive, East York, Ontario M4G 3V1

SWITZERLAND: Hogrefe Publishing, Länggass-Strasse 76, 3012 Bern

Printed and bound in Canada

ISBN 978-0-88937-568-0 (print) · ISBN 978-1-61676-568-2 (PDF) · ISBN 978-1-61334-568-9 (EPUB)
https://doi.org/10.1027/00568-000

Preface

According to the US National Institute of Mental Health (NIMH), in 2017, almost one in five (46.6 million) adults lived with a mental health challenge. Of concern is the fact that young adults between the ages of 18 and 25 years have the highest prevalence, among whom over one in four experience mental health challenges (NIMH, 2019). Mental health challenges are therefore in need of further discussion toward subsequent action. Service providers have a range of modalities, approaches, and treatments available to them, and this handbook explores a range of practical tools and strategies to address such challenges.

The purpose of this handbook is to provide a hands-on guide that discusses the *how* of person-centered approaches. It can be seen as an extension to Rudnick and Roe's 2011 book *Serious Mental Illness: Person-Centered Approaches* (Rudnick & Roe, 2011), in that it builds on theoretical material presented there, to provide practical examples across clinical care, research, education, and health care leadership. This handbook is intended for service users and service providers alike. Often books on person-centered approaches have mostly addressed theory and neglected to give enough detailed advice on practicing this approach. The authors of this present work have therefore endeavored to provide concrete examples, techniques, tools, and resources to assist service users and service providers to use on their own and/or in practice. There are a variety of approaches that put the service user at the center of care, and this handbook explores a number of these approaches.

The book is divided into six chapters: foundations, clinical care, research, education, health care leadership, and a conclusion chapter. This text looks to address the main areas of mental health care. Within each of these realms, practical person-centered strategies are illustrated using detailed case vignettes within diverse service user–service provider clinical relationships. The application of tools and resources are illuminated using the information from the case vignettes in each section for the reader to gain real-life insight into using the person-centered approach. The same tools and resources are also provided as blank handouts in the Appendix, which can be printed out for personal or clinical use.

The case examples included in the book do not report real cases or use the names of real persons, but they are based on the experiences of the authors in their clinical work.

The clinical care chapter (Chapter 2) is further divided into: clinical relationships, clinical communication, cultural care, family-centered care, co-occurring (concurrent) disorders, adolescents, dual diagnosis, forensic care, and older adults. These sections were chosen because they represent some of the most common areas for exploration in the therapeutic realm. These topics were discussed in Rudnick and Roe (2011) and this book will delve into them in greater detail.

The research chapter (Chapter 3) is divided into: research relationships, collaboration in research, planning and implementation of research, and research communication, as these sections mirror person-centered approaches to these areas. The chapter starts with relationships as a basis and moves to collaboration as a concept that reflects a less hierarchical concept. Planning and implementing of research are traditional phases, and communication reflects the final phase of the research process so that others are aware of the results.

The education chapter (Chapter 4) is divided into: shared decision making, family education, education of health professionals, and public education. The rationale to include these sections is the vast nature of the topic area of education. When thinking about education pertaining to person-centered care (PCC), one can conceptualize the need to engage with those making the decision (the service user involved in shared decision making), the possible extended support systems that exist (e.g., family), those providing information for the service user to make decisions (most often service providers), and the broader population who require information to make informed decisions (e.g., the public).

The health care leadership chapter (Chapter 5) is divided into: person-centered leadership, becoming a reflective leader, developing and leading service user–centered teams, emotional intelligence, generative relationships, collaboration leading change, project methodology, change models, and system change. This chapter recognizes the present challenges to health care delivery and the need for a person-centered approach to much-needed health care transformation. The chapter leads the reader through a collaborative administrative process, providing a selection of tools that may be utilized to enable successful, strength-based aspirations and results.

Although much of the knowledge about person-centered mental health care addresses serious mental health challenges, it also applies more generally to all mental health challenges; this book addresses a wide range of mental health challenges.

The authors of this book have varied educational backgrounds as well as clinical and nonclinical experiences in health care. The information provided in this handbook draws on the experiences of what has contributed toward effective health care, research, education, and health care leadership.

Acknowledgments

For service users and all others involved in their care and in related services such as research, education, and leadership.

Special thanks to our families – at work and at home.

Contents

1 Foundations

Mental Health Challenges and the Person-Centered Approach

Mental health challenges (MHCs) may be defined in different ways. The National Survey on Drug Use and Health (NSDUH) defines an MHC as "a mental, behavioral, or emotional disorder (excluding developmental and substance use disorders)" that is diagnosed within the year, meets *Diagnostic and Statistical Manual of Mental Disorders,* 5th edition (DSM-5) criteria, impedes function, and restricts day-to-day activities (Substance Abuse and Mental Health Services Administration, 2015, p. 1). There are some who view mental health challenges as the suffering that comes from pain to one's self-worth or identity (Abramson, Metalsky, & Alloy, 1989; Beck, 1967). This may include diagnoses such as schizophrenia, major depressive disorder, bipolar affective disorder, obsessive-compulsive disorder, anxiety disorders (such as panic disorder), and others.

A person-centered approach (PCA) – also referred to as client-centered care (CCC) or person-centered care (PCC) – has been a relatively modern attitude in the provision of services and care. PCAs are widely used in the care of individuals with dementia (Mitchell & Agnelli, 2015). PCAs are also used to counsel individuals experiencing depression (Sanders & Hill, 2014). For almost 20 years, the UK has incorporated PCA into legislative policies along with best practice guidelines (Department of Health, 2001, 2005, 2006, 2009). In Rudnick & Roe (2011) PCA is discussed as a multidimensional construct (which includes the PCA process), person-focused (with the service user as the primary beneficiary), person-driven (the service user makes choices on the course of care actions), person-sensitive (specific to service user needs), and person-contextualized (past and present experiences are taken into consideration).

The fundamental characteristics of PCA that service providers embody in a clinical relationship include those of understanding, compassion, authenticity or a genuine nature, acceptance, and unconditional positive regard, as well as empowerment or the supporting of the autonomy of the service users in their own lives (Rogers, 1949, 1956). Service providers embody these characteristics as a way of being to create a safe space where service users can work through their challenges. This may require service providers to cultivate themselves in a way that aligns with these qualities. The service provider has a sense of connectedness to the service user as a human being. Compassion involves getting into another person's world regarding their experience, where the service provider becomes present to the associated thoughts and feelings of the service user. Of importance, compassion involves taking an action, however small, which is in line with the service provider's intention to support the service user towards recovery. Interestingly, this in turn allows for the delivery of person-centered care while being a resilient service provider (Thibeault, 2020). PCA also involves developing and maintaining supportive relationships with service users, along with (self-)respect for service users, their experiences, strengths, knowledge, and autonomous choice (Hammell, 2013).

Little et al. (2001) developed a model of patient-centeredness that includes five elements:

1. Looking at the service user's experience with MHCs and their effects
2. Considering the person as a whole, including their emotions and environmental context
3. Common ground between the service user and service provider to decide upon a care plan
4. Health promotion and taking preventative measures
5. Improving the service user–service provider relationship through shared power.

The person–environment–occupation (PEO) model is another tool that may be used to consider personal (physical, cognitive, affective), environmental (cultural, physical, social, institutional), and occupational (self-care, productivity, leisure) components that contribute to the uniqueness of an individual (Law et al., 1996). This model is person-centered in that it requires collaboration with service users and is directed by their abilities, needs, interests, contexts, and more. PCA may be applied through several different methods across health care disciplines. The key is putting the individual at the center of care.

Benefits and Challenges of the Person-Centered Approach

PCAs are methods that may be applied when working with service users. Involvement of service user preferences throughout the duration of the relationship is important. PCA may foster a sense of empowerment in the service user's life, which may lead to increasingly effective interventions (Ladd & Churchill, 2012). In them, we discuss achieving a balance between the dominant medical model approaches, with that of PCA. At times, there are acute psychological symptoms that may effectively be treated with medication. At the same time, PCA is useful to address the various factors that may have contributed to MHCs in the first place.

PCA lends flexibility for both service users as well as service providers. It can be employed by new and seasoned professionals, may be used regardless of age, can be applied to different health challenges, and provides a framework from which professionals can hone their skills when working with service users (Brown, Thornton, & Stewart, 2012). PCA applies to service users who experience all kinds of challenges, whether it is mental, cognitive, intellectual, or otherwise. It is accessible to different cultures and disciplines, which means that PCAs have a broad applicability in the field of mental health (Cooper, O'Hara, Schmid, & Bohart, 2013).

PCA helps to validate a person's needs, wants, preferences, beliefs, values, and more, and is shown to have mental, physical, and economic benefits (Ekman et al., 2011). These approaches support service users to develop and maintain their strengths and abilities, promoting self-efficacy, confidence, and the ability to make their own decisions (Fors, Taft, Ulin, & Ekman, 2016). PCA may help service users to maintain all or part of their independence and begin or maintain effective health behaviors (Innes, Macpherson, & McCabe, 2006). The PCA of shared decision making is rated higher among service users in the domain of quality of care when compared with those who have not experienced shared decision making during their care (Solberg et al., 2014). Ultimately, with PCA, service users may have an improved quality of life (US Department of Health and Human Services, 2010).

It has been reported that service providers who employ PCA may provide more effective care emotionally, physically, and even spiritually (Puchalski, Vitillo, Hull, & Reller, 2014). PCA helps to maintain an awareness of the person being supported rather than the service provider's attention shifting to the symptomologies of various diseases (van der Laan, van Offenbeek, Broekhuis, & Slaets, 2014). It builds trust and mutual respect, which may create greater ease in the clinical relationship (Cloninger, 2011). Brown et al. (2012) have illustrated the utility of PCA through various experiences and interactions of service users and service providers, and ways to address challenging situations. They explore the service user's experience with MHCs by looking at the person as a whole, and searching for a common denominator between the service user and the service provider, which may enhance the clinical relationship.

PCAs have been shown to improve the overall operation of health care settings (Epstein, Fiscella, Lesser, & Stange, 2010). Bertakis and Azari (2011) also found that PCA is associated with decreased annual medical charges as compared with a non-PCA in primary care. PCA supports service users in improving their understanding of the challenges they are experiencing, to the extent that they access emergency services less frequently (Epperly et al., 2015). It has been shown that service users are also thereby more likely to adhere to their treatment plan (Robinson, Callister, Berry, & Dearing, 2008). After all, with PCA, service users are involved in the process to develop the treatment plan; therefore, their preferences have already been taken into consideration.

In spite of all of this evidence, however, PCA faces challenges for several reasons. There has been some discussion as to the alignment between PCA and evidenced-based decision making and care. PCA may be seen as the *goal* of care, while evidence-based care may be considered the *guidelines* of care (Good & Rogers, 2012). The goal is what service providers aim to achieve in their care provision, whereas the guidelines are the standard to be upheld. Depending on the situation, PCA may be more or less appropriate to apply in service provision, based on the criticality of the situation. For example, if a service user with a mental health challenge is experiencing an episode of psychosis and is a risk to themselves or others, it is of crucial importance to stabilize the service user through a combination of medication and psychosocial interventions. However, when the same individual has stabilized, the strategies that are put in place to maintain service user wellness using PCA become increasingly important.

There tends to be a push toward empirically supported therapies, or therapies that are proven effective through research trials, where service users have little say in the course of their treatments and interventions (Cooper et al., 2013). In a way, the very basis of such research revolves around non-PCA principles. This is not to say that PCA cannot be empirically validated, rather, what we view as the "gold standard" seldom considers PCA. However, PCA can be integrated into research and evidence-based practices. There have been countless studies comparing non-PCA with PCA practices that continually demonstrate the effectiveness of PCA.

Moore et al. (2017) found that existing organizational frameworks and the continuation of traditional models of practice hinder the implementation of PCA. In Canada, even when there is support for PCA in theory, there are competing factors such as attempts to reduce costs and waste, and to maintain the health care system, which impede the application of PCA in practice (Kuluski, Peckham, Williams, & Upshur, 2016). Even at the local level, in Germany, Hower et al. (2019) found that individual factors and the work setting of health and social care organizations – for example, communications between staff and employee well-being – may impede PCA implementation. Davidson, Tondora, Miller, and O'Connell (2015) acknowledge that beyond the service provider, additional resources, time, and infrastructure are needed to facilitate PCA.

Lack of clarity around what PCA entails has also been a deterrent to research and its application in practice (Louw, Marcus, & Hugo, 2017). It is argued that the notions of unconditional positive regard, compassion, and congruence are elements that ought to be practiced by any effective service provider. In the UK, while exploring the current applications of personhood in dementia care, it was found that, although there were some effective examples of PCA, service providers were not availing themselves of all opportunities to implement PCA in their practices (Clissett, Porock, Harwood, & Gladman, 2013). This may suggest a lack of understanding between the principles of PCA and its day-to-day practice.

Person-Centered Approach Applications

We are seeing changes on a societal level that are making it possible for PCAs to be realized more easily. For example, technology is developing incredibly fast, and there is now an array of assistive devices designed with the end user in mind, so that devices, interfaces, platforms, and so on meet the particular needs of the user. Assistive technologies that are person-centered may consider aspects that enhance the retention of information, orientation to the environment, maintenance of safety, and the provision of activities or occupations that are meaningful to the user. Examples include the plethora of mobile applications or apps that continue to be developed to meet needs-related challenges such as organization, the breakdown of tasks, or addressing communication barriers.

The work of Carl Rogers on PCAs was not only limited to the field of mental health; he worked on applications to other fields as well, including education, group work and conflict resolution, leadership, and business (Kirschenbaum, 2004). In terms of education, Rogers discussed the similarities between educational and psychotherapeutic behaviors, as they may both appear to be based on the foundations of unconditional positive regard, compassion, and congruence (Lemberger & Cornelius-White, 2016).

PCA in education recognizes that the learner's experiences are important elements that affect how the learner perceives their environment (Cornelius-White, Motschnig-Pitrik, & Lux, 2013). Educators adjust their role to meet the needs of the learner, based on the learner's point of view. This requires compassion on the part of the educator to have an understanding, not just of the individual as a learner, but as a whole person. Here, educators assist in making learners aware of their own realizations and newfound understanding (Cornelius-White et al., 2013).

Within the realm of health, PCA abounds. For example, PCA can be used as a means to prevent or limit the "othering" that may occur with service users with dementia (Doyle & Rubinstein, 2014). Viau-Guay et al. (2013) discusses person-centeredness as an approach that increases the quality of care in long-term care homes. PCA in long-term care homes may also influence the communication between staff and residents, which may replace patronizing and directive interactions that foster dependency and may compromise personal identity, with communication that allows for service user preferences and takes into consideration a person's life history (Savundranayagam, 2014). The use of narrative as a PCA in geriatric care may be helpful to understand the life story of a service user, along with their challenges with mental health (Clark, 2015). Gillick (2013) discusses the need for caregivers to be educated and trained in PCA as an element in the provision of high-quality, cost-effective health care.

A systematic review from Li and Porock (2014) found that changes in the residential culture toward using PCA benefited residents' psychological well-being, and PCA specific to dementia decreased challenging behaviors and the need for pharmacological therapy for those in long-term care. Terada et al. (2013) found that PCA in geriatric health care facilities correlated with quality of life improvements in service users with dementia and correlated with improved cognitive performance and function of activities of daily living in hospitals. Additionally, PCA can have a beneficial impact on staff working with individuals who have dementia in residential care facilities, decreasing stress and burnout while increasing job satisfaction (Barbosa, Sousa, Nolan, & Figueiredo, 2015).

PCA can help to shape health care facilities, such as in the Cleveland Clinic health system, where their nursing model was guided by the "patients first" principle to provide high-quality care (Small & Small, 2011). Lavoie, Blondeau, and Martineau (2013) found that integrating PCA into a palliative care setting led to a decrease in task-focused care, an increase in respect for the needs and wants of service users, along with improved listening, autonomy of, and respect for the service user. Edvardsson, Winblad, and Sandman (2008) add that when working with service users with Alzheimer's disease, PCA may require viewing the personality of a service user as being not as easily accessed rather than as being lost. Other elements of PCA in this population include tailoring health care services to the unique needs of the individual, looking at clinical decisions from the service user's point of view, and shared decision making.

The term *recovery* is used widely, but what does this really mean from the perspective of PCA? Recovery may involve a number of elements, including having an awareness of what is getting in the way of one's day-to-day activities, respect for self and others, possibility for a newly created future, being grounded in current circumstances, learning new skills, taking personal responsibility for one's life and actions, moving beyond challenges with mental health, setting and working toward personal goals, a sense of belonging to a community, receiving support from peers, and meaningful activity (Andresen, Oades, & Caputi, 2003; Jacobson, & Greenley, 2001).

Within mental health services, Rogers presented the nondirective method of care with the underlying notion that individuals have the ability to understand their own suffering, along with the ability to adjust their own disposition in life toward greater consciousness to alleviate painful experiences (Rogers, 1956). This approach toward care requires attentive listening by the service provider, meeting service users where they are, fostering a safe space, and reflecting the thoughts and feelings of service users in order for them to have insights, make realizations about their situation, and take subsequent action. This was a shift from the more typical approaches of asking questions, analyzing, and giving advice and suggestions to the service user (Kirschenbaum, 2004). The service provider's attitude is also a vital component of PCA and requires that they show genuine understanding, empathy, and acceptance so the service user truly feels understood and heard. This requires service providers to embody these characteristics as a way of being.

Chapter Conclusion

Person-centered approaches focus on the relationship between the service user and service provider. Through the service provider's practice of compassion, unconditional positive regard, authenticity, and empowerment, the service user develops a newfound sense of self. Despite some of the challenges that PCA faces in terms of uptake and implementation, the benefits of such approaches are clear. The applications of PCA are widespread and can be found inside and outside of health and mental health settings.

References

Abramson, L. Y., Metalsky, G. I., & Alloy, L. B. (1989). Hopelessness depression: A theory-based subtype of depression. *Psychological Review, 96*, 358.

Andresen, R., Oades, L., & Caputi, P. (2003). The experience of recovery from schizophrenia: Towards an empirically validated stage model. *Australian and New Zealand Journal of Psychiatry, 37*, 586–594. https://doi.org/10.1046/j.1440-1614.2003.01234.x

Barbosa, A., Sousa, L., Nolan, M., & Figueiredo, D. (2015). Effects of person-centered care approaches to dementia care on staff: A systematic review. *American Journal of Alzheimer's Disease & Other Dementias, 30*, 713–722. https://doi.org/10.1177/1533317513520213

Beck, A. T. (1967). *Depression: Clinical, experimental, and theoretical aspects.* New York, NY: Hoeber Medical Division, Harper & Row.

Bertakis, K. D., & Azari, R. (2011). Determinants and outcomes of patient-centered care. *Patient Education & Counseling, 85*(1), 46–52. https://doi.org/10.1016/j.pec.2010.08.001

Brown, J. B., Thornton, T., & Stewart, M. (Eds.). (2012). *Challenges and solutions: Narratives of patient-centered care.* New York, NY: Radcliffe.

Clark, P. G. (2015). Emerging themes in using narrative in geriatric care: Implications for patient-centered practice and interprofessional teamwork. *Journal of Aging Studies, 34*, 177–182. https://doi.org/10.1016/j.jaging.2015.02.013

Clissett, P., Porock, D., Harwood, R. H., & Gladman, J. R. (2013). The challenges of achieving person-centred care in acute hospitals: A qualitative study of people with dementia and their families. *International Journal of Nursing Studies, 50*, 1495–1503. https://doi.org/10.1016/j.ijnurstu.2013.03.001

Cloninger, C. R. (2011). Person-centred integrative care. *Journal of Evaluation in Clinical Practice, 17*, 371–372. https://doi.org/10.1111/j.1365-2753.2010.01583.x

Cooper, M., O'Hara, M., Schmid, P. F., & Bohart, A. C. (Eds.). (2013). *The handbook of person-centred psychotherapy and counselling* (2nd ed.). New York, NY: Palgrave Macmillan. https://doi.org/10.1007/978-1-137-32900-4

Cornelius-White, J. H. D., Motschnig-Pitrik, R., & Lux, M. (Eds.). (2013). *Interdisciplinary applications of the person-centered approach.* New York, NY: Springer.

Davidson, L., Tondora, J., Miller, R., & O'Connell, M. J. (2015). Person-centered care. In P. W. Corrigan (Ed.), *Person-centered care for mental illness: The evolution of adherence and self-determination* (pp. 81-102). Washington, DC: American Psychological Association. https://doi.org/10.1037/14644-005

Department of Health. (2001). *National service framework for older people.* London, UK: Stationery Office.

Department of Health. (2005). *Everybody's business: Integrated mental health services for older adults; A service development guide.* London, UK: Stationery Office.

Department of Health. (2006). *Dignity in care public survey.* London, UK: Stationery Office.

Department of Health. (2009). *Living well with dementia: A national dementia strategy.* London, UK: Stationery Office.

Department of Health and Human Services. (2010). *Multiple chronic conditions – a strategic framework: Optimum health and quality of life for individuals with multiple chronic conditions.* Washington, DC: Author.

Doyle, P. J., & Rubinstein, R. L. (2014). Person-centered dementia care and the cultural matrix of othering. *Gerontologist, 54,* 952-963. https://doi.org/10.1093/geront/gnt081

Edvardsson, D., Winblad, B., & Sandman, P. O. (2008). Person-centred care of people with severe Alzheimer's disease: Current status and ways forward. *Lancet Neurology, 7,* 362-367. https://doi.org/10.1016/S1474-4422(08)70063-2

Ekman, I., Swedberg, K., Taft, C., Lindseth, A., Norberg, A., Brink, E., . . . Lidén, E. (2011). Person-centered care – Ready for prime time. *European Journal of Cardiovascular Nursing, 10*(4), 248-251. https://doi.org/10.1016/j.ejcnurse.2011.06.008

Epperly, T., Roberts, R., Rawaf, S., Van Weel, C., Phillips, R., Mezzich, J., . . . Appleyard, J. (2015). Person-centered primary health care: Now more than ever. *International Journal of Person Centered Medicine, 5*(2), 53-59.

Epstein, R. M., Fiscella, K., Lesser, C. S., & Stange, K. C. (2010). Why the nation needs a policy push on patient-centered health care. *Health Affairs, 29,* 1489-1495. https://doi.org/10.1377/hlthaff.2009.0888

Fors, A., Taft, C., Ulin, K., & Ekman, I. (2016). Person-centred care improves self-efficacy to control symptoms after acute coronary syndrome: a randomized controlled trial. *European Journal of Cardiovascular Nursing, 15*(2), 186-194. https://doi.org/10.1177/1474515115623437

Gillick, M. R. (2013). The critical role of caregivers in achieving patient-centered care. *Journal of the American Medical Association, 310*(6), 575-576. https://doi.org/10.1001/jama.2013.7310

Good, E. D., & Rogers, F. J. (2012). Patient-centered management of atrial fibrillation: Applying evidence-based care to the individual patient. *Journal of the American Osteopathic Association, 112*(6), 334-342. https://doi.org/10.7556/jaoa.2012.112.6.334

Hammell, K. R. W. (2013). Client-centred occupational therapy in Canada: Refocusing on core values. *Canadian Journal of Occupational Therapy, 80*(3), 141-149. https://doi.org/10.1177/0008417413497906

Hower, K. I., Vennedey, V., Hillen, H. A., Kuntz, L., Stock, S., Pfaff, H., & Ansmann, L. (2019). Implementation of patient-centred care: Which organisational determinants matter from decision maker's perspective? Results from a qualitative interview study across various health and social care organisations. *BMJ Open, 9*(4), e027591. https://doi.org/10.1136/bmjopen-2018-027591

Innes, A., Macpherson, S., & McCabe, L. (2006). *Promoting person-centred care at the front line.* York, UK: Joseph Rowntree Foundation.

Jacobson, N., & Greenley, D. (2001). What is recovery? A conceptual model and explication. *Psychiatric Services, 52*(4), 482-485. https://doi.org/10.1176/appi.ps.52.4.482

Kirschenbaum, H. (2004). Carl Rogers' life and work: An assessment on the 100th anniversary of his birth. *Journal of Counseling and Development, 82*(1), 116-125. https://doi.org/10.1002/j.1556-6678.2004.tb00293.x

Kuluski, K., Peckham, A., Williams, A. P., & Upshur, R. E. (2016). What gets in the way of person-centred care for people with multimorbidity? Lessons from Ontario, Canada. *Healthcare Quarterly, 19*(2), 17-23. https://doi.org/10.12927/hcq.2016.24694

Ladd, P. D., & Churchill, A. (Eds.). (2012). *Person-centered diagnosis and treatment in mental health: A model for empowering clients.* Philadelphia, PA: Jessica Kingsley.

Lavoie, M., Blondeau, D., & Martineau, I. (2013). The integration of a person-centered approach in palliative care. *Palliative & Supportive Care, 11*, 453–464. https://doi.org/10.1017/S1478951512000855

Law, M., Cooper, B., Strong, S., Stewart, D., Rigby, P., & Letts, L. (1996). The person-environment-occupation model: A transactive approach to occupational performance. *Canadian Journal of Occupational Therapy, 63*(1), 9–23. https://doi.org/10.1177/000841749606300103

Lemberger, M. E., & Cornelius-White, J. H. D. (2016). Introduction to the special issue on person-centered approaches in schools. *Person-Centered and Experiential Psychotherapies, 15*(1), 1–4. https://doi.org/10.1080/14779757.2016.1148918

Li, J., & Porock, D. (2014). Resident outcomes of person-centered care in long-term care: A narrative review of interventional research. *International Journal of Nursing Studies, 51*(10), 1395–1415. https://doi.org/10.1016/j.ijnurstu.2014.04.003

Little, P., Everitt, H., Williamson, I., Warner, G., Moore, M., Gould, C., . . . Payne, S. (2001). Preferences of patients for patient centred approach to consultation in primary care: Observational study. *British Medical Journal, 322*(7284), 468–472.

Louw, J. M., Marcus, T. S., & Hugo, J. F. (2017). Patient- or person-centred practice in medicine? A review of concepts. *African Journal of Primary Health Care & Family Medicine, 9*(1), 1–7. https://doi.org/10.4102/phcfm.v9i1.1455

Mitchell, G. & Agnelli, J. (2015). Person-centred care for people with dementia: Kitwood reconsidered. *Nursing Standard, 30*(7), 46–50. doi:10.7748/ns.30.7.46.s47 https://doi.org/10.7748/ns.30.7.46.s47

Moore, L., Britten, N., Lydahl, D., Naldemirci, Ö., Elam, M., & Wolf, A. (2017). Barriers and facilitators to the implementation of person-centred care in different healthcare contexts. *Scandinavian Journal of Caring Sciences, 31*(4), 662–673. https://doi.org/10.1111/scs.12376

National Institute of Mental Health. (2019). *Mental illness.* Retrieved from https://www.nimh.nih.gov/health/statistics/mental-illness.shtml

Puchalski, C. M., Vitillo, R., Hull, S. K., & Reller, N. (2014). Improving the spiritual dimension of whole person care: Reaching national and international consensus. *Journal of Palliative Medicine, 17*(6), 642–656. https://doi.org/10.1089/jpm.2014.9427

Robinson, J. H., Callister, L. C., Berry, J. A., & Dearing, K. A. (2008). Patient-centered care and adherence: Definitions and applications to improve outcomes. *Journal of the American Academy of Nurse Practitioners, 20*(12), 600–607. https://doi.org/10.1111/j.1745-7599.2008.00360.x

Rogers, C. R. (1949). The attitude and orientation of the counselor in client-centered therapy. *Journal of Consulting Psychology, 13*(2), 82–94. https://doi.org/10.1037/h0059730

Rogers, C. R. (1956). Client-centered therapy: A current view. In F. Fromm-Reichmann & J. L. Moreno (Eds.), *Progress in psychotherapy* (pp. 199–209). New York, NY: Grune and Stratton.

Rudnick, A., & Roe, D. (Eds.). (2011). *Serious mental illness: Person-centered approaches.* London, UK: Radcliffe.

Sanders, P., & Hill, A. (Eds.). (2014). *Counselling for depression: A person-centred and experiential approach to practice.* Thousand Oaks, CA: Sage.

Savundranayagam, M. Y. (2014). Missed opportunities for person-centered communication: Implications for staff-resident interactions in long-term care. *International Psychogeriatrics, 26*, 645–655. https://doi.org/10.1017/S1041610213002093

Small, D. C., & Small, R. M. (2011). Patients first! Engaging the hearts and minds of nurses with a patient-centered practice model. *Online Journal of Issues in Nursing, 16*(2), 2.

Solberg, L. I., Crain, A. L., Rubenstein, L., Unützer, J., Whitebird, R. R., & Beck, A. (2014). How much shared decision making occurs in usual primary care of depression? *Journal of the American Board of Family Medicine, 27*(2), 199–208. https://doi.org/10.3122/jabfm.2014.02.130164

Substance Abuse and Mental Health Services Administration. (2015). *National Survey on Drug Use and Health.* Retrieved from https://www.nimh.nih.gov/health/statistics/prevalence/serious-mental-illness-smi-among-us-adults.shtml

Terada, S., Oshima, E., Yokota, O., Ikeda, C., Nagao, S., Takeda, N., . . . Uchitomi, Y. (2013). Person-centered care and quality of life of patients with dementia in long-term care facilities. *Psychiatry Research, 205*(1-2), 103–108. https://doi.org/10.1016/j.psychres.2012.08.028

Thibeault, R. (2020). *Implementing peer support resources for physicians in the context of the COVID-19 crisis* [PowerPoint Slides]. University of Ottawa, ON, Canada. Retrieved from https://med.uottawa.ca/international-global-health-office/sites/med.uottawa.ca.international-global-health-office/files/peer_support_-_april_8_2020_webinar_0.pdf

van der Laan, M. E., van Offenbeek, M. A. G., Broekhuis, H., & Slaets, J. P. J. (2014). A person-centred segmentation study in elderly care: Towards efficient demand-driven care. *Social Science & Medicine, 113,* 68–76. https://doi.org/10.1016/j.socscimed.2014.05.012

Viau-Guay, A., Bellemare, M., Feillou, I., Trudel, L., Desrosiers, J., & Robitaille, M. (2013). Person-centered care training in long-term care settings: Usefulness and facility of transfer into practice. *Canadian Journal on Aging, 32*(1), 57–72. https://doi.org/10.1017/S0714980812000426

2 A Person-Centered Approach to Clinical Care Related to Mental Health Challenges

Introduction

Clinical care is an integral part of what service providers do to facilitate the recovery of service users who experience mental health challenges (MHCs). This chapter on clinical care includes sections that address different aspects of care (clinical relationships, clinical communication, cultural care, and family-centered practice) and different populations with MHCs (including those with co-occurring disorders, adolescents, those with a dual diagnosis, the forensic population, and older adults) through a lens using a person-centered approach (PCA). This approach includes building rapport with the service user and family; assessing service user MHCs; providing education and promoting insight; actively listening to service user values, preferences, and experiences; developing and supporting the service user in reaching recovery goals; and partnering with service users to pick treatment option(s).

Each section opens with a clinical case that will be used to guide the reader through the different aspects of the section (whether that is about different aspects of care or a particular client group) and to illustrate the service user's and service provider's experiences. Then, there is an introduction to the area of focus. The clinical cases are developed throughout the chapter to demonstrate how theoretical principles, models, and frameworks apply in the clinical setting. Exercises completed by the service user of the given clinical case are included throughout the sections, to provide the reader with realistic applications of the tools that service providers can use when working with service users. Alternatively, service users may complete the exercises independently to apply the learned information to their own situations. The sections are designed to focus on the particular area of interest in a concise manner. Some exercises, although placed in a particular section, may be applicable to various contexts of care.

Clinical Relationships

Wally is a 26-year-old man who lives in an apartment with his fiancée, Liz, whom he has been with for the past six years. Recently, Wally has begun to show signs of psychosis. Liz first noticed these signs when he was increasingly on-edge and nervous. She found it difficult to follow what he was saying. He was also taking less care of his personal hygiene, and no longer seemed to care about making himself look presentable when going out in public.

Wally was experiencing mounting pressure at work as an engineer and began missing work, until he took a stress leave. He had been distant from friends for some time, leaving few friends with which to spend time. He would sometimes shut out Liz as well. Wally was beginning to show signs of paranoia; he would sometimes mention to Liz that people were following him.

His fiancée was very concerned for him and encouraged him to seek help. He did not think he needed help and thought he was simply overwhelmed with work and wedding preparations. He thought he needed a break to de-stress. To put her at ease, he eventually looked for counseling support. She was willing to attend any sessions with him, as needed.

Wally never liked the idea of talking one-on-one with a counselor and sharing his thoughts and feelings. He thought it was a waste of time and too personal for his own comfort. He received a referral to a counselor named Sabrina.

Three Phases of Clinical Relationships

According to Peplau (1952, 1997) there are three phases to clinical relationships: the orientation phase, working phase, and resolution phase. These phases may increase one's awareness of the factors to consider in the formation of a therapeutic clinical relationship.

Orientation Phase

The first phase, the orientation phase, involves addressing any preconceived notions about one another before meeting, and requires that both people move past their assumptions and see each other for who they are as unique individuals. In Table 2.1, you can see how Sabrina completed the handout "Catching Our Own Assumptions" (Appendix 1).

Wally did not think that this counselor, or any counselor for that matter, would be very relatable and was unsure of how long he would attend. Based on Wally's medical and personal history, Sabrina pictured him to be introverted; she thought that it would take some time for him to open up about his experiences. She also thought that building trust would be a challenge based on his symptoms of paranoia. She was expecting someone who looked disheveled.

When Wally met Sabrina for the first time, she was not as reserved as he had imagined, and had a friendly nature. She told him that he could call her Sabrina, which was not what he expected. When Sabrina met Wally for the first time, she found him to have an outgoing personality, which she did not anticipate. He was presentable and had a sense of humor.

Regardless of the approach taken to build a clinical relationship, it is important to develop a relationship where service users are able to discuss their thoughts and feelings, gain new insights about their situation, trial new behaviors in a safe space, and maintain the

Table 2.1   Catching Our Own Assumptions: Sabrina's Notes on Her Preconceived Ideas About Wally Before Meeting Him.

Ask yourself – what preconceived ideas do I have about this person? This can be based on, or in relation to:	
Name	I associate the name Wally with someone older, maybe 60+.
Age	He is a millennial. This appears to be the first episode of psychosis and may be quite unsettling for him, his partner, and his family.
History	I wonder if there is a history of psychosis in the family.
Race/ethnicity	I assume he is of European descent, specifically German.
Mental health challenge and diagnosis	His symptoms are quite typical of psychosis.
Family	It seems like he has a strong support system that will help him through this experience.
Cognitive ability	He appears to have been high functioning before this episode based on his employment and his personal relationships.
Gender	Male, may be reluctant to share his feelings.
Religion	He may have been born Christian. He may practice the religion as he is getting married earlier than is typical in this society.
Culture	I would assume that he has adapted to American society.
Lifestyle	He seems to live independently and, until recently, has been able to participate in activities that he enjoys.
Vocation	He works as an engineer, where he is likely doing well financially.
My previous relationships (personal or professional)	None, although his name reminds me of my father's friend with the same name whom I saw on occasion — he was quite a character.
Other	He may be experiencing low mood given that he is not working and on stress leave; he may be lacking meaningful activities at this time.

sense that change is possible. PCA relationships are person-focused, person-driven, person-sensitive and person-contextualized (Rudnick & Roe, 2011), and focus on the service user's unique goals and needs throughout care.

Few would argue that one of the foundational elements of all relationships is mutual trust. This may not be an easy task, especially for those experiencing MHCs. However, building trust is possible by focusing on the goals and needs of the service user. The service user can work in collaboration with the service provider to shape the overall nature and process of the clinical relationship and recovery. Consistency in terms of the therapeutic approach taken, scheduled meetings, and the role of each person in the clinical relationship may also help to foster trust. This may take time and may be cultivated in conversation, through the inclusion of phrases such as:

- We can work together on whatever goals are most important to you.
- You can share with me as much or as little of your experience as you feel comfortable.
- Feel free to talk about any thoughts or ideas you have on your mind, as our discussion will stay only between us.

Instead of:
- Tell me what is bothering you.
- I can only help you if you talk to me about the problem.
- You can trust me.

Force or coercion in an attempt to foster trust in a clinical relationship may lead to mistrust and hinder the process of working together toward recovery. The service user may test the service provider to see their commitment to the clinical relationship. Testing may be typical behavior and may be a part of the process in the development of trust. Service users may not have had a reliable figure to depend on, and the individual may want to ensure that the service provider is committed to the clinical relationship (Morrison-Valfre, 2016).

Sabrina's method of PCA involved making sure that care focused on Wally's needs and goals. Sabrina began the conversation by asking what brought him to seek counseling and what he wanted to get out of the time they would have together. Wally began by saying that he was there for his fiancée's sake and that he wanted Sabrina to tell her that he was fine, and that there was no need for him to be there.

Sabrina acknowledged what Wally was saying and proposed that in order for her to be able to tell that to Liz, she would have to get to know Wally better, which would take some time. He reluctantly agreed but he was concerned that this would take too much of his time, which he needed to spend on his return to work. When Sabrina asked about his work situation, he would ask Sabrina questions about her life and he would bring up topics other than himself. She recognized that he was tentative about sharing too much information with her.

Wally would also test Sabrina by saying that he knew that she shared his information with his fiancée, and that he knew that she could not wait to have him off her caseload. To this, Sabrina said that she would stay committed to the terms of the clinical relationship to which they had agreed, which included confidentiality. She recognized that Wally was looking for someone reliable before he would trust her. To build trust with Wally,

Wally would guide the conversation and would discuss topics, within the boundaries of their clinical relationship, so that they were both able to better understand one another. She emphasized that, in order to get to know him well enough, she would have to see him consistently. Sabrina recognized the nature of Wally's challenges with mental health, and how symptoms such as paranoia could make building trust take longer or pose more of a challenge. Although Sabrina did not learn as quickly about Wally as she would have liked, she was confident that gradually building trust in their clinical relationship would set the stage for a healthy dynamic.

Sabrina asked a number of questions to build the clinical relationship with Wally. In Table 2.2, you can see what Sabrina asked in "Points for Discussion to Build a Therapeutic Clinical Relationship" (Appendix 2).

Table 2.2   Points for Discussion to Build a Therapeutic Clinical Relationship: Working to Build Trust Between Wally, a Service User, and Sabrina, a Service Provider

The following are points for discussion that the service provider can ask to further the initial conversation and build trust:	
What brings you to seek support?	Wally comes to therapy because of the concerns of his fiancée. He has been told that he is being overly cautious and making decisions that are unlike him.
What would you like to get out of counseling or therapy?	Wally is aware that work pressures have been mounting and these are taking a toll on him. He wants to de-stress so that he can get back to work.
What do you want me, as your service provider, to know about you?	Wally is hesitant to share about himself. He wants Sabrina to know that he is here for Liz and that he will do what it takes to get back to work.
What would you like me to do while working with you?	Wally is not clear on how these sessions will go or what he would like Sabrina to do, besides help him get back to his regular way of living.
What would you like me to avoid doing while working with you?	Wally does not want to answer too many questions or go way back into his past or childhood. He values his privacy.

Wally observed Sabrina closely to see if she was someone he could trust. She only spoke of experiences that she had had with other service users when it related to his circumstances and did not give away any of their personal details. She also emphasized working together on his goals, rather than talking about things that he was not interested in discussing or telling him that there was something wrong with him. There were times when she brought up topics with which he was not going to engage, but she recognized when this was the case and was respectful enough to not probe any further. She kept a positive attitude, was a keen listener, and seemed genuine in her discussions with him. These observations made Wally feel like she was someone who he could trust.

The service user, service provider, and other environmental factors may all play a role in shaping a clinical relationship (Forchuk, 1992; Peplau, 1997). Factors of service users that impact the clinical relationship include how open they are to care services, their insights into thoughts and feelings, and their active participation in the recovery process (Coatsworth-Puspoky, Forchuk, & Ward-Griffin, 2006; Forchuk et al., 2000; Passer, Smith, Atkinson, Mitchell, & Muir, 2003). The number and length of hospitalizations, which may reflect the severity of the MHCs, may be a factor in the clinical relationship. Further, the notion of power differences between the service user and the service provider may also influence perceived trust, preconceptions, and anxiety (Coatsworth-Puspoky et al., 2006; Frank & Gunderson, 1990). In addition, the fit between the challenges of the service user and the type of care is important to consider when building the clinical relationship (Beutler, Machado, & Neufeldt, 1994). Service users who experience anger, anxiety, or delusions may be more guarded, for fear that others will hold these experiences against them. Such symptoms inherently make the clinical relationship a challenge to develop due to the gap in trust and communication.

Service provider factors that influence a clinical relationship include preconceptions and first impressions. Such notions may influence personal attitudes, including professionalism, hopefulness, respect, connection, teamwork, and humanity (Coatsworth-Puspoky et al., 2006; Forchuk et al., 2000; Rydon, 2005). The exercise "Catching Our Own Assumptions" earlier in this section (Table 2.1) may address these assumptions. Commitment, understanding, listening, respectful responses, compassion, problem solving, appropriate exploration, trustworthiness, warmth, acceptance, and genuineness result in service users feeling safer and more secure in their clinical relationships (Forchuk & Reynolds, 2001; Hörberg, Brunt, & Axelsson, 2004).

Other factors such as age of the service user, cultural differences, when the service user began to experience challenges with mental health, and cognitive abilities (which vary depending on the individual, e.g., the ability to express themselves, or that were lost, e.g., sight or hearing loss) can affect the clinical relationship (Forchuk et al., 2000; Rydon, 2005). Such loss, if unaccounted for by the service provider, may make the service user less willing or less able to engage in care. Ideally, the physical environment will suit the needs of any service user who has difficulty with mobility, hearing, vision, or otherwise. The arrangement of where the sessions take place, lighting, and other factors are also considerations. When trust is not present, and there is modest progress, a transfer to another provider may be a consideration, recognizing that the challenge was in the clinical relationship instead of the service user or service provider.

Working Phase

The working phase, according to Peplau (1952, 1997), is the second out of the three phases in the clinical relationship. The working phase involves what we normally picture when we think about a clinical relationship – identifying and working on challenges brought up by the service user, and collaboratively discussing suitable interventions. Patience is required with the information that a service user shares (or lack thereof); trust has to deepen before more complex challenges are revealed. Service providers may be able to demonstrate their commitment and helpfulness to service users through supporting them in challenges that may not, at first, directly relate to the MHCs.

Sabrina was aware that work was currently a challenge for Wally, and that he was hesitant to talk about himself. In the following session that took place a few weeks later, Sabrina talked about previous experiences that she had had with service users who faced challenges in the workplace, as well as how she worked with them to overcome those challenges. Wally had a knack for solving problems and would talk with her about the different options that these service users would have had in their situations. She asked if he had ever had similar experiences, and after a few sessions, Wally began to talk about the difficulties he was having at work. This included his difficulty focusing on and organizing his projects, which was slowing him down and making the amount of unfinished work grow. Sabrina stated that they could think of strategies together so that he could better manage his workload, to which Wally agreed. Looking back at his original impressions about counseling, Wally had thought they would focus on past events that had led to his current feelings. He had no idea that it would have led to something as useful as problem solving his current challenges at work.

Over the weeks, Wally became more and more talkative about his situation, allowing Sabrina to learn more about his thoughts, feelings, and experiences. He mentioned that he was also getting distracted at work because he thought so-called colleagues were constantly watching him. Sabrina was glad that Wally trusted her enough to discuss this personal challenge.

Clinical relationships, like all relationships, require boundaries so that the focus is clearly and consistently on the service user's needs. This involves maintaining boundaries when it comes to roles, time, money, place, space, gifts, services, language, clothing, self-disclosure, and physical contact (Gutheil & Gabbard, 1993). Boundaries are the responsibility of the service provider and are to be in the best interest of the service user to prevent mismanagement of power imbalances. Policies, guidelines, and standards across different health care professions regulate and maintain such boundaries. When service providers use their role in the clinical relationship to meet their own needs rather than those of the service user, this may be a transgression of boundaries. Signs of boundary transgression include the sharing of unnecessary personal information, sexual behavior, and more.

Sabrina had developed a positive clinical relationship with Wally, but there were times where she felt like she had to be careful to uphold professional boundaries. For instance, when scheduling a meeting was a challenge, he had suggested that they meet for coffee with Liz in the evening. He would also offer tokens of appreciation such as treats when he came for appointments. In both instances, she clearly stated that meeting outside of the defined hours of her work and accepting gifts were not appropriate given the nature of their clinical relationship. She clarified that Liz was welcome to attend appointments as long as he wanted her to do so. When he insisted that she keep the gifts and that he had no use for them, she thanked him and told him that she would leave them in the main area to share with other service users and service providers. Keeping such professional boundaries ensured that Sabrina was meeting Wally's needs, rather than her own.

Resolution Phase

The third and final phase, the resolution phase of Peplau's phases of clinical relationships (1952, 1997), is from the time of discussion of the last topic or challenge through to when the term *service user* no longer applies to the individual accessing support. Here, it is important to identify resources that the service user can access to maintain wellness, gain further self-awareness of symptoms of the MHCs and their management, and build lasting supports in the community.

> Since they had tackled his experiences of paranoia and discussed reality checking, Sabrina knew that they were coming closer to the end of the clinical relationship. During this time, she talked with Wally about recognizing the symptoms that could signal signs of relapse – distancing himself from his friends and fiancée, difficulties with focus and organization at work, increased levels of stress, a lack of self-care, and an increase in mistrustful thoughts. She discussed the different organizations that were available to provide support if he wanted future assistance. She offered to connect him with these places before the end of their clinical relationship so that he knew exactly where he could go if in need. They also reviewed routines that he could keep to maintain his own well-being, which included exercising regularly, eating well, avoiding illicit drugs and alcohol, reality testing with those close to him, and getting enough sleep. Table 2.3 includes a list of Wally's wellness strategies and warning signs (for a blank copy of the handout, see Appendix 3).

Table 2.3   Resource Sheet for Wellness Self-Management: Example of Information to Gather for Wally to Manage His Own Wellness.

Routines or things that I can do to take care of myself	Going to the gym, making a meal plan to ensure healthy eating, staying away from recreational drugs and drinking alcohol, asking Liz's or a close friend's perspectives on situations rather than jumping to conclusions, and having a restful night's sleep.
Symptoms or signs telling me that challenges with mental health are returning	Ignoring Liz or friends, having trouble completing my work, feeling stressed, grooming in the morning that is not complete, feelings of being alone and not being able to trust anyone.
Community resources that I can access if I am in need	Local mental health organizations. Schizophrenia society in my area and their support group. Telehealth line.

Conclusion

Person-centered approaches for clinical relationships involve building trust, focusing on the service user's needs and goals (which shape the course of care), and ensuring that adequate supports are in place at the end of the clinical relationship. Following such an approach can build a strong clinical relationship where having trust and positive regard for one another can support the service user in the process of recovery.

Clinical Communication

Dani is a 19-year-old woman diagnosed with borderline personality disorder. She grew up in a rural area with her parents. She is an only child. She identifies as lesbian, and when she told her parents, they had a difficult time coping with this information. Though supportive, they did not understand what their daughter was going through.

Dani moved away from home and currently lives in an apartment in a larger city with her partner, Stella. Dani works part-time in retail. She and Stella are finding it difficult to make ends meet financially.

Dani has challenges with managing her anger; she tends to blow up at Stella and then storms off. She can also be impulsive in her words and actions, and periodically cuts herself. She and Stella have a network of friends; however, there are often fights within the group that lead to further tension in Dani's relationship with Stella. Dani attends outpatient care with Shaun, a psychiatrist.

Clinical communication between a service user and a service provider is needed to gather pertinent information, facilitate service user understanding of their experiences, ensure service user needs or uncertainties are met, agree on the plan of care, and strengthen and maintain the clinical relationship (Forchuk & Coatsworth-Puspoky, 2011). In line with developing a clinical relationship, clinical communication involves skills such as expressing compassion, active listening, articulating, clarifying, and reflecting the service user's thoughts, feelings, and underlying commitments, meeting service users where they are, accurately interpreting nonverbal communication, and skillfully addressing emotions that arise. Communication in PCA also includes listening to the service user's experiences and concerns, respecting culture and beliefs, and providing information about the MHCs that may be of interest to the service user and potentially loved ones, along with using straightforward language. PCA can lead to higher levels of service user trust and contentment with the care experience (Rudnick & Roe, 2011). It is important that the clinical communication between both parties enables service users to take control of their own care. Communication can be especially difficult for those who experience MHCs, as symptoms can influence a service user's ability to communicate effectively. It is important for service providers to adapt to the needs of the situation and have different strategies to ensure effective dialogue.

The Four Habits Model

One person-centered tool for communication is the *four habits model* (Frankel & Stein, 1999). According to this model, there are four parts to a health care encounter: (1) investing in the beginning, (2) eliciting the service user's perspectives, (3) demonstrating empathy, and (4) investing in the end. This model begins by encouraging the discussion of topics outside of challenges with mental health, which is a conversation that may help to increase the comfort of the service user when providing input on personal experiences and to address any concerns. The second habit looks at understanding service user challenges and their effects on daily living from the perspective of the service user. The third habit involves being compassionate and acknowledging how the service user feels in relation to their experiences. The fourth habit ensures that the service user has an understanding of the plan of care and any alternatives. This may include using straightforward language to explain information, checking for understanding, and addressing any concerns that the service user may have.

Dani sat in silence with Shaun for the entire initial session. Shaun knew that in order to remain person-centered and for Dani to work toward recovery, she would need to provide more information to personalize the plan of care. He kept his words simple and straightforward. He began by asking what she hoped to get out of the sessions. She continuously gave no response and simply stared at him.

Shaun took a multifaceted approach. He started to talk about the change in weather and the commute to the clinic, and asked for her opinion and to see if she had any challenges. "Fine," she replied. He asked if she had any immediate questions or concerns, to which she was silent. Moving forward, Shaun summarized his understanding of Dani's challenges based on the referral information. He asked her if she wanted to add or correct anything that he had said. She did not respond. He recognized that she was likely not going to provide lengthy answers at this time and then shifted his approach to ask yes or no questions. "If you could tell me, yes or no, if there is anything else that is important for me to know, that would be very helpful." To this, she shook her head, signaling that she did not.

Dani was silent for a few reasons. It took a long time for her to open up to people, and the same was true while working with Shaun. She was concerned about being judged and was embarrassed by her past behaviors. The whole experience of living with Stella, working, and managing money for food and rent every month was overwhelming for Dani. She could not quite figure out how to express all of the emotions that she felt. She liked having structure to her day, and attending appointments gave her a reason to get out of the apartment, especially when she needed time away from Stella. Shaun seemed nice to her, and because she felt confused about her situation, she preferred to hear his ideas about what she could do.

Motivational Interviewing

Motivational interviewing (MI) is a technique that focuses on the service user's personal drive to bring about change in a person's life (Miller & Rollnick, 2012). Principles for service providers include maintaining a compassionate attitude, skillfully highlighting that a service user's current behaviors may be misaligning with the goals, finding alternative strategies to move past resistance, and encouraging service user self-efficacy. Using MI, the service provider may be able to get a better sense of how committed the service user is to working toward their goals. MI can help build rapport, and it is useful for those seeking awareness or insight into their challenges with mental health. MI can also help to structure conversations by first gauging how willing a service user is to hear information; followed by providing information, opinions, or suggestions; and finally asking follow-up questions to see whether the service user understands and accepts the information provided. MI involves four techniques represented by the acronym OARS (Miller & Rollnick, 2012), which stands for

- **O**pen-ended questions – questions that leave room for discussion, where the service user is able to provide a narrative about their experiences or challenges; not simply answered with a yes or no response.
- **A**ffirmation – highlighting service user strengths, pointing out successes from the past.
- **R**eflections (reflective listening) – repeating, rephrasing, and paraphrasing service user statements, along with reflecting the feelings and commitments of the service user. This can help to demonstrate service provider understanding of what has been said, clarify as needed, and prompt self-reflection and further exploration of the subject.
- **S**ummaries – putting the information together to help the service user focus on key points, make sense of their experiences, see the bigger picture, and be motivated to bring about change.

Dani found that sharing her experiences was a challenge. Shaun began to think about how her challenges to manage emotions might affect her day-to-day life: "I would imagine that you and your partner are having difficulty communicating, is this the case?" or "Living on your own for the first time can be difficult for many people – emotionally, financially...does this sound familiar?" Every so often, he would ask open-ended questions, but he seemed to get the most input from Dani through more directed questions. Through this approach, they were both able to decide on their focus for discussion and plan for care. The goal that they both agreed to was to improve her relationship with her partner through managing her emotions, especially anger, and by improving her ability to communicate with her.

Shaun demonstrated compassion by saying things like, "It must be frustrating when you are having trouble getting along with someone that you care about" or "I am getting the sense that you are worried, is that accurate?" to further build trust. He also looked for opportunities where he could acknowledge Dani. She was always present for her appointments, and Shaun pointed this out: "Coming to these sessions and talking about some of your current challenges is not easy. I want to acknowledge you for putting in the work." He maintained a calm and welcoming demeanor through his facial expressions, being with the silences and welcoming her responses when she felt comfortable enough to share.

Although Dani said very little, her continued presence and her attentiveness during sessions made Shaun think that she was motivated to bring about change. Shaun made some observations of patterns of behavior that were hindering her relationship and explored these observations with Dani.

Shaun: "As we discussed, you want to improve your relationship with Stella. I notice that when she says something that hurts your feelings, you tend to feel angry with what she says and then leave the room. I wonder how this affects the relationship."

> Dani: "It's not good. But Stella said that we might have to sell some things that I bought her, for the money, so I freaked out."
> Shaun: "It sounds like you found the suggestion that Stella made quite hurtful."
> Dani was attentive but did not provide a response.
> Shaun: "I can only imagine how difficult that must be. It sounds like Stella wants you two to be able to afford everyday expenses and is willing to sacrifice something that she likely values quite a bit so that you two can continue to remain in the apartment. Perhaps we could talk about ways to let her know how you feel so she understands what is bothering you. You sound very committed to the relationship and willing to do what it takes to make things work."

Shared Decision Making

As was mentioned previously, service users have a large role in setting and working toward their personal goals. Therefore, communication with the service provider is imperative so that both parties have a clear understanding of what the service user wants. Tools such as MI or the four habits model can facilitate service users and service providers to engage in shared decision making (SDM). SDM is a collaborative PCA that focuses on how service users and service providers can work together during care (Charles, Gafni, & Whelan, 1997). SDM emphasizes open communication and active participation of the service user for input in the decision-making process, from appointment timings through to addressing any concerns they may have. In SDM, the service user and service provider work together to address the service user's needs and values when deciding on a care plan.

SDM posits that service user needs, values, and preferences are distinct and important to inform the most effective course of action for that service user. Discussions involve finding a fit between the service user's needs – for example, those related to life plans – and the various avenues for care that are available to the service user, all the while considering the associated risks and benefits of each. Care plans are typically a long-term commitment,

Table 2.4   Soliciting Service User Input: Prompts for Dani to Share Her Input Regarding Her Plan of Care

Verbally or in written form, the service provider can offer service users guiding prompts to express their thoughts more easily and inform the care plan. When it comes to discussing and working through my care plan:	
I am concerned about	*Medication side effects, failure, therapy not being of any help.*
I want/need/value	*Time, support, freedom.*
I would appreciate it if the service provider would	*Understand where I am coming from, be patient, explain the process step-by-step.*
I would appreciate it if the service provider would not	*Pressure or force me, judge me, or provide too much information at once.*

which requires that the service user be agreeable and willing in the recovery process. Scientific knowledge and personal preferences and experiences combine to reach an agreement on the plan of care. The service user makes the final choice about treatment or care. The topic of SDM is also covered in the Education chapter (see the section "Shared Decision Making" in Chapter 4).

Table 2.4 provides prompts for service users to share their ideas on what is important to them (Appendix 4). These discussions can help to ensure that the course of care is person-centered and that the selected treatment options are the right fit for the service user.

> When it came to planning for care, Shaun would gauge Dani's opinion by providing a number of treatment options, along with the reasons he thought they might be helpful for her, and the risks and benefits of each. "There are a number of options for moving forward," he said, "and we can start some of them at the same time. One option is a (re) evaluation of your medication. This can help to stabilize your mood, but there can be side effects depending on the type of medication we choose. Another option is skill development, where you would attend a group regularly to learn different ways to manage body sensations and express your emotions. This can be very helpful to improve communication with Stella, although the group setting can be a bit daunting – but everyone is there to learn. Do you think one, or both, of these options could work for you?" He also had all of the information concisely written down so that she could review the options at her own pace and think about any questions or concerns she might have. Below, in Table 2.5, is a template to organize Dani's treatment options (see also Appendix 5).

Table 2.5   Treatment Options Template: Example of One of Dani's Treatment Options

Treatment option	Skill development group
Risks	Potentially intimidating or overwhelming environment as there will be a maximum of 10 people present; requires participation in the group.
Benefits	May learn valuable skills that I can apply long after the group is over; may meet new people; may have new perspectives on myself and my situation.
Questions or concerns	Can I leave the group at any time?
Why this option may work for me	I might learn techniques to manage my anger and to get along better with Stella.
Why this option may not work for me	I do not like speaking in groups. I don't know what this is going to be like.

> Dani expected Shaun to tell her exactly what she should do, but instead, he left her with a lot of opportunity for her thoughts and input. She did not like this at first, but over time came to appreciate how much he valued what she had to say. She also thought he would try to convince her to do whatever he thought was best, but instead he listened, asked questions, made some suggestions, and left the choices to her.

Challenges to Applying SDM

There are various challenges for SDM when working with people who experience MHCs. It can be challenging to work toward the service user's goals when there is a lack of awareness of how the challenges with mental health may be impeding the service user's ability to reach the goals. Some service users may be unfit to make personal care decisions. Additionally, symptoms of MHCs, such as paranoia, difficulty with focus, or disorganized speech can directly affect decision making (Karnieli-Miller & Salyers, 2011). Some service users may express the opinion that they do not want to participate in planning their care. In addition, a lack of follow-through on the part of the service provider to use the principles of SDM can be a challenge; this may shift the focus away from the service user's goals for recovery. Another challenge is that in keeping service users in a safe place, service providers may be limiting their recovery. There may also be a lack of transparency as to why a service provider suggests care options, which can also affect levels of trust in the clinical relationship (Karnieli-Miller & Salyers, 2011).

Overcoming Challenges to SDM

SDM requires that the service user and service provider actively work together in the clinical partnership. Advance directives are documents prepared ahead of time that legally allow moving forward with health decisions at the wishes of the person in question. This may be useful if the individual or the service provider anticipate that the service user will reach a point where they demonstrate incapacity (Appelbaum, 1991). Service users who tend to be passive can be encouraged to play a more active role through improved communication between the service user and service provider. It is important to keep in mind that each person processes information differently, and that using multiple modes of communication, whether verbal, written, visual images, and/or otherwise, can help increase service user and service provider understanding of the information (Karnieli-Miller & Salyers, 2011). Decision aids can also help to convey information regarding care and related decision making, as covered here in the chapter on education (see the section "Shared Decision Making"). Written plans about care decisions between service users, service providers, and others may prove useful. An example of this is a *wellness recovery action plan* (WRAP), which outlines what a service user is like when they are well, what strategies help them to stay well, signs of MHCs, and what to do about those signs, which can include a crisis plan (Copeland, 1997). Improved communication skills, as demonstrated by the service provider, include listening and understanding the service user's values, attitudes, beliefs, and life plans; the ability to identify the service user's current knowledge, areas for discovery, and level of motivation; and providing information on the MHCs and care options. Additionally, discussing risks and benefits of each option, encouraging service users to share their opinions, and negotiation toward agreement may also be useful (Takhar, Hiaslam, McAuley, & Langford, 2011).

Now that Dani was communicating more with Shaun, this information helped to ensure that any choices or conversations reflected Dani's thoughts, feelings, and concerns. Dani was open to multiple routes of treatment and opted to take medication and attend the group skills sessions.

Dani had mentioned that she was not sure if the medication she was taking was causing oversleeping. Shaun addressed this concern of hers by posing a few options: slightly lowering the dose, providing her with a tracking sheet to determine whether it was the medication or if there were other events that were occurring in her life that were leading to oversleeping, or any other course of action she may be able to identify. Dani was unsure of what to do. Shaun discussed the pros and cons of each, saying that adjusting the dose could reduce her sleepiness but might also no longer effectively stabilize her mood; the tracking sheet could be helpful to pinpoint the cause of oversleeping if it was due to lifestyle factors. However, it requires a bit of work to observe your own behaviors and record them daily. Dani, now knowing the risks and benefits of each, decided that they could do both, but begin with the tracking sheet and then lower medication based on what they found – to which Shaun agreed.

Through a multimodal approach to communication, Shaun and Dani were able to work collaboratively to improve her relationship with her partner. She found that a lower dose of medication stabilized her mood with fewer side effects, and she was able to learn new skills in the group sessions she had agreed to attend. Through the group, she realized that when she unconsciously let go of control over her own actions, she, as well as her loved ones, suffered the most. With time, she was able to express herself in the group and receive ongoing feedback from other group members. She was also able to learn from other people's experiences and receive advice from those who had gone through their own challenges.

She discovered that she was out of tune with what her body was trying to communicate with her before getting upset – her palms would get sweaty, her mind would begin to race, and her heart would beat faster. Once she realized that these were signs that she was getting upset, she consciously practiced detecting these signs. When they would occur, she would leave the room, drink a glass of water, or get some fresh air. She realized that she was not alone and that others were going through the same sorts of challenges, even though their situations were different. She was able to test the boundaries to see how others would respond to her comments, and she learned what was effective and what was not. Also, she was able to listen to what others were going through and, on occasion, give advice which made her feel like she had something to contribute. This experience helped her to apply skills such as effective interpersonal communication, impulse control, and personal distress management to her own life, and especially in her relationship with Stella.

Conclusion

Clinical communication is vital during all stages of the clinical relationship; it is important in any approach to clinical practice. There are a number of models and frameworks that follow PCA, such as the four habits model, MI, and SDM. In these, there is an emphasis on collaboration and active participation of both parties so they have a mutual understanding of goals when working toward the service user's recovery.

Cultural Care

Laila is a 23-year-old woman who has recently immigrated to Canada from Pakistan. She traveled by herself after being sponsored by her husband, Kashif, a few years earlier. Her in-laws also migrated from Pakistan within the last 10 years. She currently lives with her husband and his parents in a joint family system, where they uphold their Pakistani Muslim traditions. She has been experiencing feelings of helplessness on a regular basis and has lost a lot of weight since she arrived in Canada. She is not able to sleep well at night, which makes tending to household responsibilities, as well as to her in-laws, difficult. She experiences exhaustion and aches. Focusing on household tasks is a challenge for her. Laila knew that she would have to take equivalency courses to be able to work in her field as an accountant, but she has been lacking the motivation to do so. She sometimes goes on outings with her husband and his parents, which is typically the only time she is motivated to leave the house. She does not usually take time for herself unless her in-laws tell her to do so. She does not have any family or friends in Canada besides her in-laws. She keeps in contact with her social network in Pakistan every day using her phone but is lonely and homesick. She receives a referral by her family physician to outpatient mental health services at a hospital for the second time – this time to a therapist, Nadia.

Culture is the collection of knowledge, skills, and practices that makes a community distinct, the attributes of which may be passed along through the generations (Avruch, 1998). These can include language and religion. An individual's culture may shape their values. The experience of MHCs can present differently based on the influence of a person's culture (Desjardins, Gritke, & Hill, 2011). For those experiencing MHCs, there may be personal values that influence the manifestation of symptoms or behaviors – for example, faith-based delusions. Culture shapes the way individuals view their environments, which in turn influences how information is processed, shaping their realities. Therefore, it is important to consider culture, as it can have an influence on an individual's experience of MHCs and on the recovery process.

PCA aligns with incorporating cultural care by considering a person's social and cultural context, understanding challenges with mental health that are informed by culture, and including culture in the recovery process as relevant for the individual (Desjardins et al., 2011). Culture is a topic of discussion that the service user and service provider can have, to understand how it plays a role in the service user's life. Service providers must acknowledge their own culture as a potential influence on the clinical relationship, as service providers may be looking through a different cultural lens than that of service users.

Acculturation

When someone from one culture enters a new, dominant culture, the individual can choose to acculturate (adapt or change to the new culture) to varying degrees. Identifying this change can provide insight into how strongly one identifies with the native (original) versus mainstream (dominant) culture.

Five basic levels of acculturation have been identified (Garrett & Herring, 2001): (1) *traditional* (the person continiues to follow their native culture, customs, and practices); (2) *marginal* (speaks language of both cultures but may not completely accept either the native culture or the mainstream culture); (3) *bicultural* (accepted in dominant society and practices both cultures); (4) *assimilated* (accepted in dominant society and follows mainstream culture); and (5) *pantraditional* (returns to, or participates in, native culture, although the individual may not have been raised with such traditions). The service provider would work with the service user to find a balance between both cultures that fits the values as defined by the service user. It is important to avoid making assumptions on how acculturated an individual may be. As previously mentioned in the section "Clinical Relationships," we tend to make assumptions about the people we encounter, which may not necessarily be accurate. Catching those assumptions is important to avoid labeling or stereotyping a service user. Continuously assuming that another culture plays a large role in the service user's life can be counterproductive and may make the service user feel alienated, which can hinder the recovery process. As well, treatment for an individual who closely identifies with their original culture may not necessarily focus primarily on those cultural aspects (although these aspects may be considerations when working through service user challenges and throughout care planning).

Laila has been to one other therapist, who referenced her culture occasionally. She did not expect him to be familiar with her culture, but Laila felt it was difficult to implement potential actions that he discussed because they simply did not fit with the dynamics of her relationships at home. For example, the suggestion of having her husband temporarily assist with household responsibilities was simply not a possibility – doing so would mean that she was not fulfilling her responsibilities as a wife and daughter-in-law, and she did not want to disappoint her new family. She did not want her in-laws to think that they had made a poor choice by choosing her to marry their son. She was also uncomfortable having a male therapist but was unsure if requesting a female therapist was a possibility.

Cultural Context

Cultural context can encompass a variety of elements. It may be useful for service providers to learn how the culture of the service user explains challenges with mental health – and whether the service user adheres to those beliefs. This knowledge can be useful to ensure that the plan of care is in line with the service user's understanding of the MHCs. Additionally, it can be beneficial for service providers to inform themselves of the historical context of individuals who have lived in areas that have experienced war or the like, to understand how these events may affect the service user's perspective (Desjardins et al., 2011).

Laila's new therapist, Nadia, was quite open with her. Nadia asked her to share any information on Pakistani culture so she could better understand Laila's perspectives and experiences. Nadia also informed herself through discussions with a colleague from the same culture (he had immigrated to Canada when he was a young child and therefore was able to provide information), and through some reading. She also followed international news but was cautious about assuming Laila's experiences.

Nadia was aware that most cultures hold a stigma toward – and frown upon discussing – challenges with mental health. She asked Laila how she, and her culture, viewed people who experienced challenges with mental health. Laila said that the word 'depression' is used commonly when someone is feeling down. In more extreme cases, she had heard stories of people whose behaviors were under the influence of possession by jinn, or spirits, or of people who did not wish them well. In terms of treatment, she had heard of doing additional prayers. Nadia had not heard of these cultural perspectives before and asked Laila to elaborate in order to learn more. Laila herself was unsure of the details and did not feel it was necessary for them to explore the topic further.

Nadia explained the idea of recovery, where individuals work through psychological, pharmacological, and rehabilitative care to undertake roles that they find meaningful. Laila was hesitant about the medication aspect of care. She mentioned that her culture had many remedies using foods or herbs that cured different ailments. She did not know, however, about items that were useful for challenges with mental health. Nadia expressed how appreciative she was that Laila was willing to share these cultural aspects with her. She emphasized that medication, like any other aspect of treatment, was a choice, and that Nadia would inform Laila of the risks and benefits of each. This explanation made sense to Laila, and she agreed to consider this course of treatment.

A culture's worldview is generally either sociocentric (interdependence, collectivism, cooperation among people) or egocentric (individual freedoms, competition, valuing the self before others). Knowing whether a culture follows a dominance hierarchy (rankings based on traits such as race or gender) or egalitarianism (equality for all people) can also give the service provider further insights into the service user's perspective (Pope-Davis & Coleman, 2001).

Nadia was aware that Pakistani culture has more of a sociocentric worldview, as seen in Laila's living arrangement and the responsibilities that she carries out, such as tending to the home and caring for her in-laws. Nadia also had an idea that Laila's culture followed a gender hierarchy, where men are usually dominant heads of households, and women, generally, tend to be more submissive. However, Nadia did not know how true this was for Laila. Nadia wanted to learn more about Laila's relationship with her husband, and observed that she tended to go along with whatever her husband (or her in-laws) requested, without question or complaint. It seemed to Nadia that Laila had the responsibilities of a wife carved out for her. Laila had agreed to that arrangement, had anticipated these responsibilities before marriage, was skilled in such tasks, and enjoyed doing them – but all of these changes had taken a greater emotional toll on her than she had expected. Laila stated that, despite how she had been feeling since she arrived, she knew that her parents wanted a better life for her, so she had accepted her current situation as it was. Although Laila did not seem to mind or see a problem with the current dynamic at home, Nadia was concerned that her depressive symptoms would continue if the situation did not change in some way.

Nadia also asked about how the politics of the country affected Laila's lifestyle and outlook. Laila told her that many of the places that have recently been considered dangerous areas of Pakistan were north of where she lived, and that those who were financially comfortable were less likely to be directly impacted by such political events. Violence in public places would occur at times, which had prevented her from shopping or traveling to visit family while she still lived in Pakistan. Nadia also asked about the transition to Canada and Laila's experiences with that. Laila discussed the fact that she had not known what to expect in moving from a place where "everyone was the same" to a country with a mix of different people and cultures. Since arriving, though, she has had overall positive experiences while in the community.

Values and Traditions

Identifying a person's values and traditions can occur over the course of treatment as the clinical relationship strengthens. Religious or spiritual beliefs of the individual and/or the native or dominant culture may also influence values. Service providers must recognize the individuality of each service user. Cultural elements that are important to one person may not be relevant for another person of a similar background. This can vary due to a number of factors, including the level of acculturation, regional differences within a culture, the individual's family culture, or simply personal preferences (Desjardins et al., 2011). When family members or partners are present at appointments, with the express consent of the service user, these individuals may support the service provider in better understanding the service user's situation, culture, and context.

Family and unity were central to Laila. Also, prayer and her belief in God seemed to play a large role in Laila's outlook on life. Even though her situation was less than ideal, Laila told Nadia that she would remind herself that there were people who were in much more difficult situations, and she wanted to remain grateful for what she had. She also valued harmony and ensuring that everyone was happy, even if she herself was not happy at the present time. It was very clear that, in the past, Laila had looked forward to being a wife along with the thought of being a mother. She said that it was becoming more and more difficult to look forward to the future because of how she felt physically and emotionally. She felt very guilty for feeling this way.

Laila was not used to talking with people who knew little about her culture – she did not know how Nadia would respond. She did not think that Nadia would be able to understand what she was going through. To Laila's surprise, Nadia seemed quite interested in learning more and was not afraid to ask questions to understand Laila's experiences.

Nadia was sometimes unsure if Laila would take offense to some of her questions, as she might find them too invasive, but Nadia made sure to clarify the reasons for her questions. This way, Laila would know that Nadia's questions were simply so she could learn and to help inform recovery, rather than to offend or question her culture.

Nadia also made a point of welcoming Laila's husband to an appointment if they were interested in doing so. Laila told her that he knew that she was seeking outside support and would drive her to appointments, but she did not want to create more stress for him by making him attend appointments with her. Nadia clarified that it did not have to be on a regular basis and that it might help him understand what Laila is experiencing. Still, Laila did not like the idea, so Nadia respected her choice and told her that they could revisit the idea later if Laila wanted to do so.

Nadia herself was of US origin, with a cultural descent from Greece a number of generations before. She understood the cultural importance of family, and although she would have liked to involve Laila's husband in their meetings, she respected Laila's request to work through her challenges on her own. Table 2.6 is a compilation of Laila's cultural considerations (see also Appendix 6).

Table 2.6   Environmental Scan of the Influence of Culture: Example of Taking a Closer Look at Laila's Situation

Cultural context	Native culture: Recently moved from Pakistan.
	Views of challenges with mental health in culture: Culture tends to have little discussion about challenges with mental health, she seemed ashamed that she was feeling the way she was. There may be the belief that MHCs stem from possession (by spirits) or is brought about by those who are ill-wishers of the individual. Natural remedies are common in her culture, but are more common for physical ailments.
	Service user views of MHCs: Laila did not seem to hold on strongly to her native culture's health beliefs. She was also not seeking alternative treatments that were in line with her culture's explanation of challenges with mental health. Laila is open to Western treatment, other than pharmacotherapy.
Historical context	Major occurrences or events in the culture: Colonialism occurred until the mid-20th century, which may influence the clinical relationship.
	War (past or present): Areas of Pakistan currently experience violence somewhat regularly; however, Laila does not indicate that there have been many direct impacts on her from such events.
Worldview	Sociocentric (collectivist) or egocentric (individualist): Pakistani culture holds a sociocentric or collectivist view, which shows in Laila's actions of living with and caring for her in-laws.
	Hierarchical (rankings) or egalitarian (equality): Laila's culture is hierarchical in that females tend to be more submissive to males and elders, which shows in Laila's attitudes.

Table 2.6 Continued

Values and traditions	Religion/spirituality: Laila's culture has a basis in Islamic beliefs — monotheism, emphasis on prayer, patience, and gratitude.
	Family: Family is very important in her culture and to Laila personally. She consults with her husband on most matters.
	Gender roles: There is more emphasis on traditional gender roles, which Laila practices.
Acculturation and identity	Length of time in Canada: Less than 1 year.
	Similarities vs. differences of native and mainstream cultures: Laila lived in a metropolitan area in Pakistan, which has some similarities to the mainstream culture in Canada, such as in socializing (but typically with the same gender) and a focus on education.
	Level of acculturation: She speaks her native language at home and is fluent in English as well. She does not show clear signs of her native culture in her clothing or through conversation. At the same time, she has not had a lot of exposure to the mainstream culture and so has not had the opportunity to observe and/or learn mainstream cultural practices. Laila may fall under the marginal level of acculturation.
Verbal and nonverbal communication	Although Laila experienced depression, she did not physically present this way — she was friendly, presentable, and had a faint smile throughout the session.
	Service user statements on the impact of culture on life: Her culture and religion are important to her. That is the only lifestyle that she has known until recently.

Note. MHC = mental health challenge. Adapted from Desjardins, Gritke, & Hill, 2011.

Nadia worked together with Laila to address Laila's desire to meet new people, and improve her sleep and her mood. Laila wanted to hold off on pursuing education that would allow her to work in her field, until she was feeling better. In order for Laila to be active in the community, Nadia discussed options of public transport or learning how to drive. Laila said that this was something that she would work on. Nadia also recommended medication for her sleeping difficulties, but Laila informed Nadia that she would not be taking prescription medication. Instead, her discussions with Nadia about cultural herbal remedies reminded Laila of a few items that she would try. Personally, Nadia did not think that this was the most effective option for Laila, but she respected her decision and provided her with some information on sleep hygiene to improve her likelihood of improved sleep.

Because of Laila's limited social network in Canada, Nadia wanted her to consider a female activity group based on her interests, such as cooking, or to develop a new interest, like reading in a book club. She recognized that it was important for Laila to spend time with people outside of her household to build new relationships in the community and so that she could participate in activities that she enjoyed without the pressure of being a wife or caretaker. Recognizing that Laila's faith was important to her, she recommended that she attend psychotherapy, yoga, and mindfulness meditation that integrates spirituality in order to address her depressive symptoms in a way that would align with her values. Nadia wanted to connect Laila to a newcomer resource center in her area. This would provide Laila with information on familiarizing herself with various systems in Canada. They would also have a hub of resources that she could access even after the clinical relationship with Nadia was over. Laila was in agreement with these interventions and was appreciative of Nadia integrating cultural elements that were important to Laila.

Conclusion

Culture can play a very influential role in a service user's understanding of the environment, others, and themselves. This understanding may include perspectives on MHCs, which may differ from those of the mainstream culture. Service providers also have to take into consideration how their own culture may affect their perspectives or view of the beliefs of service users and/or how they provide care. Service providers can research cultures to gain a deeper understanding of longstanding views and perspectives that people of that culture may have. Open dialogue about the service user's culture, and its importance to them, can better inform a plan of care that meets the needs of the individual who identifies with another culture.

Family-Centered Care

A single mother, Tanya, accompanies her 30-year-old son, James, to visit a community counselor. James has been living in the family home all of his life. He had earned a university degree and since then has been unable to secure stable employment. He spends most of his time in his room.

James has been to mental health care providers before and does not trust them – he has had countless experiences where he talked but stated that they were too distracted by their computer and e-mails to provide anything useful to him. He did not feel listened to at all. Diagnoses have included depression, anxiety, and bipolar disorder. He is not sure what to believe anymore.

James has also had difficulties in the past with health care providers because of the issue of medication. He has been on many different medications of varying doses, most with side effects that were getting in the way of his daily life. Because of this, he has not been able to remain on any medication long term. He has been turned away from a service provider when he refused to take medication.

He is angry about his situation, and at everyone around him. Most of his interactions with family members involve yelling, and he states that he does not want to associate himself with his family, and that he would move out if he could financially afford to do so. Tanya does not know how to deal with James's emotions and is desperate to find her son help. The situation has taken a toll on her – she appears worn down and does not have a lot of energy.

"I want to see him live his life and to know that he will be able to take care of himself after I am gone," she says. In fact, Tanya wanted to attend a few counseling sessions for herself to manage her own worries.

The health care provider, Natasha, has seen many situations like this before. Having had decades of experience in the field, she is quite aware of James's sort of experience in the health care system. The negative interactions that James has experienced with the health care system may have even been the result of practices that Natasha herself had previously used before she began adopting a more person-centered approach in her work.

The role of family is important to consider throughout the care of a service user. Family members are sometimes the ones to provide emotional and financial support. Family typically has inside knowledge of their loved one's day-to-day functioning. They may carry a great deal of stress and burden, while sometimes lacking knowledge of their loved one's challenges with mental health and what effective treatment might involve (Mueser & Gingerich, 2011). This can have a negative impact on the individual experiencing challenges with mental health, as well as on the entire family unit.

When it comes to family, the family as a service user is distinct from the service user in the context of their family. When the family is the service user, they will be together for meetings, and the family dynamics will be the focus. In family as context, the service user is the individual, and information from the family supports an understanding of the service user's challenges. Family may also attend separate educational groups, which can provide insight into ineffective behavioral patterns (Center for Substance Abuse Treatment, 2004). For the case example in this section, we will look at the individual in the context of family. We will illustrate how one can achieve the four main goals of family work – collaboration with family, giving family basic information, teaching family members how to monitor mental health of the service user, and reducing stress of family members along with improving their quality of life – using this example (Mueser & Gingerich, 2011).

Goal 1: Establish Collaboration With Family

Goal 1 is to establish an authentic, collaborative relationship between the family members and the care team. In this example, where the service user is the individual in the context of family, the clinical relationship will be primarily established with the service user, where the extent of family involvement is to the service user's discretion. Focusing on the service user's goals requires an effort on the part of the service users, family members, and service provider. Requesting that service users create a detailed plan of their goals inside or outside of the meeting time can allow individuals to have ownership of their own recovery. When there are shared goals with the service provider and family members, individuals can work collaboratively to discuss realistic steps that service users may take toward reaching their goals.

James was unwilling to have his mother present while speaking with Natasha, while Tanya had made it quite clear that she wanted to be involved. Natasha wanted to clarify his concerns about having his mother in the room. He stated that he would not be able to say what was on his mind, and that she would put on an act and defend herself. Tanya said she would never do that. James pointed out that this was exactly what he had been saying. Natasha wanted to use PCA, and recognized that family members are important to the recovery process. Therefore, she proposed an agreement. If James was open to the idea, Tanya could remain in the room during a few sessions as long as everyone spoke in turn. Given that he is the service user, the choice was ultimately up to him.

Tanya agreed to such terms, but James was still not convinced. "I don't trust her," James said. Natasha then asked what would make James comfortable in that moment. He shrugged and said that he would proceed with the session as it was currently set up, but that he would decide, from week to week, who would be attending appointments.

James was hesitant but agreed to have his mother in the room during this conversation with Natasha. Instead of asking first about his symptoms, Natasha asked James about his daily routine. She wanted to get a holistic understanding of his situation by asking what a typical day looked like for him, in detail. James stated that he usually woke up about 10 a.m., made himself coffee with a light snack for breakfast, and stayed in his room most of the day, except for preparing meals, which he ate in his room. He watched videos, communicated with others online, browsed the Internet, and read various articles. Natasha asked which articles, and he mentioned some on world history. He also followed some business affairs. He occasionally looked for work online. He did not socialize much in person, and he left the house mainly for walks and for the gym.

Natasha then asked about any goals that he was thinking about or was currently working on. James said that he wanted to move out, and knew that he would need to get a job to do so. Natasha said that his goal of finding work and moving out was something that both she, as well as his mother, Tanya, could support.

Nearing the end of the appointment, Natasha highlighted the fact that both James and Tanya had done an excellent job of respecting the communication boundaries set at the beginning of the session. Natasha also pointed out that Tanya had put in a lot of effort in staying involved in James's recovery and thanked her for doing so. They decided that Tanya would attend the next session to delve into goal setting. James acknowledged that to reach his goals, his mother would be an important part of the process in continuing to provide a place to live and providing financial assistance as needed. Tanya was more than willing to take part in this process and left the session with the sense that she could work as part of the team to support James in his recovery.

Family members may feel that they do not have the knowledge and skills to contribute to their loved one's care. Supporting their loved one in relation to goals, on the other hand, can be more tangible. This can help to empower family members and to promote the positive role they can play in recovery.

When collaborating with families and establishing the clinical relationship, it can be helpful for the care team to contact the family to provide updates on the service user if in hospital, given that the service user has provided consent to do so or the family are the sub-stitute decision makers. Ongoing communication, with the service user's consent, can en-sure that everyone understands the current situation, and the steps going forward. These conversations can also include shared goals and goal setting for the service user and fam-ily members, to ensure the well-being of everyone involved. The service user as well as the family can add valuable insights into care planning, which can increase service user inter-est, and lead to desired outcomes for everyone involved (Mueser & Gingerich, 2011). Also, encouraging family collaboration can help to increase the social support that service users receive. Focusing on the service user's strengths as well as validating concerns of the fam-ily may alleviate family stress and provide a sense of what is possible moving forward.

With James's permission, Tanya agreed to take part in care planning. This was helpful to keep open communications between Natasha, James, and his mother while working toward James's goals. Since Tanya was a team member in her son's care, it was impor-tant that she be knowledgeable about what care steps were planned and taken, and why. This knowledge could help Tanya feel involved in James's recovery and could act as a reminder to focus on what works in the situation.

Natasha made sure that she also asked Tanya about any concerns she had with the current situation. Tanya was concerned about how James would care for himself when she would no longer be there to support him. Natasha reassured Tanya, saying that her concern was understandable. She reminded Tanya that she could only tackle the situa-tion that was currently in front of her. Natasha stated that it was quite clear that Tanya was doing all she knew to currently support James. They discussed that planning and taking actionable steps at present would better serve the situation, rather than focusing on worrying thoughts about the future.

Natasha made a point of acknowledging the strengths of both James and Tanya. James was an intelligent, capable individual. He also showed determination from one session to the next to reach his goals. Tanya showed a great deal of patience in the situation, along with compassion. Natasha also talked about resiliency, which meant that even though they had both been through a number of challenges, they had both continued to move forward and could derive strength from their experiences rather than allowing the difficulties to get the best of them. Both were also willing, rather than willful, meaning that they were open to developing new habits and replacing old ones that were imped-ing the recovery process.

Goal 2: Provide Basic Information to Family Members About the Nature of MHCs

Providing information to the service user's family members about the challenges with men-tal health and the principles of care can be useful for a number of reasons. These include the ability to understand and recognize the symptoms as well as clarify any myths they may have heard regarding MHCs. Education can also involve personal goal setting and main-tenance for one's own self-care while supporting a loved one with MHCs, information on medication and rehabilitative interventions, external resources, coping with stress, and improving communication. Learning more about the MHCs and their causes can also help to lessen the blame that the family may feel is directed toward them. Service providers may also provide a sense of what is possible, through anonymous examples of previous service users, their families, and their recovery journeys (Mueser & Gingerich, 2011).

Natasha noticed Tanya's confusion about her son's behavior. Beyond the care that James received, Natasha thought it would be helpful for Tanya to learn more about her son's challenges with mental health. This included his symptoms, along with clarifying any myths or misunderstandings that she might have about the MHCs. This knowledge may be provided in a few different ways. Natasha could address any questions Tanya might have, one-on-one, and give her information sheets that they can review together or she can review on her own. This can be helpful to address any immediate questions Tanya might have. Natasha could also recommend family educational sessions so that family members could better understand the challenges with mental health. This sort of group can also be helpful to answer questions regarding the role of medication and the process of rehabilitation; to improve communication; and to support family members to alleviate stress, gain perspective, and recognize that there are others going through similar situations (Mueser & Gingerich, 2011). Such groups can also be helpful for family members to stay on track with their own personal goals so that they continue to move their lives forward and maintain their own well-being, which can help to reduce burnout while supporting their loved one.

At James's individual appointment with Natasha, he discussed his frustration with his situation. He felt like he had no control over his life, and anything that he felt was in his control, his mother tried to take over – for example, what he should be doing during the day, what he ate, and where he went. Natasha said that it might be very frustrating to feel as though someone is making decisions on his behalf when he feels as though he already has little control. James continued, saying that he knew that his mom wanted him to be more independent, which was what he wanted for himself as well. The process for reaching this goal had been much more challenging than he had imagined, and at this point, he had few ideas on how to reach this goal on his own. Natasha inquired as to why he wanted to reach his goals on his own rather than with the help and support of his mother, or others. James said that he wanted to prove that he did not need anyone to be successful. Natasha was interested in knowing more about his way of thinking: "What would happen if you were to get help from her?" Natasha asked. "Then it would prove that I still need her and that I'm not able to make it on my own," James replied. To this, Natasha said, "Well, James, I have to be honest – I cannot think of a person who has been able to be successful without the help and support of at least one other person, such as a family member, friend, or mentor. I do not know if I would be where I am today without the support of others. I understand what you are saying in that you do not want help because you want to be independent. I see your commitment to making it on your own. What if, instead, you looked at the support as a means to become independent? For example, if she were to drive you to an appointment you have, instead of spending a sizable amount of time walking or using public transit to be independent, that time saved could be spent applying for positions, or doing anything that brings you closer to your goals. This way, the support that you are getting may lead to more independence in the long run." James had a hard time accepting the idea of his mother's help, and Natasha encouraged James to reflect on their discussions.

Tanya discussed her feelings of guilt privately with Natasha. She felt as though she had let her son down and did not give him the attention he needed while he was growing up. She did not feel like she was the parent he deserved, and felt like James's current situation was her fault. Natasha discussed that a person can only draw on one's own knowledge and experiences to deal as effectively as possible with a situation, and that Tanya could not have expected herself to behave any differently with the knowledge and skills she had at that time. Natasha emphasized that Tanya was currently taking steps forward to learn, adapt new habits and approaches, and cope, such as through mindfulness, support groups, exercising, and regular communication with her mother. Tanya felt reassured that although she could not change past events, she was taking action toward a positive future for both James and herself.

Natasha described the situation of another family that she had seen in the past. She mentioned the changes in communication that she saw between family members from the beginning to later on in care, which had made a big difference for their relationships. She emphasized that this was gradual and not without trial and error, but became easier and more routine for everyone over time. Natasha also described that the previous service user, with the support of both her care team and her family, was well on her way to achieving the goal of returning to school. Such stories served as a reminder to Tanya that recovery is possible.

Goal 3: Teach Family Members How to Monitor the Course of MHCs, and Develop a Relapse Prevention Plan

Education may also play a role, where family members gain knowledge of the signs of the MHCs, and what to watch for in case of relapse. Developing a relapse prevention plan, including what to say and how to react, what resources to access and what strategies to implement, can be very helpful to manage and de-escalate stressful events.

After Tanya was more familiar with the symptoms of depression, anxiety, and bipolar disorder, it made it easier for her to identify when James was showing some of these signs, such as changes in sleep (too much or too little), restlessness, anger, irritability, and difficulty concentrating. Instead of questioning or fighting with him, she took steps to lessen his symptoms and prevent distressing events from occurring in the house. She began to separate her son from the symptoms of the MHCs and stopped reading meaning into his words and behaviors – for example, that the words and actions were directed toward her. This way, she was able to stay calm and think about what she was going to say or do, before acting. She would make his favorite meals when he had little energy or motivation to do it himself. She and James also made sure that there was open communication, so that if Tanya thought James showed signs of challenges with mental health, she could discuss this with him, along with what they could do about it: whether that was to seek outside support together, devote some of his time and energy toward something that he enjoyed doing, such as exercise, talk to someone about anything that was bothering him, or see if there needed to be any adjustment in medication.

Goal 4: Reduce Stress on Everyone in the Family and Improve Their Quality of Life

Reducing stresses on the family, such as worries about their loved one (Rudnick, 2004), is important. The provision of resources and strategies to lessen that burden on the family may help all family members to have a sense of accomplishment in other areas of their lives. Reaching the point of burnout is counter-productive, and it is therefore important for all family members to take care of their own well-being while caring for their loved one. This in turn may reduce the service user's frequency of relapses and hospitalizations.

During care, Tanya became more and more skilled at learning how to respond to James as effectively as possible to have the best-case scenario occur in situations, even if the event seemed like nothing positive would result. This not only helped James's symptoms, but also lessened Tanya's stress levels as well. She became less fearful of the future, and she focused on what she could do in the present to make life more manageable. This included things like anticipating James's needs, setting boundaries in their relationship so that she did not overextend herself toward burnout, and setting time every day for her own self-care. She also made a conscious effort to stay focused on possibilities and on signs of progress, such as an enjoyable conversation she had had with her son, or anything they did together as a team, such as household tasks.

Tanya also discussed her feelings about James's need for independence. It became clear that as much as Tanya wanted her son to be independent, she felt comfort in knowing that he needed her in some way. She was scared that once he gained his independence, he would leave her, and she would not see him again. Natasha pointed out that gaining independence for oneself might be a part of growth for James. She prompted Tanya to think about when she was her son's age, and any experiences that she had had which made her feel like an independent, competent person. Tanya began to recognize that James might not have had those experiences – she did not want her fear of him leaving to hinder his full potential.

Tanya also recognized that she could only support James as long as she took care of herself throughout the process. This took some time for her to accept, as she felt guilty about spending time on herself rather than on her son. She realized that her own stress was affecting how she responded to James. For instance, she noticed that she was increasingly anxious when she did not practice mindfulness strategies for a few days, which in turn made conversations with James more difficult. Tanya thought about taking some time off work to support James full-time, but then realized that it was in their best interest for her to have some physical and mental separation from the household environment, where she could continue to develop in another area of her life.

Tanya also realized that she felt resentment toward James for his lack of appreciation of her. Upon further reflection, she distinguished her thoughts on forgiveness in a letter that she wrote for herself:

"There are circumstances in life that are beyond our control. They will occur in the way that they are meant to happen, in order to teach us what we need to learn in life. These are challenges we have to accept. We also have to accept (but not agree to) the way people behave in reaction to *their own* challenging circumstances, as we do not have control over the actions of others. We can suggest and provide guidance, but the decisions of others are not ours to make. We may feel angry at the behaviors of others, as it may appear to be unjust and unfair. Whether or not we know *why* others behave the way they do, we must know that, for certain, it is for a reason. There *is* a cause. If we knew the reason, we may then understand the behavior, and instead of anger, frustration, or hurt, we would feel empathy for others. Therefore, even though we may not know the cause for their behaviors, it is more effective if we manage our expectations of others. Forgive them. They are already going through a tough time. Even when the choices they make seem to have a negative impact on us, the universe will find a way to help us get through it, and even thrive from it. Hone the character that we wish to achieve."

From James's perspective, he noticed that his mother was acting differently from before. She seemed to be much calmer, and more accepting, instead of trying to micromanage situations like before. He was skeptical at first that these changes would last, but she continued to respect his space and independence which he needed to figure things out on his own. He did not feel angry as often as he used to, which allowed him to get more things done in the day and have conversations with his mom that did not end in arguments. He also liked that he was trusted to take care of the household when his mother was away. Some symptoms of his challenges with mental health would persist or recur, but both James and his mom were able to identify when he needed to refer to the relapse prevention plan to manage symptoms and stay on track toward recovery.

Goal Setting

As previously mentioned, working toward one's goals can be a large part of the recovery process (Rudnick & Roe, 2011). There are times when goal(s) that the service user poses cannot be accomplished within the period of care. Nevertheless, maintaining the service user's goal(s) as something to work toward can help to develop habits and routines that will be beneficial regardless of what the service user pursues in the future. For example, if an individual's goal is to become a renowned artist, habits such as how to structure one's daily routine, which includes waking up at a set time, preparing food, and showering and getting dressed, are all useful to have, no matter what the service user's goals are.

James, along with Tanya, returned for his next appointment with Natasha. Natasha asked James if he was okay with his mother sitting in on the session, reinforcing that everyone would speak in turn. He did not have a preference; Tanya chose to remain in the meeting. Natasha suggested that together they come up with a more detailed plan, to break down, systematically, how James was going to achieve his goals, and identify any supports that might be helpful along the way. Both James and Tanya agreed to this.

Natasha provided James with a goal-setting template and asked if he would write down what they created. James restated his goals of getting a job and moving out on his own. Natasha asked what this looked like – such as the kind of living arrangement, the location, and estimated costs. This helped to inform the goals related to finding work, such as whether it would be part-time or full-time, to cover his expenses. She also asked what kind of work he was interested in and what aligned with his skills. He had a Bachelor of Arts degree in history, and said that, at this point, he was unsure of what he could do with this training. Natasha then asked about any job or career goals that he had, which did not have to relate to his degree. To this, James said that he would like to be some sort of analyst. Natasha questioned him further and learned that he was skilled at identifying patterns as well as observing how past events might influence future occurrences. Natasha was glad to hear that James had ideas of what he wanted to do in the future. She also wanted to be realistic about how much they could achieve together.

Townsend and Polatajko (2007) speak to the importance of collaborative goal setting, where action-based objectives are identified. Table 2.7 and Table 2.8 are examples of courses of action for James, which can clearly identify what is needed to help him achieve his goals of moving out and making new friends (see also Appendix 7). Table 2.9 is a weekly schedule, broken down hourly, to support James in taking action on his goals (Appendix 8).

Table 2.7   Step-by-Step Goal Setting – Example 1: Goals and Objectives Toward James Living Independently

This exercise can be done by the service user alone, with significant others and family members, or with a health care provider. This template breaks down goals into more manageable objectives and steps.	
Main goal	Move out in 1 year's time to rent an apartment
First action-based objective	James will seek and maintain employment within the next 4 months to fund the costs of renting an apartment
Steps to be taken	• Visit school's career counseling office that is open to alumni and develop and improve his resume and cover letter, and learn skills to tailor the resume to the jobs that he applies for • Learn about tips on navigating applications, networking, and building his online professional profile with guidance from the school career counseling office • Apply to at least one position per day on-line, and make follow-up calls and in-person visits, as needed • James will practice his interviewing skills with a career counselor, as well as with online interview practice sites and with friends • Upon securing employment, identify needs or concerns with the employer as soon as possible to improve chances of on-the-job success
Second action-based objective	James will seek out an appropriate housing arrangement

Table 2.7   Continued

Steps to be taken	• Save enough funds for first and last month's rent (estimate based on current apartment rental values) • Narrow down the number of apartments he can rent by picking a location and a particular price range that he can afford with his earnings, after factoring in all other expenses (food, transportation, furniture, utilities, and recreation) • Search and identify apartments that fit his needs and preferences (number of rooms, layout, view) • Call prospective owners or landlords to set up and attend viewings • Identify preferred choice, inform owner, and come to an agreement — read lease carefully and understand rights and responsibilities as well as the owner's obligations

Note. Adapted from Townsend & Polatajko, 2007.

Table 2.8   Step-by-Step Goal Setting – Example 2: Goals and Objectives Toward James Making New Friends

Main Goal	Have two more friends (not on social media) in half a year's time
First action-based objective	Attend a social gathering of interest at least once per month
Steps to be taken	• Browse events or gatherings on social media or meet-up sites, taking safety into consideration • Select a gathering that is of interest to James such as attending the movies, sports activities or events, fitness class, or a dinner • Arrange for transportation through public transit by purchasing tickets beforehand (or through carpooling with the event organizer if applicable)
Second action-based objective	Initiate and maintain contact with new connections
Steps to be taken	• Initiate at least one conversation with a new person by discussing a topic of shared interest — for example, movie, sport, etc. • Keep in touch with those who seem willing through obtaining phone, e-mail, and/or social media • Attend future events or independently initiate a meeting with new connections, as applicable

Table 2.9   Scheduling: Using a Structure to Manage One's Daily Activities

Having a daily, weekly, or monthly calendar can help service users to plan for and meet their commitments. It may also serve to show accomplishments thus far. Similarly, a chart like the one below may help to organize daily and weekly objectives to achieve one's goals. Digital calendars may also work well.

	Sunday	Monday	Tuesday	Wednesday	Thursday	Friday	Saturday
7 a.m.							
8 a.m.							
9 a.m.							
10 a.m.							
11 a.m.							
12 noon							
1 p.m.							
2 p.m.							
3 p.m.							
4 p.m.							
5 p.m.							
6 p.m.							
7 p.m.							
8 p.m.							
9 p.m.							
10 p.m.							
11 p.m.							
12 mid-night							

With both Natasha's and his mother's support, James has been working toward his goals by breaking down the tasks into manageable steps. He also gained the skill of goal setting to apply to other areas of his life. Tanya was sad to see her son working towards moving out, but she knew that it would be the best outcome for everyone. James needs his independence, but he is thankful to his mother for supporting him in where he is today.

Conclusion

Family-centered care is an approach to care that can increase the satisfaction and success of service users. Four goals for family work include establishing a genuinely collaborative relationship between the family members and the care team; providing information to family members about the nature of the MHCs; teaching family members how to monitor the course of the MHCs, and developing a relapse prevention plan to help them; and reducing stress and improving the quality of life of all family members (Mueser & Gingerich, 2011). Involvement of family members as care team members can improve their knowledge, understanding, and choice of behaviors so that service users are better supported and better able to reach their recovery goals.

Co-Occurring (Concurrent) Disorders

Daniel is a 42-year-old man who lives with bipolar disorder and has challenges with alcohol use. He sometimes finds it difficult to go about daily tasks that were previously not a problem. His mood episodes tend to last a few months each time; when experiencing mania, Daniel typically spends excessive amounts of money and jumps from one home project to the next before completion. When experiencing depression, he drinks alcohol excessively and remains in bed. He gains or loses weight depending on whether he experiences a depressive or manic episode, respectively. He has trouble remembering what people have said and in expressing himself.

Daniel is married with two children, and his wife is seriously considering filing for divorce. His overspending has put the family into a great deal of debt, which is causing a lot of tension in their relationship. She no longer knows how to handle his mood swings – between being lively and energetic, to retreating to their room for extended periods – while she looks after the household and children. In the past, his substance use has put the safety of himself, his children, and others at risk while he was driving under the influence.

He has maintained a stable job for a number of years, and his employer is aware of his challenges with mental health, but not of the alcohol addiction. They have made accommodations for him at work, but they have started to notice that lately he has been absent more frequently and that his productivity has declined significantly. He had a group of friends with whom he and his wife spent time. However, with talk of a divorce, his social network has shrunk, and he has fewer people to talk to for support. One close friend convinced him to go to psychiatric emergency services after Daniel mentioned that everyone might be better off without him.

Co-occurring (concurrent) disorders may be classified as a condition that involves both MHCs and a *substance use disorder* (Center for Substance Abuse Treatment, 2005). The repeated use of substances that gets in the way of day-to-day functioning is considered a substance use disorder, and may be of two kinds: dependence or abuse. Substance *dependence* can be physical or psychological; in physical dependence, a person needs a larger amount of the substance to reach the same effect (tolerance) or has symptoms of withdrawal. With psychological dependence, a person spends a large amount of time trying to obtain the substance instead of engaging in daily activities (Mueser & Drake, 2011). There may also be a number of failed attempts to limit substance use. On the other hand, substance *abuse* is the use of a substance that causes or worsens a mental health challenge, or does something that puts the person or others at risk or in harm's way.

The *stages of change model* highlights phases that an individual may go through while undergoing changes in their thoughts and behaviors. The stages are *precontemplation* (lack of awareness of the need for change), *contemplation* (considering change), *preparation* (getting ready to make changes), *action* (taking the steps needed to make lasting change), *maintenance* (ensuring that change is upheld), and *termination* (change has been made) (Prochaska et al., 1994). Often 12-step programs, such as those in place for substance use, stem from this model and may be an effective means toward recovery.

The care for those with substance use disorders can be organized into six stages: (1) screening, (2) education, (3) establishing personal preferences, (4) care planning, (5) implementation, and (6) monitoring participation and outcomes (Mueser & Drake, 2011).

The first stage, screening, identifies persons with a substance use disorder. Self-identification or probing questions will likely be the most common method of screening. Urinalyses may reveal substance use, as appropriate. Then, discussion of details such as the frequency of use, tolerance, symptoms of withdrawal, and attempts to limit use may be informative. This information may come from loved ones, as needed.

> When Daniel was admitted to hospital, his friend told staff that he had a drinking problem. Daniel admitted that he drank a bottle of vodka every day after work, and would sometimes begin drinking during the early afternoon on weekends, without his wife's knowledge. He had been drinking more over time to get the numbing effect that he craved. Doing so has made it difficult to attend to his family's needs, take care of himself, or get anything done around the house. When he was not drinking (during previous attempts to quit), his depressive symptoms deepened, and he would become sluggish.

The second of the six stages, education, can help to explain that no one is to blame for the circumstances involved and that the MHCs may be linked to biological factors, which can lessen any perceived shame and guilt and may encourage service users to learn more. Service providers can also educate service users on the symptoms and consequences of substance use. For those who experience challenges with mental health, it is important to be aware that their vulnerability to undesirable outcomes from substance use can increase (Mueser & Drake, 2011). There may be more consequences for individuals with MHCs compared with when they did not have challenges with mental health. It is important to emphasize and instill the idea of the possibility for recovery.

Daniel was feeling extremely guilty for what transpired with his family. He felt that it was because of him that they were struggling to get by financially, and he was ashamed that he was not being the father that his children needed or deserved. He thought that everyone was going to judge him as a terrible father and husband. Jay, the psychologist who began to work with Daniel, explained that a person's biological make-up may increase the likelihood of substance use and that no one is to blame in the situation. Jay explained that Daniel drank alcohol as a way to cope with stresses and challenges, and that, when he was ready, they could work together to develop new habits and coping strategies that did not involve drinking. Daniel felt a small sense of relief from hearing this, but he was unsure if things could actually change. He had tried to stop drinking in the past, and although friends and family were supportive at first, they grew tired of dealing with his relapses. Eventually, they no longer provided the support he needed, and he would continue to feel miserable.

To ensure that the plan of care is in line with service user wants and needs, the third stage considers the personal preferences of the service user. Service providers can educate service users on common reasons for use, in the second stage, which can help service users understand their particular situations, along with the resulting negative outcomes that they experience. However, beware of providing too much information, as this can be off-putting and lead to confusion, disengagement, and the feeling of being overwhelmed (Mueser & Drake, 2011).

Jay wanted to provide more material to Daniel regarding the symptoms and consequences of drinking, but Daniel refused. Daniel was not in a mindset to have someone tell him this information; he was already experiencing major life challenges that were partially the result of the substance use. With PCA in mind, Jay reevaluated his approach and asked open-ended questions to delve deeper and learn why Daniel would drink in the first place.

Intensified mood swings between mania and depression, financial difficulties, work stress, marital challenges, and the responsibility of children were some of the major problems that Daniel and Jay were able to identify as stressors. Jay reassured him that his situation would be a lot for anyone to handle, and that developing alternative skills and strategies to manage his stresses and emotions could lessen the urge to drink. For Daniel, coping skills and strategies that might be effective included recognizing the urge and changing his focus to something else entirely by engaging in another activity – for example, exercise, deep breathing, eliminating all alcohol from his environment, keeping a picture of his children with him, having a brief conversation with a friend, or changing his physical environment to get a new perspective and to remind himself of where he wants to go and how drinking would not fit into that picture.

The pros and cons of substance use versus nonuse may help to inform service users in their decisions about next steps (Janis & Mann, 1977), as seen in Table 2.10 (Appendix 9). It is important for service users to know their options and make choices based on personal preferences. This can increase motivation and follow-through and build trust with the service provider for care planning.

Table 2.10 Decisional Balance: Daniel's Decisional Balance for Drinking Heavily

Pros of not engaging in the behavior:	Cons of not engaging in the behavior:
• Would be able to be there for his children • Better manage work • Save money • Better able to manage his challenges with mental health • Better for his physical and mental health	• Would not be able to temporarily forget about his problems • Would lose the social aspect of drinking • There is a risk of failure (again)
Pros of engaging in the behavior:	**Cons of engaging in the behavior:**
• Get away from his problems temporarily • More social with others • Feels good in the moment • Relaxes him	• Takes a toll on his physical health (weight gain) • Not able to function well for a while afterwards • Makes symptoms of the mental health challenge worse • Headaches • Safety of himself and others may be at risk • Seriously affecting his marriage

In the fourth stage, care planning related to co-occurring disorders is ideally the integration of treatment for MHCs and substance use disorders. Integration of treatment is an important element of care planning with this population to ensure that the various needs of a service user are addressed in a cohesive manner (Mueser & Drake, 2011).

In the fifth stage, the implementation of interventions can involve a combination of group therapy, motivational interviewing, cognitive behavior therapy, medication, housing, and more, while maintaining a focus on recovery goals.

It was becoming clearer to Daniel that eliminating drinking would remove some of the problems he was having. Jay worked with him to figure out the interventions that would be effective for him. A con of giving up drinking was that he would lose a social network. Joining a support group of people who were overcoming similar challenges, on the other hand, would exemplify that recovery is possible.

Daniel was hesitant because he did not want anyone else to know about his situation, but said he would try. Jay reassured Daniel that the group is confidential and that every participant would likely feel the same way he did.

Setting goals could motivate Daniel to focus on where he wants to be in the future. It was difficult to develop some of these goals because of the uncertainty Daniel faced about divorce. Nevertheless, he set goals to consistently attend work and increase his productivity back to levels of the past; better manage his finances with the help of a financial planner, where he would develop and keep to a budget to manage his debts; and maintain relationships with his children by sharing an experience with them every weekend. For every week that he attended the support group, he would reward himself with an evening where he would go on a drive with friends or have a nonalcoholic treat.

When monitoring service user participation and outcomes in stage six, it is important to identify which interventions are working, and which are not. This can be helpful to streamline or identify key ingredients that are bringing about change, so that efforts of the service user and service provider focus on interventions that work toward the goals of recovery (Mueser & Drake, 2011). Standardized and nonstandardized assessment tools can track progress. Nonstandardized tools can include journaling the frequency of urges to use substances, and strategies that are successful to avoid acting on such urges.

With the support of Jay, his close friends, and a sponsor from a 12-step program, Daniel was making strides in managing his challenges with mental health and his addiction. Daniel was able to work toward his goals and remain sober for 27 days. He experienced relapses, but the positive experiences he had with his children while sober were motivations to persevere. He accepted the relapses as a part of the recovery process – he saw it as a signal to somehow change and improve the skills and coping strategies he had for himself so there was less chance of relapse in the future. In line with an integrated therapeutic approach, Daniel received assistance with education on how to manage his finances, and continued to attend individual therapy for specific challenges. He saved the money that would otherwise have been spent on alcohol, to help manage his debts. He also put limits on money withdrawals and purchases on all of his credit and debit cards to avoid large, impulsive purchases. He continued to attend psychotherapy to improve his mood; however, he was not consistent in that. He was able to feel more joy when spending time with his family, which helped take his mind off drinking. His wife was not convinced that these changes were permanent, but tried to support him where she could.

Conclusion

Co-occurring or concurrent disorders are the combination of challenges with mental health and a substance use disorder. Ideally, care is to be cohesive and integrate elements that address both challenges. Six stages can be followed to identify and treat service users undergoing such challenges: screening, education, establishing personal preferences, care planning, implementation, and monitoring participation and outcomes (Mueser & Drake, 2011). Of note is the importance of person-centered care, which ensures that the service user's values and opinions remain central to the care plan and to the recovery process.

Adolescents

Monica is a 16-year-old female who has experienced psychosis for the first time. She is the second of four children, and her parents are extremely concerned about her. She has been distant from her family since she entered her teen years. She continuously argues with her parents, and looks to her friends for advice. She attended a party where she tried marijuana for the first time. Since then, she has been acting out at school and at home, and has begun to hear voices. She believes that she has special powers to know what other people are thinking. Her academic performance has declined, and she has had major fights with her group of friends. She is engaging in increasingly risky behaviors, including drinking and sexual activities, and shows a lack of awareness and insight.

Based on Monica's behaviors, her parents requested the service provider to assess her capacity. She was found to be incapable of making personal care decisions; therefore, these decisions were the responsibility of her parents. They decided to bring her to psychiatric emergency services, where she was admitted to hospital for additional support. A therapist, Josh, meets her, among others. She remains in the inpatient unit, where her parents visit her every day.

Between the ages of 15 and 24, the risk of a first episode of psychosis is relatively high. Early intervention programs are important to address addictions and psychotic and mood disorders (Amminger et al., 2006). Using PCA can be helpful to remain focused on the needs of the young service user and to encourage service user participation. This approach may facilitate a shift from precontemplation to contemplation as per the stages of change model (Prochaska et al., 1994) as described in the section "Co-occurring (Concurrent) Disorders." Working with adolescents is distinct from working with other age groups, in that adolescents rapidly continue to develop socially, cognitively, and emotionally throughout the clinical relationship (Fisman, 2011). Furthermore, discussing whether the adolescent service user is able to make care decisions, which may be at odds with those of the guardian(s), can pose additional challenges.

Capacity and Consent

In order for an adolescent to be able to take part in personal care decisions, they must be deemed to have the capacity to give consent to (or decline) care. *Capacity* involves the ability to understand the relevant information as well as appreciate the consequences of making a care decision (Health Care Consent Act, 1996). In situations of incapacity, the guardian or other appointed persons for informed consent make the decisions. This, however, may be in opposition to the principles of PCA, which leaves room for other considerations when assessing an adolescent's ability to provide informed consent. Consent can fall into four categories: *implied consent* (service user gets routine assessment), *presumed consent* (service user is unconscious and in need of emergency treatment), *substitute consent* (service user is not deemed capable, and an appointed person decides on their behalf), and *voluntary/competent/informed consent* (service user understands and appreciates the risks, benefits and consequences of receiving [or not receiving] care) (Health Care Consent Act, 1996).

Considerations such as the adolescent's level of cognitive development, emotional maturity, and even reading ability can inform a service provider's decision on whether an adolescent can provide informed consent. Respect for autonomy (independence), beneficence (do good), nonmaleficence (do no harm), and justice (fairness) are four ethical principles that can also be used to evaluate a person's ability to provide consent (Spencer, 2000). Additional factors to consider in the matter of consent include the notion that adolescents are aware of their autonomy, their right to make personal decisions, and their right to privacy with the service provider.

In some jurisdictions, there may be a minimum age in order to provide consent. Service providers must bear in mind that respecting the wishes of an adolescent can be counterproductive for the individual's overall ability to recover. As well, the adolescent's development can affect capacity, as the ability to make informed choices often matures in midadolescence (Thorne & Lambers, 1998). Family input may also be a consideration, although this can be at odds with the adolescent's autonomy.

"You can't keep me here! I should be able to choose if I want to be here or not!" Monica screams. She refuses to attend any group sessions or activities in the inpatient unit. She says that she will be leaving as soon as she possibly can, whether her parents know about it or not. She addresses Josh by saying, "I don't want to talk to you. Why should I? I know what you're thinking anyway."

"And what is that?" Josh responds.

"That my parents were right in bringing me to this hell hole, and that there's something wrong with me. Well, guess what? It's all of you who are messed up! I'm perfectly fine. I don't need you, or anybody."

Josh takes a pause, and then replies, "Well, there are some thoughts that I have which you may have missed. You are correct in saying that you have a choice as to whether you are going to remain on the unit or not. Your parents were very concerned about you and so they brought you here. The reason for your admission was that the physician thought that your safety was at risk and that you may not have been in the most effective state of mind to be making choices about your care. But you seem to be doing better now, and I think it's time that we have a conversation about the next steps. It is very important that you have a say in what happens, because, after all, it's all about you."

"So, tell me, Monica," he continues, "if there's anything that you want to get out of our time together, what would it be? Is there anything that is bothering you and/or that has been a challenge lately?"

"You, and my parents, obviously," Monica remarks.

"What is it that your parents are doing that is frustrating you?" Josh asks.

"What you are doing right now – assuming that something is wrong when it's not!" says Monica.

Adolescent Development

During the adolescent development period, three phases have been described to further elucidate the developmental changes that are occurring throughout adolescence (depending on the individual's rate of development): early adolescence (ages 12–15), midadolescence (14–18), and late adolescence (17 to maturity) (Fisman, 2011). Understanding these phases can help service providers recognize and address adolescent challenges and build a clinical relationship that is person-centered.

Typical development in the early phase involves physical growth as well as cognitive maturation from concrete operational to formal operational thinking, which allows for increased problem-solving abilities (Fisman, 2011). This allows adolescents to look to the future, and for some, to experience feelings of hopelessness. Erikson's stage of identity versus role confusion is apparent in this phase (Thorne & Lambers, 1998), where they begin to separate themselves to be an individual (Erikson, 1963). Depending on geography, culture, and other considerations, the influence of peers can play a role that can overshadow that of the family or guardians. In this phase, adolescents can experience confusion, impulsivity, and moodiness, which can manifest as rebellious behavior. In this phase, they may question the values and perspectives they currently hold. Service providers may observe in them, neediness, demanding behavior, and/or a lack of empathy or reciprocity. A service provider who is stable, consistent, and warm will likely be able to engage an early adolescent in care planning (Fisman, 2011).

Midadolescence involves new beliefs, values, and ideals; role models can be of influence (Fisman, 2011). The influence of peers may continue to overshadow that of the family or guardians. Argument and debate allows this group to express their sense of separation and independence while learning from others. There may be ongoing changes and uncertainty in terms of what an adolescent in this phase values. Self-examination or soul-searching, where the adolescent withdraws into their thoughts and reflections, is common. For midadolescents, it is important to respect the service user as an individual and, at the same time, demonstrate the service provider's own sense of separateness and individuality. A service provider needs to be more participatory in their conversations – the adolescent will be expecting to hear the service provider's views, personal values, and ideals. Service users can learn from the new perspectives of service providers, which may challenge the adolescent's viewpoints (Fisman, 2011).

Erikson's stage of intimacy versus isolation is apparent at the late adolescence stage. Identity in terms of moral, sexual, political, vocational, and other elements becomes clearer. The individual is better able to cooperate with others and deal with uncertainty. MHCs at this stage can increase feelings of isolation. In the late stage of adolescence, the service provider's approach will be typical of that for an adult. The individual fluctuates between the need for independence and reliance on others (Fisman, 2011).

"Okay. So school is fine. There are no problems with friends at school," Josh states.
Monica is silent.
Throughout this process, Josh was aware of the difficulties she was having, and kept in mind her family's wishes for her to remain in hospital until progress was made. "You know what I think? Even though you may feel that everything is okay, make the most out of your time here. It doesn't hurt to think about what you want in life, and how you're going to get it."
"What do you mean – what do you think I want?" Monica asks.

"That is something that only you can answer for yourself, but it could be anything from strengthening relationships with others, being captain of a sports team, improving grades, or having new experiences."

"And how would I do that exactly?" Monica wonders.

"Well, once you've figured out what you want to work toward, then if you want, I can help with breaking things down into manageable steps so that you can more easily reach your goals."

Monica stares at him, and then looks away. "I used to get along with my friends, and I was a pretty good student ... I don't know what happened."

To reach a place where all parties are working toward recovery, it can help service providers to remain person-centered by attending to adolescent service user needs and experiences, along with focusing on their goals. In Table 2.11 and Table 2.12, you can see how Monica journals her thoughts and feelings, and the roles of those in her social network (Appendix 10 & Appendix 11).

Table 2.11 Journaling What Is Important to You: Example of Monica Exploring Her Thoughts and Feelings Through Journaling

Monica enjoys writing. Josh encouraged her to think about and write down answers to these questions to get a better idea of how she feels, what is important to her, and what she envisions for herself. He assured her that he would not look at them, and that they were just for her to help establish goals that they would work on together. This template may clarify what is important to service users, which can help to identify goals and objectives to work toward.	
Rate, out of 10, how I am feeling and why.	4/10, I don't know what I am doing here or with my life, whether my friends are still there for me . . .
What do I want?	To be happy, have friends, do well in school, get along with my siblings and parents
Who do I want to be?	A good person — who cares for others; a leader — I want my voice to be heard
Whom do I look up to? Why?	My classmate, Taylor — she is pretty, confident, works hard, not afraid to say what she thinks
What do I value?	Connection with others, freedom, independence, trust, control
What do I believe?	Everything happens for a reason; I believe in myself and not what other people are telling me

Table 2.12 Social Network Roles: Example of Reflecting on the Roles of Others in Monica's Life

This exercise can be helpful to promote reflection to recognize roles that family and friends play in an adolescent's life.	
What my family provides or does for me that is unique	*Makes me food, provides a place to live with my own room, gives me an allowance*
What my friends provide or do for me that is unique	*New experiences, fun, support*
What only I can provide or do for myself	*Be strong, stay true to my opinions, self-esteem*

Monica decided that she would focus on doing better at school – her friends were important to her, but she was not sure if she could do anything to make them change their minds about their arguments. She also prided herself on doing well in school, and she wanted that to continue to be a part of her identity. While in the inpatient unit, she worked with Josh to figure out exactly what had changed – her ability to concentrate, organize, and understand information, along with distractions from the voices she hears. Together, they figured out solutions to address each of these challenges such as taking breaks during homework, developing an organizational system for her notes, and talking with her teachers and peers about the information itself to check her understanding of the material.

There were group sessions offered in the hospital that addressed how to manage the voices she heard while going about day-to-day activities, so those did not influence her thoughts and behaviors as easily. She was eventually discharged home to her family, where she attended outpatient care to manage the challenges with mental health through further skill development. This experience enabled Monica to develop a renewed sense of self as a resilient individual.

Conclusion

Adolescents experiencing MHCs are a distinct group in that they are simultaneously undergoing major physical, cognitive, social, and emotional development (Fisman, 2011). These changes can make service providers question whether these individuals are capable of providing consent for their own care, especially when respecting their need for autonomy is in conflict with other ethical principles of beneficence and nonmaleficence. Different developmental stages of adolescence may require different approaches to care. Service providers can engage young service users by addressing their needs, respecting them as individuals, and focusing on their goals, which aligns with person-centered care (Rudnick & Roe, 2011).

Dual Diagnosis

Adam is a 43-year-old man who meets the diagnostic criteria for autism spectrum disorder, level 1. This level describes individuals who require support and demonstrate inflexible behavior and difficulty with planning, organizing, and switching from one activity to another, which interferes with overall functioning. He is verbal, and has difficulties with social interactions with others. He has few friends and has difficulty initiating communication with others. He has sensory sensitivities to light, sound, and touch.

He also exhibits obsessive-compulsive symptoms with handwashing and preoccupations with cleanliness. He becomes easily agitated from changes in routine or the unexpected. He has also demonstrated inflexibility in his behavior, which may be seen as stubbornness.

He has also recently been diagnosed with schizoaffective disorder. He had a delusion of snakes in his living space that he has not had since. More often, he displays extreme anger toward everyone around him. He lives in the basement of his parent's house. He works as a car mechanic, which he enjoys. Adam was referred to outpatient mental health services after having a physical confrontation with a coworker. His workplace is aware that he is on the autism spectrum and has demanded that he address his anger with a counselor, Maria, before returning to work.

Dual diagnosis can refer to the condition where a person has a cognitive (developmental) disability, such as intellectual disability or autism, in addition to MHCs or behavioral challenges (Centre for Addiction and Mental Health, 2012). A developmental disability can be referred to as "significant limitations in cognitive functioning and adaptive functioning," which involve (a) "a person's intellectual capacity, including the capacity to reason, organize, plan, make judgments and identify consequences" and (b) "a person's capacity to gain personal independence, based on the person's ability to learn and apply conceptual, social and practical skills in his or her everyday life," respectively (Services and Supports to Promote the Social Inclusion of Persons with Developmental Disabilities Act, 2008, pp. 2–3). As well, a developmental disability typically originates before 18 years of age, persists throughout one's lifespan, and affects major life activities – for example, learning and language abilities. Note that some jurisdictions may refer to dual diagnosis as the co-occurrence of substance use with mental health challenges. This section will look at the former, including adaptation, information processing, and sensory modulation disorders, as well as psychiatric and social-environmental influences. The service provider when working with persons with a dual diagnosis may consider such factors. Those with cognitive impairments have a greater chance of experiencing mental health challenges (Menolascino, Levitas, & Greiner, 1986). This area of practice may be challenging, as there is a lack of agreement on the most effective methods of care, including assessment and intervention options.

Bradley and Burke (2002) outline four questions, asked in sequence, that service providers can think about to determine if there are MHCs in addition to a developmental disability:

- *Is there a medical issue?* This involves identifying if there are any untreated physical health ailments – for example, uncommunicated pain or discomfort that causes the individual to experience anger or to be easily frustrated.
- *Is there an issue with supports and appropriate expectations?* This question probes whether the assistance that the individual receives (from family, the service provider, the community) meets their needs, and/or it identifies what is missing to ensure that those needs are met.
- *Is there an emotional issue?* Emotional challenges can be brought on by events, whether internal (e.g., feelings of failure) or external (e.g., experiencing a loss). Various coping strategies can be used to manage such emotions; however, MHCs may be present if these strategies are not successful in adequately addressing the emotional challenges.
- *Is there a psychiatric disorder?* Providing a diagnosis of an MHC may be helpful to determine and narrow the range of treatment options. At the same time, there is no definitive guide for diagnosis of individuals with a developmental disability (Lunsky & Weiss, 2012).

Adaptation

Adaptation, as described above, requires efficient information processing, including accurately gathering and evaluating relevant information, making choices, evaluating results, and storing this information for the future. It is proposed that low frustration tolerance and difficulty modulating one's affect are due to the inability to adapt to internal and external environments (Leyro, Zvolensky, & Bernstein, 2010; Rao, 2011). As an example, changes in routine, noise, and interpersonal conflict may lead to and aggravate dysregulated behaviors. A person's experiences, social and environmental, can shape the ability to adapt to the environment. A person with a cognitive impairment may not have an optimal environment from which to acquire cognitive skills. Persons in this situation are more likely to experience stressors such as illness, separation due to hospitalization, uncommunicated pain, and negative school experiences. All of these factors can lead to a person's inability to adapt effectively to the environment.

Adam blamed others for what had happened to him. He was angry with his coworker for calling out his "mistake," and blamed his manager for making him take leave from work and undergo counseling sessions. He did not feel he had any reason to be there and thought that this was going to be a waste of his time, so he skipped the first few appointments. Once again, his manager told him that if he did not attend the sessions, he would not be able to return to work. At the time he spoke to his manager, again he was furious. After some time when he was calm, his parents spoke to him about what it would mean if he did not attend the sessions – he would lose his job, income, and may then have to find a new place of work with new people and routines. He enjoyed his job and disliked change, so after a week, he came around to the idea of attending sessions if that meant he could get back to work.

Information Processing

For those with cognitive impairments, a number of factors may hinder information processing. Attempts to avoid distress, discomfort, or pain, along with habitual thinking patterns, and life experiences can all influence how information is processed (Rao, 2011). Other influences include one's ability to problem solve and foresee consequences. Deficits in regulating behavior and emotions, along with difficulties in problem solving due to neurodevelopmental challenges, are also known as executive dysfunction. The added challenges with mental health and environmental or physical stressors may lead the individual to become dysregulated. See Table 2.13 for a breakdown of the manifestations that may result from various cognitive challenges (Appendix 12).

Table 2.13 Taking a Closer Look at Behaviors: Behaviors That May Be a Result of Cognitive Challenges

Observation of service user behaviors may help to identify aspects of cognition in which the service user may be having challenges. Identifying such aspects may guide care planning.	
If there are signs of	**They may be experiencing challenges with**
Difficulty perceiving or integrating experiences	Attention
	Sensations
	Problem-solving abilities
	Generalizing abilities
Disorganized behavior and perseverating on ideas	Flexibility of thought
	Sequencing
	Logic
Executive dysfunction or metacognition (inability to execute goal-directed, purposeful behavior by regulating behavior; Gioia, Isquith, & Guy, 1996; Rao & Hall, 2009) resulting in maladaptive behaviors – for example, aggression, perseveration, anxiety, and self-injury	Impulse control
	Managing frustration
	Judgment
	Memory
	Emotional dysregulation

Those with difficulties in modulating sensory input are at a higher risk of anxiety, depression, decreased confidence, and aggressive behavior. Sensory modulation disorders may be of three kinds (Schoen, Miller, Brett-Green, & Nielsen, 2007):

- Sensory overresponsivity (strong emotional reactions to stimuli which are not necessarily aversive – for example, sound, lights, or touch. Persons may have difficulty with attention, organizing behavior, and difficulty adapting to their environment).
- Sensory underresponsivity (less aware of the environment and is not motivated to seek stimulation, whether social or environmental).
- Sensory seeking (potentially reckless behavior to find experiences that fulfill the need for necessary stimulation).

Maria knew that working with individuals who have a dual diagnosis can be complex. She sought to understand Adam's way of thinking (which may be considered concrete), and how this affected his ability to problem solve. She also had to be careful to differentiate Adam's cognitive challenges, if any, from the symptoms of MHCs. She reminded herself that Adam's cognitive challenges are a consideration that they would both acknowledge and work with to address his day-to-day challenges. She recognized that ignoring his underlying cognitive challenges and focusing solely on challenges with mental health might not be fruitful. She had done this with a previous service user, and in retrospect, realized that he had become frustrated with counseling because she was asking him to reflect and execute cognitive processes that he was not equipped, or had not been taught, to handle. She made sure that she incorporated strategies that addressed these cognitive challenges, and gave him concrete ways to assess and evaluate information. This included ways of organizing the information around him so that he could process information accurately and take effective courses of action. She made a referral to a supported employment agency that provided ongoing on-the-job support.

Adam was extremely angry about the situation with his coworker. He told Maria a number of times that the coworker had deserved to be hit and that he did not know what his coworker was talking about. Maria noticed that it took Adam until the next session, or later, to consider various points of view that she had previously suggested. She recognized that he had limited flexibility in his thinking. When recounting details of this coworker interaction and previous events he had experienced at work or elsewhere, the details were not in any particular order. It was clear to Maria that Adam struggled with impulse control and had difficulty regulating his emotions. In the situations he described, he consistently responded quickly in anger, likely without thinking about the repercussions of his actions.

Biopsychosocial Influences: The Multifactor Approach

Personal and environmental factors – including school, work, social network, family, health status, and temperament – shape, and are shaped by, a service user's behavior (Frankenhaeuser, 1989; Rao, 2011). Social and environmental factors may trigger, modify, and maintain behaviors that are maladaptive to the situation at hand. The accumulation of challenging environmental factors and events may lead to a lack of effective adaptation to the environment. This maladaptation reveals itself through poor interpersonal relations, inability to cope, and personal challenges (Rao, 2011). Table 2.14 (Appendix 13) highlights the various elements that may be affecting Adam's situation and considers personal, environmental, and occupational elements as per Law et al. (1996).

Table 2.14 Multifactor Assessment of a Service User's Current Situation: Factors Including the Person, Environment, Occupation, Motivation, and Risks in Adam's Situation

A multifactor assessment for Adam would address the following, accounting for both strengths and challenges:	
Person	• Physical or biomedical: *celiac disease* • Cognitive: *challenges with perspective taking, emotion regulation, impulsivity* • Psychiatric: *schizoaffective disorder, obsessive–compulsive symptoms* • Developmental: *autism, level 1* • Affective: *anger, frustration, easily overwhelmed*
Environmental	• Social: *supportive parents* • Institutional: *currently accessing care, supportive work environment* • Cultural: *others have some awareness of his challenges* • Physical: *challenges with sounds, lights, and touch*
Occupational	• Self-care: *independent* • Productivity: *works as a mechanic; shares household responsibilities* • Leisure: *solitary activities — for example, reading*
Motivation	• *Selective motivation related to employment*
Risks	• *Impulsive behaviors* • *Aggression*

Note. Adapted from Law et al., 1996.

To address the cognitive challenges that Maria observed while working with Adam, she decided to incorporate a number of different strategies, both restorative (addressing the root of the challenge) and compensatory (working around or with the challenge). To address emotion regulation, she talked to Adam about identifying body sensations, which were physiological cues that he might be getting upset. After some discussion, they learned that he tended to have a rapid heartbeat and clenched his jaw during times of stress. Having him recognize these sensations might cue him to leave the situation in order to collect himself before addressing the issue (Lieb, Zanarini, Schmahl, Linehan, & Bohus, 2004).

Groups such as psychotherapy, mindfulness, or recreational groups were another option, where he could learn how to better manage his thoughts and emotions in a safe space (Hesselmark, Plenty, & Bejerot, 2014; Spek, Van Ham, & Nyklíček, 2013). Technologies that can elucidate facial expressions and tone of voice to understand how another person may be feeling can also be useful (Golan & Baron-Cohen, 2006).

For impulse control, she discussed counting to five before reacting to stressful situations. This would encourage him to take pause before acting, in order to have a more favorable result. For difficulties with sequencing and logic, writing down his thoughts on situations and challenges could help Adam organize and identify effective courses of action. Adam was encouraged to use a simple template (paper or electronic) with an ABC approach – that is, antecedents (causes of his feelings and thoughts, or what is happening from his perspective as well as from a different perspective), behaviors (what he does and/or wants to do, or why this is happening with at least two different explanations), and consequences (the results and expected results, or what may happen that includes at least one positive and one negative result for every action he is considering) (Schall, 2010).

To address inflexible or black-and-white thinking, Adam could use the template in Table 2.15 as a guide to gain insight into another person's perspective. Maria provided Adam with this template of short questions to help guide him through looking at a situation from another person's point of view (see blank version in Appendix 14).

Table 2.15 Understanding Another Person's Perspective: Example of Looking at Adam's Situation From a Different Perspective

When there is conflict with another person, it can be difficult to see the other person's point of view. The questions below can help to better understand an event, and the person(s) involved. The service provider can work through events with the service user.	
What was said?	Coworker said that he had made a mistake in a car's repairs.
Who said it?	Coworker who works as a mechanic, who has more years of experience than Adam does.
Where was it said?	In the garage, one other mechanic present but working on another repair. Manager was absent at the time.
When was it said?	A few days before customer pick-up.
Why was it said?	Repairs had to be fixed before customer returned to the shop.
What might the other person be thinking?	Coworker wants to ensure the repair is done correctly to avoid the customer being dissatisfied and having to return.
What might the other person be feeling?	Frustrated (e.g., may have been falling behind schedule, long day).
What is important to the other person?	Excellence, getting things right, customer satisfaction.
How might the other person behave?	Assertive or aggressive (e.g., delivery of tone, volume).

Maria discussed the fact that it can be quite a task for anyone to use these strategies in the moment. To start, she recommended thinking about and using these strategies before and after such events occurred. Reviewing these kinds of strategies – such as impulse control techniques – beforehand may help to avoid potentially challenging situations. She reminded him about getting in touch with the body sensations he was experiencing. This might help him to understand how he was feeling at that moment.

Reviewing strategies related to looking at another person's point of view, after he had calmed down from a challenging situation, could help to promote perspective taking and understanding the consequences of his choices.

Adam did not like the idea that he had to do all of this work to get his job back when his coworker was the problem. When he first worked with Maria, he thought that she was going to be against him – telling him that what he had done was wrong and that he needed to change his behavior. Instead, he found her to be understanding of his perspective, and she told him that his responses made sense, given the circumstances. She framed the strategies that they discussed as something that Adam could practice so that he would be less frustrated in general, rather than having to learn these strategies for others.

After discussing alternative ways of thinking about, and responding to, the incident at work, Maria wanted to ensure that Adam would be able to apply what they had talked about to future situations. She knew that it was important to discuss various circumstances so that Adam effectively managed different situations. This way, he would be able to think through effective responses ahead of time, rather than be in a situation that overwhelmed him, and where he returned to ineffective behaviors. They talked about how he could respond to scenarios where customers or his manager became frustrated or angry.

Similar prompts to the above exercise may support service users to determine the most effective approach when speaking with others.

Situation: A customer is angry about the cost of repairs that she had previously agreed to pay.

- What do I want to say? *"This is the cost that we had agreed to. If you still have concerns, you can speak to the manager."*
- How should I say it? *Stay calm. Even though the other person is angry, it does not mean I have to be angry too. Practice techniques to stay calm – for example, deep breathing, excuse myself from the conversation to control emotions.*
- Who am I speaking to? *Customer, and it is important that they are content with the service so that they return in the future.*
- Where am I going to say it? *Somewhere where there is privacy from other customers, which is not an overstimulating environment.*
- When should I say it? *I will address customer concerns as quickly as possible.*
- Why do I want to say it? *This is the agreement, and it is fair. I do not have the final say on pricing, so talking to the manager would be more appropriate.*

Integrated models in mainstream psychiatric units, where there are areas allocated specifically to persons with dual diagnoses (as opposed to mainstream units without specialist care or specialist units for dual diagnosis) generate more positive experiences from service users. In this setting, learning disability professionals who specialize in this domain provide the services. Service users have reported feeling less vulnerable and less fearful, while having an increased understanding of their prescriptions to manage their MHCs (Venville, Sawyer, Long, Edwards, & Hair, 2015).

Intervention approaches may address a number of challenges that a service user with a dual diagnosis faces. An interdisciplinary team may be effective for comprehensive care for those with a dual diagnosis (Harris, 1999). Similar to approaches to other populations, developing a clinical relationship based on trust, showing interest in the service user, strategies for communication, validating the feelings and commitments of service users' experiences, and empowering service users are of value to those accessing support (Stenfert Kroese, Rose, Heer, & O'Brien, 2013). O'Brien and Rose (2010) point out the desire for individuals to have a sense of control in their own lives, and at the same time, acknowledge that outside support is sometimes necessary. Therefore, having a sense of autonomy along with support systems in place may facilitate success toward recovery goals. Stigma, which is pervasive across mental health challenges, continues to play a role in the lives of service users; interventions in care planning ought to point out the limitations of systems and of society, which are no fault of service users (Jahoda, Wilson, Stalker, & Cairney, 2010).

Conclusion

When working with an individual who has a dual diagnosis, that is, a cognitive or developmental disability along with mental health challenges, it is important to take an integrated care approach to address both the symptoms of mental health challenges and the developmental disability. Doing so may allow for more effective care planning. Identifying key elements of cognitive challenges can lead to the implementation of strategies that may improve service user adaptation and information processing to challenges.

Forensic Care

Mike is a 52-year-old man who has been diagnosed with schizophrenia since his twenties. He shares an apartment with another man. He recently discontinued taking his psychotropic medication; he did this in the past on occasion, despite what everyone had told him about managing his hallucinations and delusions. A part of him felt as though these experiences were telling him important things and providing more insight into the world around him. In addition, he did not think he needed his medications as much as he had when he was younger. His delusions have been typically of a sexual nature, where he imagined that he was having physical relations with aliens. He had a recurrence of hallucinations and delusions that involved his neighbor, which made him think that she was interested in him sexually. He experienced hallucinations of her voice suggesting to him that he should invite himself to her apartment. He responded by forcefully entering her apartment and touching her inappropriately and was charged with sexual assault. He was found not guilty by reason of insanity (NGRI) and not criminally responsible (NCR) because he was actively experiencing MHCs at the time of the event and he was acting based on these experiences. He was subsequently admitted to the forensic psychiatry system where he is working with the rehabilitative team for an extended period before reintegrating back into the community.

The forensic psychiatry system provides care to individuals who have had encounters with the judicial system in relation to MHCs and who therefore have court orders to receive mental health care (Mejia & Vandevooren, 2011). Systems are in place in the UK, the US, and Canada, as well as other countries, so that criminal behavior related to MHCs are not penalized; instead, the person receives care with safety measures for the public. The care received may or may not be in line with PCA. For an individual to have been guilty of a criminal offense but found NGRI and/or to be considered NCR for an action, the MHCs of that individual must have impacted the person to the point where they lacked the capacity to appreciate the consequences of the criminal behavior or lacked the knowledge that it was wrong (Bloom & Schneider, 2006). It is widely held that the MHCs must have been present at the time of offense for an NGRI or NCR ruling to be relevant.

Mike worked with a team of service providers, including Mona, a social worker. The team carried out various assessments to get a clearer picture of Mike's situation, challenges, needs, strengths, and abilities. In terms of treatment, the priority was educating Mike on the importance of adherence to his psychotropic medication. Additionally, skills training was another option for Mike to further develop social skills, manage stress (which exacerbated his symptoms), and identify coping strategies to better manage his health challenges. Mike strongly desired to return to his place of residence, but did not show signs of remorse or any understanding of the consequences of his actions.

The forensic psychiatry service where Mike was admitted was a secure unit, which had locked doors to get in and out and cameras at the entrance doors. His room door was locked at certain times. He had access to a yard if he wanted to go outside. The hospital was of a newer design and the organizational structure adhered to PCA within the limitations of security measures.

Forensic psychiatry services address the MHCs of individuals who come into contact with the law. The goal of these programs is the safe reintegration of individuals back into the community; to that end, MHCs are addressed to the point that the risks of reoffending are manageable in the community (Weinstock, Leong, & Silva, 1998). As expected, those in the forensic psychiatry system demonstrate similar MHCs, symptoms, and functional impairments to those with MHCs in the general mental health system, suggesting that they require similar approaches to care, including treatment, rehabilitation, and support to facilitate their recovery (Menditto, 2002). Psychiatric rehabilitation or psychosocial rehabilitation (PSR) is person-centered and focuses on recovery, skills, and supports development for service users to be successful in the community. However, limitations within the forensic psychiatry setting include security concerns, organizational culture of public safety first, and the use of behavioral control. The focus is on assessment and risk monitoring in this practice setting. Despite these practical limitations, the concept of positive risk management is in line with PCA and involves the following elements: collaboration between the service user and service provider, a trusting clinical relationship, a focus on recovery, using service user strengths, individualized approaches, the possibility of change in risk levels over the course of care, and an interprofessional approach (Department of Health, 2007).

PCA in the forensic psychiatry setting focuses on an individualized approach that emphasizes the lowest level of restrictive measures needed to maintain safety rather than applying stringent measures for all persons, regardless of individual characteristics (Mejia &

Vandevooren, 2011). Service users are typically first admitted to medium security environments, which may put limits on service user self-determination and autonomy. Despite these limitations, there is much room for service users to practice choice within these settings. Service providers must familiarize themselves with service users and their interests to determine the security setting and goals for care planning for each individual.

Care constantly shifts based on the needs of the service user – for example, from not being ready for care; to an awareness of MHCs and offense(s); to setting self-care, productivity, and leisure goals for reintegration into the community. Other components that staff may focus on include relapse prevention, psychotherapy, and facilitating adaptive coping strategies. It is important that service users be active participants in care, as they will be primarily responsible for themselves when reentering the community.

Trauma-Informed Care

Trauma may be defined as "the often debilitating symptoms that many people suffer from in the aftermath of perceived life-threatening or overwhelming experiences" (Levine, 2008). When an individual faces a threat, they may engage in a fight, flight, or freeze response. In both fight and flight, the sympathetic nervous system is activated, preparing the body either to face the threat head-on or to escape from the source of perceived danger. This is characterized by high energy and emotion where there may be panic or rage, increased sensation, and hypervigilance. In the case of a freeze response, the parasympathetic nervous system response is blunted. Also known as hypoarousal, sensations and emotions are numbed, along with the slowing of some cognitive processes.

According to Levine (1997), trauma may occur when an individual is trapped in a fight, flight, or freeze response. In other words, the energy in the body that is generated to deal with the threat goes undischarged. Manifestations of this undischarged energy left over from hyperarousal during or after the threat may appear as constriction (attention and energy resources are focused on the threat only), dissociation (or denial or distortions where there is a lack of presence or consciousness in one's environment due to being overwhelmed), and/or immobility (inability to move or feel when there may be too much energy in the body to discharge).

Symptoms of trauma may be seen in the small bouts of undischarged energy that are released systematically, which can occur days, months, and years after the event. These symptoms may present in the form of flashbacks, hypervigilance, light and sound sensitivity, exaggerated startle responses, increased levels of stress from daily events, rage, difficulty sleeping, panic attacks, avoidance, attraction to danger, shame, amnesia, lack of connection with others, fear of dying, shyness, muted emotions, chronic fatigue, endocrine dysfunction and pain, depression, detachment, isolation, crying, and more.

The challenge arises when one continues to discharge the energy in a seemingly negative manner, which does not allow all of the energy to be discharged. Thus, the energy continues to be released in this way, and the individual's day-to-day functioning may be compromised.

In brief, to support individuals with traumatic experiences, the service provider needs to ensure that the service user is regulated and in a state to participate in therapy. This involves observing the individual for their verbal and nonverbal cues. With these observations, the service provider supports the service user in becoming attuned to their own body sensations. This way, individuals are increasingly able to watch these sensations and distinguish them from the traumatic memories. Working through feelings such as blame, anger, or grief, and finding support in one's own community or social network is another step toward healing trauma (Levine, 2008).

Another key to healing trauma is for an individual to be flexible about what they remember about the event. Individuals may become fixated on the events that occurred, which makes it difficult to move beyond the event. Instead, individuals are encouraged to use positive experiences from the past as resources to gain strength and perspective on the threatening event. When working with a service provider trained in trauma-informed care, by discussing the event and weaving experiences of strength into the narrative, service users may be able to discharge the energy from the body in a progressive manner, which may occur as shaking; sweating; tingling; bodily movements to complete the fight, flight, or freeze response; and more. Comforting memories, when associated with the difficult memories of the past, highlight one's strength, connectedness, and resourcefulness in spite of the difficult experience (Levine, 1997). For more on trauma-informed care, the works of Peter Levine, Gabor Maté, Bessel van der Kolk and others have illuminated this area of mental health.

Mona obtained additional training in trauma-informed care, which she found to be an asset, if not a necessity, when working in the forensic setting. She found that many of those admitted to the units had previously experienced traumatic events that affected their day-to-day functioning. Mona thought that Mike was no exception.

Mona spoke to Mike further, and with time, they discovered that Mike had had traumatic experiences involving physical and sexual abuse from a relative as a child. He had not shared these experiences with many people, and he did not receive formalized supports for these experiences. When Mike spoke of these events, he could not recall much of what had happened, aside from a few memories – the shadows of the relative approaching him with various objects; the sensation of suffocation and hiding in his parent's closet. His eyes were wide as he gripped his seat when recounting these events to Mona.

Mona worked with Mike to release the energy that had remained in his body from after these events to this day. She and Mike discovered other memories, even if they were not connected to the events themselves, where he had felt a sense of power, strength, and a feeling of being cared for. Memories of being held by his grandmother, triumphantly outrunning his dad, and a fuzzy childhood blanket were all memories that had comforted him as a child or gave him a sense of mastery.

There were many moments in the process where Mike was shaking, he lost color in his face, and when Mona thought he would get up and run out of his seat. Mona continuously encouraged him to be flexible about his memories of the trauma so that, alongside the troubling memories, he could draw upon those memories that gave him a sense of refuge, comfort, and strength. With time and effort, Mike was able to recall his experiences without the fear and dissociation that had previously gripped him. This was a huge turning point in his care in the unit.

Mike's realization of his actions became clear, and he went through a period of depression. He would not finish his meals, engage with staff or other residents in the facility, or participate in recreational activities, and he would sleep for most of the day. He had also lost his drive to move back to his apartment. After weeks of little progress at the facility, Mona began to ask him if there was something else he had on his mind with which the team could support him. "I'm a terrible person," he told her. She assured him that the challenges with mental health and his own traumatic experiences were the underlying reason for the events that had taken place and that, using the supports offered at the facility and by the rehabilitative team, he could acknowledge and learn from what had occurred, and move forward in his life. Mona emphasized that what Mike was dealing with would be challenging for many to handle. It was a sign that not only was he in remission from challenges with mental health, but that he was taking responsibility for what had occurred and that he could continue rehabilitation with the team when he felt ready.

Mike felt guilty about everything that had transpired over the recent past. Similar to his own history of trauma, he recalled some of the events with his neighbor, but not others. Now having realized the impact he may have had on his neighbor, he did not see himself moving on from what had happened, nor did he see a future for himself, so he remained alone in his room in the unit for weeks. Although Mona told him that the way he was feeling could be seen as a sign of progress, he was unable to accept this for some time.

Over time, though, he recognized that acknowledging his own actions was better than being aloof, as he had been previously. He was now able to "own up" to what had happened, and he could better understand his hallucinations and actions. Although there was nothing that he could do to change the past, he began to see the rest of his life as a blank slate where he could choose whatever he wanted for the future. Living in the secure unit for the rest of his life was not something that he wanted for himself, so he increasingly began to take steps to play a more active role in directing the course of his life.

After some more time had passed, Mike became more and more involved with the various services on the unit, such as cooking and outdoor activities in the yard with the recreational therapist. The staff learned that he had a passion for cooking, and they encouraged this interest by enabling him to co-lead a small culinary class with staff for the other residents. He was, after some time, moved to a minimum-security unit. Table 2.16 lists the questions that Mona asked Mike that might direct his next steps (Appendix 15).

Table 2.16 Working Toward Your Goals: Example of Exploring Mike's Goals

Service users, after understanding the implications of their actions that are deemed criminal offenses, may find it challenging to redirect themselves away from past behaviors and focus, rather, on behaviors that are conducive to setting and reaching their life goals. The following are questions to reorient service users to focus on what they can presently do to address their current situations.	
What have you learned and discovered from your current situation?	I learned that it is best to remain on medication to manage the hallucinations and to go to therapy to talk about what I am feeling and release any pent-up energy in my body.
Where would you like to see yourself in the future (related to goals)?	I have really developed a knack for cooking. It feels good to be able to make others happy while doing something that I enjoy. I would like to do this for a living.
What strategies can help to keep you on track toward your goals?	I may have to go to culinary school, get on-the-job experience at a restaurant, or volunteer somewhere. I can keep practicing where I am now and try out new recipes that I create.

Arranging supports in the community and managing activities of daily living may be helpful for fulfilling service user goals and decreasing risk of reoffending. A community forensic psychiatry outreach team may play an important role in this domain (Mejia & Vandevooren, 2011). Supportive family involvement, where available, is integral to PSR. Risk management in the community involves addressing a person's protective factors, particularly those factors that help to eliminate or at least reduce the risk of reoffending, such as people, activities, places, and other supports.

Mona ensured that she had open and honest communication with Mike. She knew that she had to report her observations to the review board for them to make a decision about his eventual discharge. After 17 months, Mike was conditionally discharged to the community. He was not able to return to his old apartment; he moved into a halfway home with supportive staff where he could continue to retrain himself in effectively coping with schizophrenia and the events that transpired while returning to the community. Mike's protective factors (e.g., strengths, coping strategies, supports) included contact with the outreach team staff and Mona, having a space to cook meals for himself and others which provided him with a sense of purpose, going for walks in the community to gain new perspective and to connect with nature, and recently, working part-time as a line cook at a restaurant.

Conclusion

Service providers striving to practice person-centered care while working in the area of forensic psychiatry face the challenge of balancing this approach with the limitations that secured units have to maintain the safety of other service users, staff, and the public at large. Trauma-informed care may be a component of PCA that requires special attention in this population. Still, there is room for service users to have autonomy in their lives by working on their goals and pursuing their interests while living in these facilities, which may lay a foundation before reentry into the community. Community outreach teams and other protective factors can help service users reduce the risk of reoffending, while building a life that provides meaning and purpose.

Older Adults

Rania is an 86-year-old woman who has been diagnosed with depression. She uses a walker for short distances and a wheelchair for longer distances. Her husband died four years ago, and her health has been on the decline since then. She has diabetes and diabetic retinopathy. She also has osteoarthritis in her hands and knees. Rania shows signs of mild cognitive impairment. She experienced a stroke three years ago which mildly affected the left side of her body. Since then, she has not been able to live on her own, so she and her family decided that living in a long-term care home would be best for her. She recently voiced thoughts of suicide, so the long-term care facility referred her to psychiatric emergency services where she was admitted to a mental health unit. There, she was met by a team of health care professionals, including a social worker, Stephen, an occupational therapist, Tina, and a psychologist, Jade.

With the aging population increasing around the world, it is important to understand ways in which to address MHCs of this population, as older adults are at a greater risk for having MHCs (World Health Organization, 2016). This section will address older adults who have MHCs and their experiences with frailty and comorbidities, despair, and suicide. Aging may be considered from a biopsychosocial perspective, where biological, psychological, social, existential/spiritual, and other environmental elements all play a role in the aging process; for those at-risk for suicide, such challenges may be more effectively addressed by a health care team (Canadian Coalition for Seniors' Mental Health, 2006; Fried & Walston, 2003; Heisel & Duberstein, 2016). This perspective lends itself to a multidimensional approach to address the many challenges that service users experience.

Geropsychology is a field that looks at the training, research, and clinical service provision of older adults (American Psychological Association, 2011). The field looks to support older adults and their families to achieve maximal physical, cognitive, and emotional wellness, as well as to address challenges as they arise. Older adults have unique challenges in the advanced stages of life, including higher rates of MHCs, bereavement, loss (of function, their home, etc.), health concerns, lack of independence, and more. Geropsychologists have specialized knowledge of the aging process to provide the support needed in this phase of life (American Psychological Association, 2011).

The attitude of the service provider is important to consider, in addition to the method of care (Portner, 2008). Skilled health care professionals who maintain a strengths-based approach to PCA, and incorporate social, physical, and intellectual activities, can assist in the enhancement or maintenance of cognitive abilities. Focusing on what the service user is able to do and understand can help provide a constructive perspective on the situation.

Jade took Rania in her wheelchair to a quiet space where they could discuss Rania's challenges. Rania weighed less than 100 pounds. She appeared frail to Jade – with a cautious and unbalanced gait, slight tremors, generalized weakness, and apparent confusion at times. Upon speaking with Rania, Jade witnessed that Rania was thinking about ending her life. Jade also witnessed Rania's confusion of people trying to steal her possessions, which were to go to her children after her death. Jade assured her that her belongings in the hospital and in the long-term care facility were safely stored away. Jade incorporated physical retraining to address the physical components of Rania's condition. Improving or maintaining her physical abilities might help address some of the psychological challenges that Rania was facing – such retraining could boost feelings of confidence and self-efficacy. As well, social interactions could provide her with new perspectives on her situation.

Despite the limitations that Rania experienced, Jade highlighted to her that she had a number of strengths, including a caring family, positive memories from her life with her spouse, and a supportive living environment that met her current needs and offered activities and socializing that was near to her family. After speaking with Rania for some time, she also noticed her quick wit, which she highlighted as a great trait to have.

Frailty may be considered a physiological state where individuals are highly vulnerable to poor health, and which may include falls, emotional dependency, physical disability, and a need for long-term care (Fried, Ferrucci, Darer, Williamson, & Anderson, 2004). This state may be due to a weakening or dysregulation of a number of internal systems. Thus, the individual is less able to tolerate adversities such as disease, environmental stressors, and injury. Frailty, as it progresses, is more easily observed through a lack of function, changes in behavior, and biological markers. Frailty may be the accumulation of physiological losses that are not clinically significant separately but are disruptive when they accumulate. Service users may exhibit characteristics such as wasting (of muscle and body mass) and decreased strength, endurance, balance, mobility, cognitive ability, performance, and activity (Ferrucci et al., 2004; Fried & Walston, 2003). Service users may not participate in the activities that they previously enjoyed because of their loss of physical and/or cognitive abilities. They may also feel a sense of loss of their previous abilities, which can lead to feelings of hopelessness and despair. Frailty may be a contributing factor to MHCs, and/or a reaction to them.

Making environmental adaptations to the hospital and home environment, as much as possible, to accommodate the service user's physical and cognitive challenges may be beneficial. Such modifications can range from rearranging the setup for ease of use of adaptive equipment in the available space, to posting reminder notes on the wall to compensate for cognitive decline (or use smartphone prompts), and more. These changes, as simple as they may sometimes be, can have a big impact on a service user's ability to maintain a sense of autonomy throughout the day. Additionally, promoting socialization is important to give a sense of connectedness with others, especially if relationships dwindle in number with age.

Physical safety was another important consideration in Rania's situation. Rania would hide items in hard-to-reach areas of her room, which put her at a greater risk for falls when she reached for them. Jade told her that when she did not take her medications, she was putting herself at further risk for injury, in addition to psychological distress. Rania grew tired of Jade speaking to the importance of taking medication, and said that she would resume taking it if she stopped talking about it, as "either way, it doesn't make a difference." Based on Rania's response, Jade needed to ensure that she was providing care that was person-centered in order for Rania to feel as though she had a stake in her own life. Jade revisited her approach to ensure it was nondirective, which would empower Rania while maintaining compassion for her. Jade also recognized that it must be difficult for someone to listen to and depend on other people after being independent for so long. So with Rania, they adapted her environment so that she could be as independent as possible. For Jade, this step was critical to ensure that Rania felt involved, if not the lead, in managing her health. Working with Tina, they incorporated changes such as having a calendar to orient her to the day of the week, and keeping her personal items close to her so that she was not concerned about others taking them. Tina also discussed strategies for readying herself in the morning – for example, dressing and grooming while remaining in bed, by planning the night before.

Tina also encouraged Rania to take part in any of the activities that were taking place in the unit. This was difficult, as most of the activities were not of interest, or there were physical accessibility challenges that seemed to be getting in the way. Rania had an interest in knitting and baking; however, there was no knitting group and navigating the kitchen with her mobility equipment was difficult. Still, Tina said that they would work around the health challenges that Rania faced that impeded her ability to bake. Together, they decided it would be most effective to have Rania combine ingredients that were on a table height that was accessible from her wheelchair. She would then pass the mixtures to other residents in the unit to bake in the oven. She enjoyed being in the kitchen – something that she could not do in the long-term care home – along with socializing with the other bakers.

Wisdom and Despair

Erikson's theory of human development across the lifespan addresses the stage of integrity versus despair during later life. In this stage, the idea of death prompts one to reflect back on one's life as a success or a failure. Aging individuals often reflect on life's meaning (Jung, 1933). Frankl (1985) discusses the notion that death prompts one to seize life's opportunities and create meaning beyond the psychological and physical. Examples of where one may derive meaning are through relationships, activities, and one's outlook (Frankl, 1985). The research of Heisel and Flett (2016) highlights the importance of *meaning in life* in potentially protecting against suicide risk in older adults. A positive resolution of this stage involves satisfaction with one's life and a sense of wisdom. Alternatively, despair may manifest as fearing death, depression, or the sentiment that life was too short.

An additional stage of Erikson's theory, the *oldest-old*, for those typically age 85 and beyond, highlights unique challenges of loss pertaining to function and autonomy (Erikson, Erikson, & Kivnick, 1986). Individuals revisit the previous stages while reflecting on the lives they lived. This may involve coming to terms with the less desirable outcomes at each stage as more apparent, e.g., recognizing increased mistrust, guilt, and isolation in their lives at this advanced age. Success in this ninth stage culminates in *gerotranscendence*, which involves a newfound understanding of dimensions of the cosmos or the universe, the self, and personal relationships (Tornstam, 1994). The life cycle then comes full circle, and a deeper understanding of concepts such as hope, purpose, and love may lead to greater wisdom. Of note is that many of those in an advanced age are accepting of the physical and cognitive changes that become a part of their day-to-day lives and use compensatory strategies to accommodate for overall functioning (Baltes & Baltes, 1990; Moody, 2009).

> Jade wanted to find out what was making Rania feel the way she did. She learned that Rania had four children and nine grandchildren, some of whom were close by. She enjoyed seeing them, when they were free to visit her. Although she admitted that it was easier residing in supported living, she was frustrated with her situation and with the reality that she was less able to function independently than she had been before. This, combined with her partner's death, contributed to feelings of hopelessness. She ceased to take her medication; this has brought about troubling behaviors that the long-term care home found difficult to handle. She did not see a point to living, as she felt like a burden on others. She felt pathetic in that she was not able to act on her desires, because of her functional decline.

Life Review

Care plans support service users who are at an advanced age and help service providers care for them. One such care plan intervention is the life review (Haight, Michel, & Hendrix, 1998). Going through a life review may reduce depression and hopelessness and increase life satisfaction in the long term.

The service provider asks a number of questions to gather information on the service user's life. Over the course of their meetings, the service provider collects information about the service user's life experiences, both positive and negative, as they relate to family, home, childhood, adulthood, and the service user's life as a whole. The significance of these events is explored to promote a newfound understanding of the service user's life. A physical copy of the accounts, whether in text, images, or a mix of various media can be helpful to remind service users of experiences, or to review as a coping strategy. Involving family in this process can be useful to obtain additional materials to personalize the life review.

Note that caution is required when exploring a life review, as it is a therapeutic intervention that demands sensitivity. As mentioned, individuals may have had positive and fulfilling life experiences as well as difficult, negative, or even traumatizing experiences. Sensitivity is paramount throughout a life review as it may remind the individual of losses, feelings of guilt, abuse, and/or other painful experiences that could actually elicit risk for suicide. Therefore, training and supervision of providers offering this service are recommended.

> Jade, in collaboration with Stephen, gathered information about Rania's life experiences to get a clear picture of her milestones, accomplishments, and things that were important to her. With Rania's permission, Stephen contacted her family to learn about some of Rania's experiences and to obtain any items that held significance for her to add to the life review. In Table 2.17, some questions for a life review are provided (Appendix 16).

Table 2.17 Life Review: Example of Rania's Life Review

Service users in older adulthood may be asked these and other questions to glean their life experiences and promote reflection. Keep the individual situation of the service user in mind to ensure this exercise is beneficial, rather than unproductive or even triggering. The following are a sample of questions that could be asked:	
Tell me about a pleasant memory that you hold close to you.	I've had a good, full life. Lots to choose from. One of the best memories is the birth of every child and grandchild. I feel at peace every time I think about it.
Describe how you met your life partner or close friend.	Jade did not ask this question given Rania's circumstances.
What is your most treasured childhood memory?	When I would be playing outside with my brothers and sisters, and then we would all run home before the sun went down.
If you could pass along advice to your children, grandchildren, and/or younger self, what would it be?	I would tell them to forgive often, love with all your heart, and to remember to be grateful for what they've got.

> Jade reflected on the experiences that Rania had discussed, and she consistently acknowledged Rania's perspectives on her situation. Over time, Rania began to feel more understood by Jade, and Rania became comfortable sharing personal reflections and thoughts. It became increasingly apparent that Rania had experienced a number of losses throughout her life for which she showed strong emotion – loss of family members, including a child at an early age, her spouse, her health, independence, and more. Rania expressed the idea that she did not want to continue to live as her abilities continued to slip away beyond her control. With Rania's current view of how her life had unfolded, the recounting of some of these experiences was quite painful for her. Jade was consistent in her positive regard and compassion with Rania, and together, through their clinical relationship, Rania recognized that although there were elements of her life that seemed to be slipping away from her, there was also much to be grateful for. She practiced giving the experiences that pained her less significance; she realized that by giving so much of her energy to circumstances that she had no control over, she remained powerless in her own life. So, instead she looked at her situation more objectively. She

practiced watching her thoughts more and more instead of identifying with them. This newfound sense of gratitude in her life, in spite of her losses, helped Rania to approach life from a new perspective.

Using a number of different approaches proved to be useful for Rania. Through sessions with Jade, she was better able to recognize when thoughts of worry or despair entered her mind, and she also maintained and even made slight improvements in physical and cognitive abilities. She developed a greater sense of possibility and understanding of her place in the world, and showed less depressive symptoms and was increasingly involved in activities held in the hospital unit. Her family noticed positive changes in her as well. These changes persisted upon her return to the long-term care facility, where, despite many limitations, she showed an invigorated sense of self.

Conclusion

A biopsychosocial approach can help service providers understand the numerous challenges that older adults experience. This approach can be useful to inform care planning to address biological, psychological, social, and other environmental barriers and issues, such as frailty, despair, lost relationships, and the need to maintain a sense of autonomy despite these changes. A life review may be helpful to address depressive symptoms and increase a sense of what is possible. Employing multiple approaches to the care of older adults facilitates person-centered care and may lead to increased contentment of service users at this advanced stage of life.

Chapter Conclusion

Person-centered approaches can be incorporated into a wide variety of mental health settings and with numerous populations. Key tenants of person-centered care may involve, but are not limited to, rapport building with the service user; assessment of the service user's mental health challenges, barriers, and goals; educating service users and their informal supports as needed; addressing the service user's values, preferences, and experiences; supporting service users in their goals toward recovery; and collaborating to select and implement care that is the most effective fit for the service user. Implementation of PCA across mental health services and other health care settings can be beneficial in a number of ways. Adopting such methods may reduce the "revolving door syndrome" where service users return to access acute care. Service users may be more satisfied with service providers who use PCA to care planning. Future work should continue to incorporate the service user perspective on care to inform clinical practice.

Acknowledgements

We would like to acknowledge all of the contributors to the previous book (Rudnick & Roe, 2011), along with the feedback of Dr. Marnin Heisel on the topic of older adults.

References

American Psychological Association. (2011). *Geropsychology: It's your future!* Retrieved from https://www.apa.org/pi/aging/resources/geropsychology

Amminger, G. P., Harris, M. G., Conus, P., Lambert, M., Elkins, K. S., Yuen, H. P., & McGorry, P. D. (2006). Treated incidence of first-episode psychosis in the catchment area of EPPIC between 1997 and 2000. *Acta Psychiatrica Scandinavica, 114*(5), 337–345. https://doi.org/10.1111/j.1600-0447.2006.00790.x

Appelbaum, P.S. (1991). Advance directives for psychiatric treatment. *Hospital Community Psychiatry, 42*, 983–984. https://doi.org/10.1176/ps.42.10.983

Avruch, K. (1998). *Culture & conflict resolution* (Vol. 31). Washington, DC: US Institute of Peace Press.

Baltes, P. B., & Baltes, M. M. (1990). Psychological perspectives of aging: The model of selective optimization and compensation. In P. B. Baltes & M. M. Baltes (Eds.), *Successful aging: Perspectives from the behavioral sciences* (pp. 1–34). New York, NY: Cambridge University Press. https://doi.org/10.1017/CBO9780511665684.003

Beutler, L. E., Machado, P. P., & Neufeldt, S. A. (1994). Therapist variables. In A. E. Bergin & S. L. Garfield (Eds.), *Handbook of psychotherapy and behavior change* (4th ed., pp. 229–269). New York, NY: Wiley.

Bloom, H., & Schneider, R. D. (Eds.). (2006). *Mental disorder and the law: A primer for mental and legal health professionals* (pp. 121–124). Toronto, ON: Irwin Law.

Bradley, E. & Burke, L. (2002). The mental health needs of persons with developmental disabilities. In D. M. Griffiths, C. Stavrakaki, & J. Summers (Eds.), *Dual diagnosis: An introduction to the mental health needs of persons with developmental disabilities* (pp. 45–79). Sudbury, ON: Habilitative Mental Health Resource Network.

Canadian Coalition for Seniors' Mental Health. (2006). National Guidelines for Seniors' Mental Health: The assessment of suicide risk and prevention of suicide. *Canadian Journal of Geriatrics, 9*(2), S65–S70.

Center for Substance Abuse Treatment. (2004). *Substance abuse treatment and family therapy*. Treatment Improvement Protocol (TIP) Series No. 39. Rockville, MD: Substance Abuse and Mental Health Services Administration.

Center for Substance Abuse Treatment. (2005). *Substance abuse treatment for persons with co-occurring disorders*. Treatment Improvement Protocol (TIP) Series, No. 42. Washington, DC: Substance Abuse and Mental Health Services Administration.

Centre for Addiction and Mental Health. (2012). *Dual diagnosis*. Retrieved from http://www.camh.ca/en/hospital/health_information/a_z_mental_health_and_addiction_information/dual_diagnosis/Pages/default.aspx

Charles, C., Gafni, A., & Whelan, T. (1997). Shared decision-making in the medical encounter: What does it mean? (Or it takes at least two to tango). *Social Science & Medicine, 44*, 681–692. https://doi.org/10.1016/S0277-9536(96)00221-3

Coatsworth-Puspoky, R., Forchuk, C., & Ward-Griffin, C. (2006). Nurse–client processes in mental health: Recipients' perspectives. *Journal of Psychiatric and Mental Health Nursing, 13*, 347–355. https://doi.org/10.1111/j.1365-2850.2006.00968.x

Copeland, M. E. (1997). *Wellness recovery action plan*. Brattleboro, VT: Peach Press.

Department of Health, National Risk Management Programme. (2007). *Best practice in managing risk: Principles and evidence for best practice in the assessment and management of risk to self and others in mental health services*. London, UK: Author.

Desjardins, N., Gritke, J., & Hill, B. (2011). Trans-cultural issues in person-centered care for people with serious mental illness. In A. Rudnick & D. Roe (Eds.), *Serious mental illness: Person-centered approaches* (pp. 99–115). London, UK: Radcliffe.

Erikson, E. H. (1963). *Childhood and society* (2nd ed.). New York, NY: Norton.

Erikson, E. H., Erikson, J. M., & Kivnick, H. Q. (1986). *Vital involvement in old age.* New York, NY: W. W. Norton.

Ferrucci, L., Guralnik, J. M., Studenski, S., Fried, L. P., Cutler, G. B., & Walston, J. D. (2004). Designing randomized, controlled trials aimed at preventing or delaying functional decline and disability in frail, older persons: A consensus report. *Journal of the American Geriatrics Society, 52,* 625–634. https://doi.org/10.1111/j.1532-5415.2004.52174.x

Fisman, S. (2011). Person-centered approaches for adolescents with serious mental illness. In A. Rudnick & D. Roe (Eds.), *Serious mental illness: Person-centered approaches* (pp. 182–188). London, UK: Radcliffe.

Forchuk, C. (1992). The orientation phase of the nurse–client relationship: How long does it take? *Perspectives in Psychiatric Care, 28*(4), 7–10. https://doi.org/10.1111/j.1744-6163.1992.tb00384.x

Forchuk, C., & Coatsworth-Puspoky, R. (2011). Therapeutic relationships with people with serious mental illness. In A. Rudnick & D. Roe (Eds.), *Serious mental illness: Person-centered approaches* (pp. 141–154). London, UK: Radcliffe.

Forchuk, C., & Reynolds, W. (2001). Clients' reflections on relationships with nurses: Comparisons from Canada and Scotland. *Journal of Psychiatric and Mental Health Nursing, 8*(1), 45–51. https://doi.org/10.1046/j.1365-2850.2001.00344.x

Forchuk, C., Westwell, J., Martin, M. L., Bamber-Azzapardi, W., Kosterewa-Tolman, D., & Hux, M. (2000). The developing nurse-client relationship: nurses' perspectives. *Journal of the American Psychiatric Nurses Association, 6*(1), 3–10.

Frank, A. F., & Gunderson, J. G. (1990). The role of the therapeutic alliance in the treatment of schizophrenia: Relationship to course and outcome. *Archives of General Psychiatry, 47,* 228–236. https://doi.org/10.1001/archpsyc.1990.01810150028006

Frankel, R. M., & Stein, T. (1999). Getting the most out of the clinical encounter: The four habits model. *Permanente Journal, 3*(3), 79–88. https://doi.org/10.7812/TPP/99-020

Frankenhaeuser, M. (1989). A biopsychosocial approach to work life issues. *International Journal of Health Services, 19*(4), 747–758. https://doi.org/10.2190/01DY-UD40-10M3-CKY4

Frankl, V. E. (1985). *Man's search for meaning.* New York, NY: Simon and Schuster.

Fried, L. P., Ferrucci, L., Darer, J., Williamson, J. D., & Anderson, G. (2004). Untangling the concepts of disability, frailty, and comorbidity: Implications for improved targeting and care. *Journals of Gerontology Series A: Biological Sciences and Medical Sciences, 59*(3), M255–M263. https://doi.org/10.1093/gerona/59.3.M255

Fried, L. P., & Walston, J. (2003). Frailty and failure to thrive. In W. R. Hazzard, J. P. Blass, W. H. Ettinger, J. B. Halter, & J. Ouslander (Eds.), *Principles of geriatric medicine and gerontology* (5th ed., pp. 1487–1502). New York, NY: McGraw-Hill.

Garrett, M. T., & Herring, R. D. (2001). Honoring the power of relation: Counseling Native adults. *Journal of Humanistic Counseling, 40*(2), 139–160. https://doi.org/10.1002/j.2164-490X.2001.tb00113.x

Gioia, G. A, Isquith, P. K., & Guy, S. C. (1996). *Behavior rating inventory of executive function: Self-report version.* Lutz, FL: Psychological Assessment Resources.

Golan, O., & Baron-Cohen, S. (2006). Systemizing empathy: Teaching adults with Asperger syndrome or high-functioning autism to recognize complex emotions using interactive multimedia. *Development and Psychopathology, 18*(2), 591–617. https://doi.org/10.1017/S0954579406060305

Gutheil, T. G., & Gabbard, G. O. (1993). The concept of boundaries in clinical practice: theoretical and risk-management dimensions. *American Journal of Psychiatry, 150*(2), 188–196. https://doi.org/10.1176/ajp.150.2.188

Haight, B. K., Michel, Y., & Hendrix, S. (1998). Life review: Preventing despair in newly relocated nursing home residents short-and long-term effects. *International Journal of Aging and Human Development, 47*(2), 119–142. https://doi.org/10.2190/A011-BRXD-HAFV-5NJ6

Harris, J. C. (1999). *Developmental neuropsychiatry.* New York, NY: Oxford University Press.

Health Care Consent Act, S.O. 1996, c. 2, Sched. A (1996). Retrieved from https://www.ontario.ca/laws/statute/96h02

Heisel, M. J., & Duberstein, P. R. (2016). Working sensitively and effectively to reduce suicide risk among older adults. In P. M. Kleespies (Ed.), *The Oxford handbook of behavioral emergencies and crises* (pp. 335–359). New York, NY: Oxford University Press.

Heisel, M. J., & Flett, G. L. (2016). Does recognition of meaning in life confer resiliency to suicide ideation among community-residing older adults? A longitudinal investigation. *American Journal of Geriatric Psychiatry, 24*, 455–466. https://doi.org/10.1016/j.jagp.2015.08.007

Hesselmark, E., Plenty, S., & Bejerot, S. (2014). Group cognitive behavioral therapy and group recreational activity for adults with autism spectrum disorders: A preliminary randomized controlled trial. *Autism, 18*, 672–683. https://doi.org/10.1177/1362361313493681

Hörberg, U., Brunt, D., & Axelsson, Å. (2004). Clients' perceptions of client-nurse relationships in local authority psychiatric services: A qualitative study. *International Journal of Mental Health Nursing, 13*(1), 9–17. https://doi.org/10.1111/j.1447-0349.2004.00303.x

Jahoda, A., Wilson, A., Stalker, K., & Cairney, A. (2010). Living with stigma and the self-perceptions of people with mild intellectual disabilities. *Journal of Social Issues, 66*(3), 521–534. https://doi.org/10.1111/j.1540-4560.2010.01660.x

Janis, I. L., & Mann, L. (1977). *Decision making: A psychological analysis of conflict, choice, and commitment.* New York, NY: The Free Press.

Jung, C. (1933). *Modern man in search of a soul.* Abingdon, UK: Routledge Classics.

Karnieli-Miller, O., & Salyers, M. P. (2011). Clinical communication with persons who have serious mental illness. In A. Rudnick & D. Roe (Eds.), *Serious mental illness: Person-centered approaches* (pp. 155–167). London, UK: Radcliffe.

Law, M., Cooper, B., Strong, S., Stewart, D., Rigby, P., & Letts, L. (1996). The person-environment-occupation model: A transactive approach to occupational performance. *Canadian Journal of Occupational Therapy, 63*(1), 9–23. https://doi.org/10.1177/000841749606300103

Levine, P. A. (1997). *Waking the tiger: Healing trauma.* Berkeley, CA: North Atlantic Books.

Levine, P. A. (2008). *Healing trauma: A pioneering program for restoring the wisdom of your body.* Boulder, CO: Sounds True.

Leyro, T. M., Zvolensky, M. J., & Bernstein, A. (2010). Distress tolerance and psychopathological symptoms and disorders: A review of the empirical literature among adults. *Psychological Bulletin, 136*(4), 576. https://doi.org/10.1037/a0019712

Lieb, K., Zanarini, M. C., Schmahl, C., Linehan, M. M., & Bohus, M. (2004). Borderline personality disorder. *Lancet, 364*(9432), 453–461.

Lunsky, Y., & Weiss, J. (2012). *Dual diagnosis: An information guide.* Centre for Addiction and Mental Health. Retrieved from http://www.community-networks.ca/wp-content/uploads/2015/11/dual_diagnosis_infoguide.pdf

Mejia, J., & Vandevooren, J. (2011). Serious mental illness: Person-centered approaches in forensic psychiatry. In A. Rudnick & D. Roe (Eds.), *Serious mental illness: Person-centered approaches* (pp. 202–212). London, UK: Radcliffe.

Menditto, A. A. (2002). A social learning approach to the rehabilitation of individuals with severe mental disorders who reside in forensic facilities. *Psychiatric Rehabilitation Skills, 6*(1), 73–93. https://doi.org/10.1080/10973430208408423

Menolascino, F. J., Levitas, A., & Greiner, C. (1986). The nature and types of mental illness in the mentally retarded. *Psychopharmacology Bulletin, 22*(4), 1060–1067.

Miller, W. R., & Rollnick, S. (2012). *Motivational interviewing: Helping people change* (3rd ed.). New York, NY: Guilford Press.

Moody, H. (2009). From successful aging to conscious aging. In J. Sokolovsky (Ed.), *The cultural context of aging: Worldwide perspectives* (3rd ed.). Westport, CT: Praeger.

Morrison-Valfre, M. (2016). *Foundations of mental health care.* St. Louis, MO: Elsevier Health Sciences.

Mueser, K. T., & Drake, R. E. (2011). Treatment of co-occurring substance use disorders using shared decision-making and electronic decision-support systems. In A. Rudnick & D. Roe (Eds.), *Serious mental illness: Person-centered approaches* (pp. 213–231). London, UK: Radcliffe.

Mueser, K. T., & Gingerich, S. (2011). Collaborating with families of people with serious mental illness. In A. Rudnick & D. Roe (Eds.), *Serious mental illness: Person-centered approaches* (pp. 78–98). London, UK: Radcliffe.

O'Brien, A., & Rose, J. (2010). Improving mental health services for people with intellectual disabilities: Service users' views. *Advances in Mental Health and Intellectual Disabilities, 4*(4), 40–47. https://doi.org/10.5042/amhid.2010.0674

Passer, M., Smith, E., Atkinson, M., Mitchell, J. B., & Muir, D. W. (2003). *Psychology frontiers and applications.* Toronto, ON: McGraw-Hill Ryerson.

Peplau, H. E. (1952). *Interpersonal relations in nursing.* New York, NY: Putnam Sons.

Peplau, H. E. (1997). Peplau's theory of interpersonal relations. *Nursing Science Quarterly, 10*(4), 162–167. https://doi.org/10.1177/089431849701000407

Pope-Davis, D. B., & Coleman, H. L. (2001). *The intersection of race, class, and gender in multicultural counseling.* Thousand Oaks, CA: Sage.

Portner, M. (2008). *Being old is different: Person-centred care for old people.* Ross-on-Wye, UK: PCCS Books.

Prochaska, J. O., Velicer, W. F., Rossi, J. S., Goldstein, M. G., Marcus, B. H., Rakowski, W., . . . Rossi, S. R. (1994). Stages of change and decisional balance for 12 problem behaviors. *Health Psychology, 13*(1), 39–46. https://doi.org/10.1037/0278-6133.13.1.39

Rao, J. M. (2011). Dual diagnosis: An individualized approach. In A. Rudnick & D. Roe (Eds.), *Serious mental illness: Person-centered approaches* (pp. 189–201). London, UK: Radcliffe.

Rao, J. M., & Hall, M. (2009). *Reconceptualizing diagnosis for the dually diagnosed.* Paper presented at the Ontario Association of Developmental Disabilities annual conference, Barry, ON.

Rudnick, A. (2004). Burden of caregivers of mentally ill individuals in Israel: A family participatory study. *International Journal of Psychosocial Rehabilitation, 9*(1), 147–152.

Rudnick, A. & Roe, D. (Eds.) (2011). *Serious mental illness: Person-centered approaches.* London, UK: Radcliffe.

Rydon, S. E. (2005). The attitudes, knowledge and skills needed in mental health nurses: The perspective of users of mental health services. *International Journal of Mental Health Nursing, 14*(2), 78–87. https://doi.org/10.1111/j.1440-0979.2005.00363.x

Schall, C. M. (2010). Positive behavior support: Supporting adults with autism spectrum disorders in the workplace. *Journal of Vocational Rehabilitation, 32*(2), 109–115. https://doi.org/10.3233/JVR-2010-0500

Schoen, S. A., Miller, L. J., Brett-Green, B. A., & Nielsen, D. M. (2007). Physiological and behavioral differences in sensory processing: A comparison of children with autism spectrum disorders and sensory modulating disorders. *Educational and Child Psychology, 24*(4), 9–19.

Services and Supports to Promote the Social Inclusion of Persons with Developmental Disabilities Act of Ontario, S.O. 2008, c. 14 (2008). Retrieved from https://www.ontario.ca/laws/statute/08s14

Spek, A. A., Van Ham, N. C., & Nyklíček, I. (2013). Mindfulness-based therapy in adults with an autism spectrum disorder: A randomized controlled trial. *Research in Developmental Disabilities, 34*(1), 246–253. https://doi.org/10.1016/j.ridd.2012.08.009

Spencer, G. E. (2000). Children's competency to consent: An ethical dilemma. *Journal of Child Health, 4*(3), 117–122. https://doi.org/10.1177/136749350000400305

Stenfert Kroese, B., Rose, J., Heer, K., & O'Brien, A. (2013). Mental health services for adults with intellectual disabilities – What do service users and staff think of them? *Journal of Applied Research in Intellectual Disabilities, 26*(1), 3–13. https://doi.org/10.1111/jar.12007

Takhar, J., Hiaslam, D., McAuley, L., & Langford, J. (2011). Shared/collaborative care for people with serious mental illness. In A. Rudnick & D. Roe (Eds.), *Serious mental illness: Person-centered approaches* (pp. 168–181). London, UK: Radcliffe.

Thorne, B., & Lambers, E. (Eds.). (1998). *Person-centred therapy: A European perspective.* Thousand Oaks, CA: Sage.

Tornstam, L. (1994). Gerotranscendence – a theoretical and empirical exploration. In L. E. Thomas & S. A. Eisenhandler (Eds.), *Aging and the religious dimension* (pp. 203–225). Westport, CT: Greenwood.

Townsend, E. A., & Polatajko, H. J. (2007). *Advancing an occupational therapy vision for health, well-being, and justice through occupation.* Ottawa, ON: CAOT Publications ACE.

Venville, A., Sawyer, A. M., Long, M., Edwards, N., & Hair, S. (2015). Supporting people with an intellectual disability and mental health problems: A scoping review of what they say about service provision. *Journal of Mental Health Research in Intellectual Disabilities, 8*(3-4), 186–212. https://doi.org/10.1080/19315864.2015.1069912

Weinstock, R., Leong, G. B., & Silva, J. A. (1998). Defining forensic psychiatry: Roles and responsibilities. In R. Rosner (Ed.), *Principles and practice of forensic psychiatry* (pp. 7–12). New York, NY: Oxford University Press.

World Health Organization. (2016). *Mental health and older adults.* Retrieved from http://www.who.int/mediacentre/factsheets/fs381/en/

3 A Person-Centered Approach to Research on Mental Health Challenges

Introduction

Research is an important foundation for providing effective patient- or client-centered care (PCC or CCC, respectively). It can help us understand strategies that are more likely to be helpful and those that are less likely to be helpful, and for whom. Research can also help us understand processes and experiences related to mental health challenges (MHCs) and effective care delivery.

Traditionally, research has been seen by some as a form of "expert opinion" that may appear counter to focusing on the needs and preferences of individuals, families, or communities. However, participatory approaches to research emphasize collaboration and equal distribution of power by engaging multiple stakeholders as equal partners. Each research partner brings their own expertise and experience to a collaborative research process.

The sections in this chapter cover:

- A discussion of research problems, including how they are identified and the integral role of understanding the research problem to develop the research plan.
- A section on research relationships, which includes discussion of the various partners in the research process, their roles, and how they can be supported. The concept of *participatory action research* (PAR) is explored in this section as a form of research that relies heavily on relationships. Participatory action research is a form of research that is particularly congruent with the concept of CCC.
- Collaborative research approaches, which discusses the bringing together of those with research expertise, lived experience including service users and their families, along with those who have a vested interest including community organizations supporting service users and others who will make valuable contributions to the research effort.
- A brief overview of issues related to planning and implementing research. There are entire books written on this topic; this discussion focuses on some pragmatics related to collaborative research approaches.

- Communicating research which includes a discussion of traditional and less traditional means of letting others know the results of the research.
- Why should people and agencies participate in research? Here we briefly identify the importance and benefits of research participation.
- Common research terms listed at the end of this chapter (Table 3.2).

Research – What Is the Problem?

Margaret was an active member of a local mental health organization for service users. With a recent rise in rent, she was having difficulty managing financially. In discussing this issue at a community meeting at the organization, she became aware that many others were experiencing similar struggles. The group was also aware of some social benefits that had recently been curtailed, and several individuals were finding fewer hours of available work.

Group members had different ideas about what might be the most effective way to approach the issue of financial insecurity. Could they invite an expert to support financial literacy and budgeting? Should they start a common kitchen to make cost-effective group meals? Could they begin a community garden to defray food costs? Would a social enterprise to provide additional part-time jobs for members be helpful? Should they focus on advocacy efforts to improve social assistance, or advocate for more rent supplements for people unable to work? How would they know where to put their energy, and how would they know whether their efforts were working? The group engaged the leadership of the organization in their concerns.

Research problems are generally issues where not enough information is known. The identification of research problems is the first step in the research process, and can emerge from many sources. In the example above, mental health service users identified the problem. Family members could similarly identify knowledge gaps. People who are working to provide direct care may also notice changing trends and emerging issues that are not addressed in their professional literature. Researchers interested in a topic may similarly find gaps in evidence. As well, a research team, which can involve multiple stakeholders, may find that their work is raising new questions, or that implications from prior work need to be implemented and tested.

The research process involves multiple stages. First, a general problem is usually identified, and then a specific research question(s) that needs answering. A review of the literature is conducted to determine what is known about the issue. Depending on the type of question(s), the research design can be qualitative and/or quantitative. Data is then collected, analyzed, and interpreted. Finally, the results are organized and findings are communicated to the target audience.

The executive director at the mental health organization, Amy, had some research experience from her own educational background, and the organization had collaborated in the past with other community agencies, as well as researchers from the local university. They had participated in program evaluations as well as some research projects in the past. Amy decided to start with a quick literature review, including looking at any literature that related to suggested strategies. She engaged some students with a placement at the agency to assist. She was disheartened to find very little evidence around many of the strategies, although an overwhelming body of literature existed around the problem of poverty and MHCs. Organizationally, Amy and the service user group decided to call together a meeting of community agencies and researchers to discuss the issue.

Amy attended the community meeting with the community agencies and researchers. She discussed the solutions that were put forth, such as a community garden or having someone visit to teach financial literacy, but highlighted that there was little research evidence around these and other proposed courses of action.

Various community agencies voiced similar concerns, in that service users were finding it difficult to make ends meet financially. They were glad to hear of this meeting so that these concerns could be addressed in a proactive manner. They were keen to be involved so that, at the very least, service users could maintain their current lifestyle.

The researchers in attendance confirmed that there was not a lot of literature on the solutions proposed. They also showed interest in exploring this issue further by framing it as a research problem for further investigation. In fact, they were ready to generate research questions to explore; however, Amy insisted that more service users were to be present to ensure that the research process had a variety of perspectives and was truly meeting their needs. With this in mind, the community agencies and researchers agreed to meet again alongside service users to establish a collaborative research process.

At the next meeting, service users, community agencies, researchers, and staff from the organization itself all came together and discussed the general problem and clearly defined a research question for further exploration. Financial difficulties were a common challenge for many; how to address this challenge was highly debated. Some individuals wanted to advocate for increased social assistance and rent supplements, but others felt this could take a long time and that the benefits were uncertain for the amount of work that it would require. In terms of bringing someone to help with financial literacy, some of the researchers thought that this might be a clear research endeavor to study. Service users thought that this would not be useful, as individuals were already stretching their dollars as much as they were able, and they did not think that budgeting advice would make a great deal of difference.

Both community agencies and service users liked the idea of a community garden; however, there were a few drawbacks. One challenge was the sustainability of the garden in the winter months. Another was finding the space to accommodate the garden. Yet another challenge was the time it would take to grow the produce. For some, it was not a solution that would provide benefits quickly enough. This was also the case for the social enterprise, though many found this to be an intriguing idea that could be pursued at a later time.

Starting a common kitchen seemed to be an idea that was liked by most. For one, it would save money on food costs, which was one of the main expenses for most service users. Additionally, the common kitchen could serve a dual function as a part of rehabilitation. Service users liked the idea of sharing recipes, learning new skills and techniques, and having an opportunity to meet new people. Researchers also saw this solution as one that could be explored through rigorous research.

From this collaborative discussion, the research question was decided: Would a common kitchen offset rising costs of living for service users of a mental health organization in New York City?

The researchers determined that this research problem could be measured through both quantitative and qualitative means, making this a mixed method research design. The main quantitative measure was the difference in food costs. Everyone wanted to know if such savings would offset the reduced social benefits. The main qualitative measure was the experience of service users participating in the initiative, including benefits and drawbacks.

Study participants would be required to track their monthly expenses both before and after the start of the community kitchen. This led some people back to the idea of bringing in someone to help with budgeting. A researcher pointed out that this would be another intervention and that double the number of participants may be required to determine which intervention was making a difference. The researchers and some community agency staff members discussed the challenges of recruitment and participant retention, so the group decided that the idea about financial literacy would not be pursued. Instead, the group agreed that those with a research background would develop an expenses document that service users and their service providers would fill out together, if required.

Discussion on how the kitchen would work – who would pitch in money; who would bring the ingredients; how to address no shows; those not paying their share; as well as where to meet and more were discussed among the group to reach a consensus.

In the authors' experience, sometimes service users, service providers, or researchers say they may feel they know the answer to a research question, but they do not actually have the "evidence" to back up that claim. And they often need such evidence for funding bodies or other groups, particularly when planning widespread interventions and solutions that cause changes to the status quo. Participation in research often allows this evidence to be gathered to support programs, policy changes, and individual care. For example, Chovanec (2016) used evidence from his qualitative research to support further evaluation of a client feedback tool for a different client population. As well, sometimes the entire research team can be surprised and question what they originally thought the answer would be, which may lead to a further inquiry to understand why the discrepancies exist. In Table 3.1, questions to catch our own assumptions as researchers are explored (Appendix 17).

Table 3.1   Catching Our Own Assumptions as Researchers: Exploring Assumptions in Research

Ask yourself, from the earlier example of poverty and mental health challenges, what are my assumptions? Is the topic of poverty among people who experience mental health challenges related to:	
Individual issues, such as poor budgeting, low financial literacy, interrupted education, absence of job skills, or limited problem-solving skills?	May be due to poor budgeting, low financial literacy, cognitive challenges, missing life skills, fewer social supports, poor coping strategies, interrupted education, upbringing.
Challenges related to mental health, such as age of onset, specific symptoms, or response to treatment and/or medication?	May be due to medication side effects, lack of coping strategies of managing the mental health challenge, hallucinations, and challenges with emotional regulation, focus, fatigue, and stigma.
Community-level factors, such as employment rates, housing vacancy rates, and available supports?	Higher demand and lower supply for employment, waitlists for community resources including mental health supports.
Policy-level issues, such as levels of social income supports, availability of social housing, availability of day care for people with young children, and supports for transitioning to employment?	Lack of policies in place to allow family to have power of attorney for financial and health decisions with ease, equal opportunity policies are not followed, subsidized housing unavailability, inflation.
How would solutions look different based on assumptions?	The solutions would be based on and guided by the assumed challenges. Other gaps outside of the assumptions may exist which would not be addressed by the proposed solutions.
How would you determine which assumptions have evidence?	Literature reviews, including systematic reviews, quantitative and qualitative research, expert opinion.

Greg, a staff member from another community organization, began to question if spending all of this time setting up a research design was worth it when the group could simply go ahead and implement the common kitchen. Some of the service users agreed with this as well.

Researchers, however, highlighted that the research process was needed to demonstrate clear financial benefits to those involved as well as to the wider community. Having a well-executed study could help to influence other community organizations to do the same when it had been empirically shown to be effective in offsetting financial constraints.

In response to this rationale, Greg and the others came around to the idea of executing the research design, even though it would take a bit longer and would require more work. For the most part, the team recognized that this could be a long-term solution across different communities. This understanding generated excitement and a sense of commitment to the process among those involved.

Research Relationships

After speaking to a number of the service users, the group found that their participation in the research would be limited due to a number of factors. A common challenge was child care. Additionally, some service users simply could not allocate the time to attend the meetings. Others worked in the evenings, so attendance was not possible. Financial costs of traveling to the location also posed a challenge. A few service users were concerned about attending meetings with strangers amid the stigma of MHCs.

A number of the concerns were tied to financial costs, and given the modest operational funding of the mental health organization, a conversation was needed around funding sources. Researchers suggested different grant funding sources for which they could apply. They noted that this would be a time-consuming process and that the funds were not guaranteed. Most did not think that this would be a timely course of action. Lori, a staff member from another community service organization, suggested that the group come up with cost-saving measures to eliminate the need for outside funding. There was skepticism at first, but as suggestions and ideas came about, this approach appeared to be a feasible option.

Grocers were approached to see if they would be willing to contribute to the common kitchen, whether as a one-time contribution or on an ongoing basis. Child care services were arranged during the research meetings and were to continue during the community kitchen so that parents could attend while their child(ren) was looked after. Child care services could be provided by high school students looking to complete their community service volunteer hours. The existing kitchen and supplies would be used as the main facility for the common kitchen. A social worker on the team emphasized that family members of service users were also encouraged to participate.

If research participation was too much of a time commitment for service users, staff suggested that participation could be counted as a session for service users (noting that participation would be voluntary). This way, service users would not have to travel to the site more than usual. Minor costs such as refreshments would be covered by the operational budget.

Although some service users were open to the idea of meeting new people, the notion of stigma came up when discussing the research meetings that were required to put the common kitchen into place. Some found it daunting to be in a room where everyone knew they were accessing the community services. They were also intimidated by the knowledge and roles of others who would be participating in the research. They felt that, in comparison, they would not have a lot to contribute to the team.

In order to address the challenge of stigma, Amy emphasized that the participation of service users was key to making this endeavor a success. Without the input from this group, the chances of the initiative meeting service user needs would be greatly reduced. Using the examples of the need for child care and challenges with time commitments, Amy pointed out that without their points of view, few, if any service users would be able to participate in the common kitchen. She reiterated that an effective initiative that fulfills what it is looking to achieve requires service user input throughout the process. Upon hearing this, service users had a better appreciation of what they could offer in the process. It also helped to highlight the importance of their commitment to taking part in the research meeting discussions.

In the example given with Margaret and Amy in the mental health organization, the issue of research relationships was already apparent from the start. Different types of research may favor different types of relationships. With the focus on CCC, *participatory action research* (PAR) is particularly important to consider. This type of relationship explicitly includes key stakeholders, such as service users, families, organizations, government bodies, and other individuals or groups who may be impacted or have an interest in the research outcomes. These stakeholders are ideally involved in all stages of the research process, from problem identification through to publication. In research promoting CCC, it would be particularly important to include users of mental health services as key stakeholders.

Service user involvement was imperative throughout the entire research process. Due to expected high attrition (dropout rates), as cited in the literature for individuals experiencing MHCs, it was important to engage as many service users and their family members as possible. All service users who attended sessions and participated in the initiative were asked if they and their families wanted to participate. It was emphasized that, in addition to the predicted financial benefits of the initiative, participating in the planning process would ensure that the initiative was reflective of their needs so that it could be a success. Refreshments were served at each meeting to encourage attendance.

Participatory Action Research

Action research is a method that is focused on creating change, rather than simply understanding the current situation. Not all action research is participatory. In PAR, a crucial element is the involvement of key stakeholders, including those with lived experience, such as individuals who experience MHCs. By involving various stakeholders in the research process, we can utilize their first-hand observations to help us understand a problem and identify the institutions, regulations, policies, practices, and attitudes that perpetuate it. A PAR approach has, for example, been used to explore the experiences of stigma among youths who were users of mental health services (Taggart, Franks, Osborne, & Collins, 2013). The youths were included as partners in the research process by being given training to interview other young service users with lived experience. The youths also had access to a filmmaker and complete creative direction to produce an animation related to their findings.

Subsequently, the researchers and stakeholders can work together to plan and implement improvements that will solve or reduce the problem(s) under consideration. The collaborative approach in PAR was, for example, ideal to inform the design of a dual diagnosis service for individuals with co-occurring mental health and substance use issues in Cork, Ireland (Connolly, MacGabhann, & McKeown, 2015). This project engaged multiple stakeholders in the process, including health care and legal professionals, academics, service users, and family, with roles evolving as the project unfolded.

PAR will ensure that the research remains grounded in local and systemic sociopolitical realities and needs. The PAR process is cyclical by design – it consists of repeated cycles of research, analysis, reflection, and action (Kemmis & McTaggart, 2005). This process increases stakeholders' understanding of existing services and their collaboration with other agencies. It allows them to discover potential improvements to current services and to design new interventions to fill gaps in service provision. For more information on how action research can differ from other forms of research, you may want to read Morrison and Lilford (2001). The valuing of firsthand experience and the partnership approach of PAR creates a close alignment of the clinical approach of CCC.

Service users voiced how helpful it was to have child care support so that they could take some time out of their week to recharge and be at their best for their children. This raised the issue of the cost of child care, which is not specific to service users. Many others on the team, including community agency staff and researchers, agreed that this was a widespread challenge. This new issue warranted further exploration so that guardians could access affordable child care at a later time. The common kitchen was the beginning of an iterative process to identify problems and collaboratively come together to take action and remove barriers.

Relationships are central to effective research processes in PAR. Just as in the clinical context, building trust is important. Having consistent and transparent processes assists in developing trust. For example, one strategy employed can be the use of an *article chart* to identify all of the potential papers that can arise from a particular study. Any team member can identify a subanalysis they feel is important and/or in which they would like to participate. This chart is circulated regularly and other team members can join various papers. This process is described in Forchuk and Meier (2014). Other guidelines for effective collaboration are available. The action research collaborative model is one guideline developed by Davis, Olson, Jason, Alvarez, and Ferrari (2006), which specifies several principles of effective partnerships, such as accommodating diverse agendas and reflecting critically on individual roles, personal values, and attitudes.

Just as in clinical care, attention to power dynamics is important. For instance, during Canada's multisite collaboration the At Home/Chez Soi project that tested a Housing First strategy, both researchers and stakeholders experienced multiple opportunities and challenges, as articulated by Nelson and colleagues (2016). Furthermore, relationships between researchers and collaborating service users and their families may involve a mixture of professional and friendship-type activities, as described by Mayan and Daum (2016). Some strategies to overcome power imbalances include having a service user as colead, ensuring adequate numbers of service users to avoid tokenism, providing an orientation to processes, and recognizing potential financial constraints by providing food at meetings and reimbursing travel costs. Opportunity for broader community input from those who may be interested, but may be unable to have regular participation, can also assist in equalizing power differentials. Examples of how this occurred for a five-year Community University Research Alliance on Housing and Mental Health are summarized in Forchuk, Csiernik, and Jensen (2011).

The meetings typically started with an introduction by Amy presenting the project status and progress since the last gathering. Then, a number of the researchers would share their thoughts on the most effective course of action. These discussions took quite a bit of time, and both staff and service users felt that they did not have adequate time to share their opinions to inform the project.

So instead, Amy decided to allocate the first part of the meeting to an open forum to hear from anyone who had any ideas, concerns, suggestions, or other comments. She also set up a suggestion box in case some participants were not comfortable openly sharing their concerns with the group.

After a meeting or two of the open forum, it was becoming clear that a lot of time was being taken with differing opinions and ideas. Not much practical progress was made. Because of this, Amy appointed a lead from each stakeholder group to ensure that all perspectives were heard. Each of the leads would meet with their respective stakeholder groups, synthesize the feedback, and share with the group to use time more effectively.

In Box 3.1, questions to clarify expectations and build trust are presented (Appendix 18).

Box 3.1   Points for Research Team Discussion: Building Trust Among Research Team Stakeholders

These are points to consider when building trust among researchers, service users, and service providers.

- What brings you to this research?
- What do you want to get out of this research?
- What do you want us to know about you?
- Is there anything that you would like, to make your participation more meaningful?
- Is there anything that you would like the research team to avoid doing while working together?

The following are the perspectives of different stakeholders for team discussions:

Service users: *What brought us to this research is the financial difficulty that we face. Based on this research, we would like to find a solution that will alleviate these financial difficulties. In terms of what is important to know about us, we would really like to see this initiative be a success. We are keen to take part in this process. At the same time, the burden of these financial stresses, along with the reasons for which we were accessing services in the first place, takes a toll; therefore, we may not always be present, physically or mentally. Listening to what we have to say and incorporating these ideas into the initiative would make our participation more meaningful. We would prefer that the research team avoid talking in jargon while working together.*

Researchers: *What brought us to this research is the expertise we possess in testing a potential solution to curtail financial difficulties experienced by service users. Based on this research, we would like to get a clear answer as to whether the proposed solution alleviates these financial difficulties, and if so, apply this solution to similar populations in other communities. In terms of what is important to know about us, we have the expertise and experience to inform the execution of this initiative. We will explain to the group why we prefer one course of action to another. We would like time and cooperation to put the research components in place to make our participation more meaningful (e.g., collecting pre-post data). We would prefer that we all avoid rushing the process while working together.*

Mental health organization staff: *What brought us to this research is the need to address the financial concerns of our clients. Based on this research, we would like to generate a sustainable solution for our clients that can be supported through the organization. In terms of what is important to know about us, we are passionate about supporting the initiative. At the same time, we recognize that there are fiscal, program, and administrative constraints that may pose challenges for this process. We would like to contribute different health care professional experiences to make our participation more meaningful. We would prefer that the research team avoid focusing on these program constraints and choose effective courses of action while working together.*

Collaborative Roles in Research

There are multiple roles in collaborative and participatory styles of research that each draw upon different, but overlapping, areas of expertise. Obviously, research expertise is one type of knowledge base required. This type of capacity is usually obtained through masters or doctoral level education that includes a research focus. Potential partners with research expertise can often be found through universities or research institutes. However, clinical agencies and community organizations may also have people with this background. An important consideration, however, is to recognize that for many types of research, you would want to maintain a degree of objectivity by including individuals not directly involved in the research problem. In particular, for a program evaluation, there would be more credibility if people were not evaluating themselves or an organization where they were employed.

In research supporting CCC, the perspective of service users and their families is important to ensure the client-centered focus is maintained. Often, recruiting team members through an organization with service users is a useful strategy. This assists recruitment by providing peer support for those undertaking this role. It also allows them to bring forward the perspective of a group of people who will usually have diverse experiences. Interested service users may also come forth from earlier research projects or public meetings. Sometimes, particularly when the research is heading into new areas, clinical team members help to identify other potential team members. The issue of tokenism must be seriously considered. Tokenism can occur intentionally, for instance, when researchers only include service users as "partners" to satisfy proposal conditions, or unintentionally, when service users are not accommodated and supported in the research process (McLaughlin, 2015). Unless the team itself is very small, it is rarely adequate to have one service user voice. Service users can hold multiple roles in the research process, including development of the question(s) and contribution to the research design, as members of steering groups and research committees, and as coresearchers (Staley, Kabir, & Szmukler, 2013). In addition, multiple community organizations supporting service users may be involved in a single project.

Practice perspectives are also important. People involved in the direct provision of care are often well aware of the potential implications of findings and specific policies that could support or interfere with recommendations for clinical practice. When considering direct service providers, it is important to consider all of the services that the person experiencing an MHC might encounter related to the issue at hand. Perhaps someone from primary health care, income support, or housing also needs to be included. It is also helpful to involve people at different organizational levels. For example, including some managers at the policy decision-making level can help ensure the findings are actually implemented, as well as providing an important context throughout the research process. Obtaining additional perspectives from local politicians, policy administrators, and funders, as well as family members and other natural supports, by invitation, may also add value.

A research advisory group is another way to broaden the perspectives of the research team. This group can be larger and commit less time to the project, while ensuring a wide base of experiences are brought to the planning and implementation stage of the research process. For example, a project that includes a policy analysis may incorporate elected or government officials to sit on an advisory group who would otherwise be unlikely to commit to being a research team member. Members of the advisory group may also have the opportunity to participate in specific papers and analyses of interest. In Box 3.2, questions to identify who may have an interest in advisory group participation are listed (Appendix 19).

Box 3.2   Research Team: Who is Missing? Identifying Relevant Stakeholders for a Research Advisory Group

- What perspectives do we have represented already on the team?
- What spheres of life are touched upon by the research topic?
- Who knows about the topic that is not here?
- Who cares about the topic?
- Who needs to care about the topic?
- Who is missing?

In the current team, representation was present from the mental health organization staff, including different health care professionals (occupational therapist, social worker, nursing) and representation by management, service users and their family members, and researchers from the local university. Areas of life that were touched upon by the research topic included finances and its impact on quality of life, and managing and mitigating stressors. Various stakeholders may have knowledge about the topic but may not be easily available to contribute, such as community service organization staff in other jurisdictions, local politicians, diverse service users, and others.

After a number of meetings with the stakeholders to design the research and ethics board approvals, the various groups handled different responsibilities – service users designed promotional posters and communicated the opportunity to participate in the common kitchen to others. Staff reconfigured the kitchen area to accommodate the influx of people that would be present and obtained the necessary supplies. Researchers oversaw recruitment and collected financial baseline data from participants.

Community organizations from other jurisdictions were consulted to provide more perspectives and to ensure that no major components of the research process were being overlooked. There were also some concerns highlighted by the mental health organization staff around funding of this initiative, including the food and replacing kitchen equipment when necessary. There were also safety concerns around the use of kitchen appliances. Amy ensured that policies would be amended to ensure that everyone was made aware of these changes and acted accordingly.

The common kitchen was tested for 3 months. There was small but statistically significant improvement in the financial state of service users who took part in the common kitchen as opposed to those who did not. Of interest was the resounding improvement in the quality of life of service users. This initiative was a new source of social networks, where they could learn, use new skills, and take part in creating something of value for themselves and their families. The initiative was popular among service users to the point that it became a part of regular day program activities.

Many service users stated that the common kitchen did help to offset changes to social service benefits. Some had stated that they were skeptical at first, but that pooling resources together made a surprising difference to curb overall living costs.

The findings of this study were communicated in a few different ways. Researchers, in collaboration with a service user and a staff member from the mental health organization coauthored a paper for publication. A presentation of this research at the university also took place during a research symposium. Additionally, a community dinner was held where people would enjoy a meal prepared by those using the common kitchen while hearing about the process, findings, and future plans. All were welcome to this event and it was well-received by community members.

Research staff and students also play significant roles in a study. Staff need appropriate background and sensitivity to the issues. Sometimes, the research staff have personal lived experience of MHCs or clinical experience to draw upon. This can be extremely helpful, but explicit discussion regarding boundaries and the difference between research roles and other roles needs to take place. For example, someone with years of clinical experience may want to quickly intervene on a personal level and forget that the purpose of the research is to understand issues on a broader scale. They could potentially create a second intervention that changes the results. If they provide support to the control group (usual care group), for example, in a study looking at a new way of providing care, then the research results might find a statistically insignificant difference between the new way (i.e., the intervention) and the usual way, when a difference actually existed. A new, more promising approach could end up being abandoned due to the faulty process. Students can support research staff, but are in learning roles as well. This means they have the potential to affect future care and research outcomes in a unique role.

It is also important to realize that roles are fluid. For example, in our five-year Community Research Alliance on Housing and Mental Health (Forchuk et al., 2011), we had people who initially joined as service users who went on to become students, and later became clinical agency staff or researchers. We also had several examples of students who became clinical staff or researchers, as well as clinical staff who went back to school and later became researchers. We had research staff (including some who were also service users) join clinical agencies as employees, and employees of clinical agencies who ended up as research staff. There was a consensus among the research team that the system as a whole benefited from this fluidity.

Planning and Implementing Research

It would be beyond the scope of this chapter to give a fulsome discussion of all the issues related to planning and implementing research. Instead, some general considerations when working with a team representing different experiences will be highlighted.

It is important to recognize that every group will have their own jargon and short forms that others may not recognize. If this is stated as an early assumption, people will feel more comfortable in asking that terms be explained or acronyms spelled out in more detail. It can be helpful in offering a brief overview or primer on research processes.

In one study, we collaborated with 16 peer support organizations throughout the province of Ontario, Canada (Forchuk, Martin, Chan, & Jensen, 2005). Some organizations had prior research experience and included service users with graduate degrees who had personally conducted research. Other organizations had no research experience at all. It was collectively decided to bring all of the organizations together to have a one-day workshop we called "Everything You Wanted to Know About Research but Were Afraid to Ask."

The study was one where 13 psychiatric units were going to implement the transitional discharge model (TDM; intervention groups), and 13 matched units would provide usual care (control groups). This model has two components: (1) hospital staff who stay involved until there is a clinical relationship with a community care provider and (2) peer support from someone with the lived experience of MHCs who has formal peer support training. The role of the peer support organizations was to coordinate the provision of peer support.

In the workshop, we specifically discussed the potential issue of contamination. Contamination is the issue of someone in the usual care group (control group) receiving the intervention. In this study, the peer support organizations would not deny peer support to an individual from a ward in the control group who showed up at their agency; in fact, that was usual care. Peer support was offered in most of the communities if a person with MHCs went to an organization asking for peer support. However, what would be unwanted would be the systematic offering of peer support to all service users of the control wards while the study was being conducted; this was certainly not usual care.

However, later in the study, as the wide difference in outcomes was becoming apparent to the staff at the various hospitals, leadership in two of the control wards contacted peer support groups to invite them to have a regular presence in their wards. It was the peer support groups who recognized the potential contamination issue and spoke to the research team, as well as explaining this issue to the hospital programs and agreeing to help them only after data collection was completed.

The study at the end found an average reduction of 116 hospital days between the intervention (TDM) and control (usual care) groups, which amounted to a cost savings of over $12 million CAD. There was increasing contamination from the control wards in the final months of the study, which no doubt reduced this outcome. This reduction in hospital stay and significant cost savings were used successfully by the team to advocate for more peer support services.

In addition, the Council of Academic Hospitals of Ontario later declared the model a best practice and promoted wider implementation throughout the province. However, if more widespread contamination had occurred, there could have been statistically no difference between the intervention and control groups – two programs may have benefited temporarily by providing peer support services to the control groups, but how many others would never have had this opportunity if this intervention had been viewed as unsuccessful?

An early issue that needs to be addressed in any research project is finding funding to conduct the research. This includes finding an appropriate funder and writing an often lengthy proposal. Sometimes, particularly with trying something very new, a pilot project is first implemented. The funding agency will generally have specific priorities that can shape the nature of the proposal. Ideally, venues will be planned for group meetings, and these costs are outlined in the proposal. For example, a general face-to-face meeting near the start for brainstorming, and some regular telephone conference call meetings are often useful. Sometimes, there is a very short window of opportunity between when the funding opportunity is announced and when the proposal is due. It is certainly not unusual for the final proposal to be over 100 pages, and if it is for some form of team funding, submissions can even exceed 1,000 pages due to the various resumes and detailed budgeting information over and above the actual research proposal. If a project has already been identified through past work, and a draft proposal is already in the works, these short timeframes have less impact on group input. However, sometimes the main body of the proposal ends up being circulated via e-mail among members of an established group, and only a few group calls take place.

Many of the research issues require choices to be made at the proposal stage. For example:
- What is the research problem?
- What are the questions to be answered?
- What methods will be used to address the questions?
- What group of people will be studied?
- Who will be part of the research team?
- How will the results be shared?

The proposal will also have sections on existing knowledge and the importance of the topic. If the key stakeholders are not included at the proposal stage, and the funding is conditional on partnerships detailed in the proposal, later changes can be difficult. Research can be described as a process of "hurry up and wait." In some cases, only 4 to 6 weeks are given for a proposal deadline, but then a waiting period of 6 months or longer can occur before the proposal is reviewed and a decision is made about funding.

When funding is secured, the real work begins. Research staff have to be hired. Research ethics reviews need to be drafted and submitted. Local agency research implementation processes also require completion. These items need to be completed prior to initiating the research project and recruiting participants. Meeting as a team early and frequently is important to keep things on track. By the time the funding and various approvals are in place, it is not unusual for a year to have passed since the proposal was submitted. As a result, people probably need reminding about what it was they were going to do!

Clinical agency staff and service users on the team often play key roles in planning the recruitment of research participants to the study. They can help with problem solving and troubleshooting emerging issues, and assist in interpreting the results from their unique perspectives. In Box 3.3, questions to consider regarding different aspects of the research process are listed (Appendix 20).

Box 3.3   How Will We Conduct this Research? Questions to Consider When Conducting Research

- What do we want to accomplish by the end of the research?
- What kind of evidence is needed?
- Who do we want to know about the research? What would they find to be important?
- How will we find the research participants?
- How will we maintain the cohort of research participants?
- How will we acknowledge the participation of research participants?
- Who will collect the data? Who will analyze the data?
- Who will review the literature?
- Who will identify study implications?
- What other analyses could be done from this data?
- How will we share the results?

Research Communication

At the completion of the research, several strategies can be implemented so that many can learn from the findings. Workshops for key stakeholder groups, including the general public, can be held to share the results. Manuscripts can be prepared for journal publications. Presentations can be held at conferences. Information can be posted on key websites. Arts-based approaches can also be used for specific purposes and audiences. For example, we have developed plays based on the qualitative results of several of our projects. Qualitative results are about stories, and fit well with this approach. For the TDM study mentioned earlier, one of our staff members set the qualitative results to music. She is a clinical nurse specialist in psychiatric nursing, and the result was very profound when she sang this in a duet with a psychiatric service user. Other arts-based approaches include poetry, photography, and drawings.

Sam was a 53-year-old man who had lived with schizophrenia for many years. He was at a point in his life where he wanted to give back to the community as a whole and help pave the way for younger people to avoid some of the early struggles he had faced. As a result, he volunteered to join a research team studying how community integration could be supported for people experiencing MHCs.

Sam has contributed greatly to the team, including some very pragmatic suggestions related to the interpretation of findings. An abstract related to this work has been accepted for a conference in a city that is a couple of thousand kilometers away. Sam has been asked to copresent with Mike, a community worker from a local mental health program, and Anya, a faculty member from the university.

The usual process for research travel is that the conference registration and airfare are paid directly from the research account; however, team members generally must pay for other travel expenses (such as taxis, meals, and hotels) personally, and then complete a travel form for reimbursement. This reimbursement can take up to six weeks.

Sam receives finances through a monthly check for social assistance and could not pay for the travel items in advance. If reimbursement was delayed, he could be in serious financial difficulty. Although he has a credit card, it has a much lower limit than those of the clinical staff or university researcher. He would love to travel to the conference, and is proud of his contributions, but is unsure how he can manage the logistics.

Many pragmatic issues can influence a person's ability to actively participate in research. If service users are involved, it is particularly important to have a chat about pragmatics that may be interfering and problem solve for solutions. We know that those diagnosed with MHCs are more likely to experience poverty (Wilton, 2004). In the example of Sam, above, arrangements could be made with the university to advance funds for travel expenses. A travel form is still required with appropriate documentation, but this would allow the money to be paid up front, rather than after the fact. Perhaps Mike, from the local community mental health agency, is also financially strapped from recently making a large purchase or from other life circumstances, so it cannot be assumed that financial constraints would only inhibit service users from participation.

The availability of a credit card is often needed to confirm hotel arrangements. Sometimes, even when the hotel is paid in advance, a credit card is needed in case of incidental costs. Sometimes an organization card may need to be used, or perhaps Anya is willing to use her card for this purpose. The solutions can vary. The important thing is to have an awareness and sensitivity to the issues that could limit the participation of some team members.

Why Should People and Agencies Participate in Research?

Effective services are required to assist in the care and recovery for people who experience MHCs. Research is needed to determine what works, and for whom. To be consistent with the CCC approach, participatory approaches to research are suggested. Participation can be empowering for both individuals and organizations (Forchuk et al., 2011). It is important to understand what is to be achieved by the research participation. Common examples include addressing problems where there is insufficient literature, where these problems impact people's lives served by the agency or those known by the individual. Community agencies often participate to gather data for future planning, and at times, to assist in program evaluation. As well, participation can be viewed as contributing to personal growth and a means of giving meaning to personal experiences.

Chapter Conclusion

Research can be an important tool to support client-centered care for people who experience mental health challenges. Research can reveal new potential approaches to old problems. It can also provide evidence to support unmet needs and the effectiveness of different approaches to care and services. Participatory approaches that include service users as well as other key stakeholders are particularly congruent with the principles of client-centered care. This chapter has included a discussion of the pragmatics related to this form of research and ends with common research terms (Table 3.2). Such participatory approaches embrace the saying, often cited by psychiatric service users, "Nothing about us, without us."

Table 3.2   Common Research Terms

Term	Definition
Contamination	A type of bias influencing experimental outcomes where participants in the control group receive the intervention.
Control group	Group that receives no intervention or receives usual care.
Experimental or intervention group	Group that receives the intervention or the new approach to care, treatment, etc. in question.
Hypothesis	A statement that predicts the relationship between two or more variables in quantitative studies.
Mixed methods	An approach that incorporates both qualitative and quantitative data collection and analyses in the research design.
Participatory action research	A research approach that aims to promote change in collaboration with multiple stakeholders throughout the research process.
Population	A large group containing a characteristic(s) of interest for investigation.
Qualitative research	Uses text rather than numbers to discover, explore, and explain subjective phenomena that occur in a naturalistic setting.

Table 3.2   Continued

Quantitative research	Utilizes numerical data to evaluate and test relationships among objective phenomena.
Random assignment	An objective process that gives participants equal chance to be in the intervention or control group in experimental designs.
Random selection	Process used to select a sample that is representative of the greater population and gives each unit equal chance to participate.
Research design	The overall plan used to investigate the research problem. This details information such as methods used to collect, analyze, and interpret data.
Research problem	The issue or topic identified as the area of focus for investigation.
Research question	Statement of the research problem in the form of a question for further inquiry.
Sample	Subset of a population selected to participate in the study. Multiple sampling methods exist for qualitative and quantitative research designs.
Stakeholders	Individuals, groups, or organizations that have an interest in research outcomes and their implications.
Tokenism	Term used to describe the superficial inclusion of underrepresented groups and populations.

References

Chovanec, M. G. (2016). Increasing client voice within involuntary groups. *Social Work with Groups, 40*(4), 1–15.

Connolly, J., MacGabhann, L., & McKeown, O. (2015). Developing a dual diagnosis service in Cork, Ireland by way of participatory action research (PAR). *Advances in Dual Diagnosis, 8*(1), 29–41. https://doi.org/10.1108/ADD-09-2014-0022

Davis, M. I., Olson, B. D., Jason, L. A., Alvarez, J., & Ferrari, J. R. (2006). Cultivating and maintaining effective action research partnerships: The DePaul and Oxford house collaborative. *Journal of Prevention and Intervention in the Community, 31*(1/2), 3–12. https://doi.org/10.1300/J005v31n01_01

Forchuk, C., Csiernik, R., & Jensen, E. (Eds.). (2011). *Homelessness, housing, and mental health: Finding truths, creating change.* Toronto, ON: Canadian Scholars' Press.

Forchuk, C., Martin, M.-L., Chan, Y. L., & Jensen, E. (2005). Therapeutic relationships: From psychiatric hospital to community. *Journal of Psychiatric and Mental Health Nursing, 12*(5), 556–564. https://doi.org/10.1111/j.1365-2850.2005.00873.x

Forchuk, C., & Meier, A. (2014). The Article Idea Chart: A participatory action research tool to aid involvement in dissemination. *Gateways: International Journal of Community Research and Engagement, 7*(1), 157–163. https://doi.org/10.5130/ijcre.v7i1.3393

Kemmis, S., & McTaggart, R. (2005). Participatory action research: Communicative action and the public sphere. In N. Denzin & Y. Lincoln (Eds.), *Handbook of qualitative research* (3rd ed., pp. 559–604). Thousand Oaks, CA: Sage.

Mayan, M. J., & Daum, C. H. (2016). Worth the risk? Muddled relationships in community-based participatory research. *Qualitative Health Research, 26*(1), 69–76. https://doi.org/10.1177/1049732315618660

McLaughlin, H. (2015). Alternative futures for service user involvement in research. In P. Staddon (Ed.), *Mental health service users in research: Critical sociological perspectives* (pp. 153–170). Chicago, IL: Policy Press.

Morrison, B., & Lilford, R. (2001). How can action research apply to health services? *Qualitative Health Research, 11*(4), 436–449. https://doi.org/10.1177/104973201129119235

Nelson, G., Macnaughton, E., Curwood, S. E., Egalite, N., Voronka, J., Fleury, M.-J., . . . Goering, P. (2016). Collaboration and involvement of persons with lived experience in planning Canada's at home/chez soi project. *Health and Social Care in the Community, 24*(2), 184–193. https://doi.org/10.1111/hsc.12197

Staley, K., Kabir, T., & Szmukler, G. (2013). Service users as collaborators in mental health research: Less stick, more carrot. *Psychological Medicine, 43*, 1121–1125. https://doi.org/10.1017/S0033291712001663

Taggart, D., Franks, W., Osborne, O., & Collins, S. (2013). 'We are the ones asking the questions': The experiences of young mental health service users conducting research into stigma. *Educational and Child Psychology, 30*(1), 61–71.

Wilton, R. (2004). More responsibility, less control: Welfare state restructuring and the citizenship of psychiatric consumer/survivors. *Disability and Society, 19*, 371–385. https://doi.org/10.1080/0968759041 0001689476

4 A Person-Centered Approach to Education on Mental Health Challenges

Introduction

Education is integral to every aspect of mental health care provision. Indeed, education is ubiquitous within any system of care. It extends beyond the didactic relationship, which is traditional in (modern Western) mental health care education. There are many parties to such education, including service users (still called *patients* by some), peer supports, front-line staff, physicians, students, and administrators, as well as family members of service users. In addition to the many individuals involved in education, there are also different types of educational activities that can occur within various educational systems. With the different permeations of individuals involved and various models of education, there are many types of such educational interactions.

This chapter addresses person-centered mental health care education. In it, we will look at how education occurs through a person-centered care (PCC) lens, pertaining to people who experience mental health challenges (MHCs). The sections in this chapter will focus on key areas including service user education, family member education, health professional education (at multiple levels such as undergraduate, graduate, and continuing education), and public education. We will do this by approaching the specific areas where educational experiences occur and providing an example for each, highlighting key principles, and suggesting exercises in relation to considering these principles. These examples are provided to assist with understanding the guiding principles, as well as to provide a tool with which to engage individuals at various levels of education.

John was a 25-year-old man who was recently discharged from an inpatient hospital stay lasting 30 days. During that hospitalization he had been diagnosed with bipolar disorder, type I, and had experienced a manic episode with psychosis.

He presented to his follow-up two weeks post discharge from hospital wanting to speak about his medications. He had been discharged on lithium and risperidone. He recalled having had many discussions with the inpatient team about possible medication adverse effects. He has been feeling much better and wants to discuss training for a triathlon, as he has always been an active person and had competed in such events previously.

Shared Decision Making

When considering service user education from the PCC perspective, shared decision making (SDM) is a core theoretical approach. SDM is a process wherein service users and service providers work in collaboration with each other to access information and/or resources that allow for service users to select and/or be actively involved in decisions impacting their care (Adams & Drake, 2006; Deegan & Drake, 2006; Drake, Deegan, & Rapp, 2010; Légaré & Witteman, 2013). The topic of SDM is also covered in the Clinical Care chapter (see the section "Clinical Communication" in Chapter 2).

Légaré and Witteman (2013) outline key elements, which they postulate need to be present for SDM to occur. These are (1) recognizing that a decision needs to be made; (2) an ability to understand the evidence related to the decision, in both the service user and service provider; and (3) incorporation of the service user's values and preferences in the decision, with support from the provider. It has been proposed that the process of SDM involves specific tools or resources that can be utilized to facilitate this approach, optimizing service user communication skills, and using visual aids and/or decision-making aids (Adams & Drake, 2006; Drake et al., 2010).

Within the SDM process, communication skills are integral. The focus of skills development may look different for service users and service providers. Adams and Drake (2006) outline ways in which these goals can be achieved, including enhancing service provider nonverbal communication with a focus on therapeutic alliance. Possible suggested approaches for augmenting service user communication skills include interventions focused on assertive communication skills and/or learning ways to communicate thoughts about health care options.

> You are the clinician working with John. He comes to you to discuss his options regarding medications, as he is unsure about the side effects. He is aware that there were discussions about this in hospital. He says he was overwhelmed during that time, and he would like to revisit his options around medication.
>
> You meet John and ask him how he has been since he was psychiatrically discharged from hospital. You take pause to give time for John to express his thoughts as he sometimes has challenges with expressing himself. You have previous experience in working with his medications, and John is able to appreciate the risks involved with modifying his medications. This is demonstrated by his initiative to discuss the possibility of changing his medications rather than simply not taking the medications without consultation. In terms of his values and preferences, John is dissatisfied with the current side effects, which affect his day-to-day activities. You find that he is having difficulty making up his mind about next steps. However, at this point he has been hesitant to state his concerns. In Table 4.1, some preliminary questions regarding SDM are listed (Appendix 21).

Table 4.1   Shared Decision Making: Eliciting Shared Understanding Between Service Users and Service Providers

When engaging in shared decision making, the process may occur in a series of steps. The following questions are examples of what may be asked when working with a service user:	
1. What are the choices to be made?	• *Whether to continue or lower the dose of medication* • *Another decision may be to consider alternative medications*
2. Do you, the service provider, feel you have the ability to understand the information that needs to be sought?	*Yes or No* If you answer *no*, what are the reasons (e.g., pharmacology out of scope of your practice)? What resources could assist in helping you to understand?
3. Does the service user have the ability to understand the information that needs to be sought?	*Yes or No*

If *yes* is the answer to all of the above questions, then you need to elicit the service user's values and preferences.

John states that he experiences drowsiness and tremors in his hands with his medications. He is cold much of the time and has ongoing stomach pains. All of these are affecting his ability to train in triathlons as he did before. Despite these side effects, he is confused. He does not want to relapse and is concerned that lowering the medication doses or changing the medication will lead to a relapse. He is very unsure of what to do.

You ask John to share more about his experiences with the side effects so that you can make a more informed decision alongside John. What are the impacts of the medication in terms of how John lives his life? John values his physical stamina, which is significantly impacted by the medication. He says that he is not himself and that he is more reliant on others while taking the medication. Participating in the triathlon serves a number of different purposes for John. There are the physical benefits of exercise. He feels stronger, more agile, and better about himself overall when he maintains his physical fitness. Not only that, but John looks forward to the challenge of the triathlon. It motivates him and reminds him that he can succeed in whatever he pursues if he keeps at it. Further, the triathlon is a source of social connectedness with others. He has formed a group of friends who all compete, share tips, work out together, and push each other to improve their performances.

The side effects do not simply limit his ability to participate in the triathlon. They affect his drive, motivation, social network, physical and mental health, hobbies, and his overall sense of self. Training takes a fair bit of John's time, and without it (due to the side effects of the medication), he lacks a sense of purpose. This has happened to John in the past, when he broke his leg, and he does not want to continue with that experience. In Box 4.1 are some suggested questions to assist in better understanding the values and preferences of the service user (Appendix 22).

Box 4.1   Possible Questions to Identify Service User Values and Preferences: Inquiry Toward Effective Shared Decision Making

- What do you enjoy doing?

John: *Exercising, specifically triathlons.*

- What activities have you done in the past?

John: *All different kinds of sports — snowboarding, swimming, soccer — to name a few.*

- What goals would you like to achieve?

John: *I like to set a higher bar with every triathlon that I complete. I want to beat last year's time.*

- What prevents you from achieving these goals?

John: *Right now, the medication is really throwing off my ability to perform. These side effects are a big barrier toward maintaining my current performance, let alone setting new personal records.*

- What has frustrated you when working toward your goals in the past?

John: *I feel more frustrated about this situation than I ever have. I have never had my body not work to this extent.*

- In the above example regarding medications, a pertinent question may be, do you have any dietary restrictions or preferences?

John: *No, I do not have any dietary restrictions or preferences when it comes to medication.*

With the information that has been gathered, what is the evidence for and against the decision and how does that influence the outcome of the decision to be made?

If John is to make a decision about whether he will seek out information about medication side effects, the chart may resemble Table 4.2.

Table 4.2   Service User Benefits and Challenges in Seeking Health Information

Reasons for seeking information (Pros)	Challenges to finding information (Cons)
This would provide John with information about the medications he is taking	Accessing information may be a challenge for John, depending on the resources he has available to him (e.g., Internet, computer skills, resources to travel to use a computer or library)
It may assist him in better understanding the medication side effects and what to expect for any improvement or worsening	
It assists in furthering his ability to make an informed treatment decision	Information that John feels he can understand would need to be found, based on his educational level and preference for learning style (e.g., visual vs. auditory)

With all of this information, you confirm that this medication at its current dose is not something that is sustainable for John. Many aspects of his life are impacted by these side effects. In your opinion, the security in knowing that symptoms will not return appears to be outweighed by the strong side effects that he experiences. The potential benefits of adjusting the dose or prescribing a different medication altogether to lessen side effects that he experiences is becoming a key option. John also has to come to a conclusion for himself. To do this, he may benefit from further information beyond what you provide to him in your short time together.

For the service provider, one mechanism to enhance SDM is through the enhancement of the therapeutic alliance. Bachelor (2013) suggests that service providers may benefit from seeking feedback from the service user about the relationship. It has also been shown that basic interpersonal skills (being responsive, empathic, expressing genuine concern) can assist in the development of a therapeutic alliance, both early in, and then persisting throughout, the clinical relationship (Heinonen et al., 2014).

When working with service users, it is important that you, as the service provider, become aware of your own values, past experiences, assumptions, and biases, and how they may impact the SDM process. If, in the past, you have observed service users to relapse after a lower dose of medication, you may be hesitant to change your recommendations, despite the side effects that are apparent for the service user with whom you are currently working. Another assumption that may occur is that service users are overly focused on the side effects rather than on the benefits of taking medication. It is important to remember that every person responds differently to medication, and the choice you recommend must take the individual experiences of service users into consideration. For John, the side effects are affecting him to the point that they significantly disrupt his quality of life. Box 4.2 gives questions for service providers to address to clarify the state of the therapeutic alliance (Appendix 23).

Box 4.2   Therapeutic Alliance Check-In: Questions for Reflection to Make the Most Out of the Therapeutic Alliance

These are some examples of questions that can be helpful for service provider reflection when working with service users:

Is the therapeutic alliance progressing? If not, why not?

With John, overall, the therapeutic alliance is progressing. There is a lack of clarity around John's options and what could be most effective for him. I can provide information, use tools, and give prompts to provide clarity as needed.

• How much effort are you contributing to the clinical relationship? The service user?

With John, there is a fair contribution in this clinical relationship. I create a space where he is able to share his concerns, and he is in communication about what he is looking to get out of the time we have together.

Another, often helpful, and very important approach is to check in with the service user. Some questions you may ask in that case are:

• What is positive about our time together?
• What would you change about our interactions?
• Is there anything you would like me to do to ensure that you are getting the most out of our time together?

A potential way to enhance service user communication in SDM is by assisting with the assertion of service user needs. One approach to this is for the service user to be prepared with questions that can assist them in gathering information to help make the final decision. Box 4.3 includes example questions that service users may have (Appendix 24).

Box 4.3   Shared Decision Making: Enhancing Service User Communication – Questions That Service Users May Wonder About Regarding Shared Decision Making

A few suggested questions for the service user to ask themselves and/or the service provider are:

- What are the choices I have to consider? Are there other options that have not been considered?
- What is my role in the decision-making process?
- What if we disagree with each other?
- How do I find information about the decisions I need to make?
- Are there other things I would like my service provider to know? (If yes, then it may be helpful to make a list so that you can be sure to remember these points when you next speak to the service provider.)

Decision Aids

Decision aids are formal tools which can be utilized to assist in making decisions as well as to understand which way (either toward or away from) one is leaning with regard to a decision (Adams & Drake, 2006; Drake et al., 2010).

For John to effectively express himself, his ideas, and preferences regarding a choice, you discuss the possibility of decision aids. John, like most service users, is unfamiliar with the process in which the service provider takes the time to obtain John's input on the choices that have to be made. He is used to receiving prescriptions for medication and simply complying with what he is told to do, even though it makes him uneasy. He questions whether he even wants to take the medication, or how and if it works. Nevertheless, he complies because he does not know of any other option. This time, however, he is surprised by the large number of options and amount of information that he receives to make a choice that works for him.

You refer John to some handouts as well as some well-known websites that provide sound medical and pharmacological information so that John can explore his options. You book an appointment with John as early as possible so that once he makes his choice, John can change the current medication or its dose to something that works for him.

The Ottawa Health Research Institute has a database of decision aids that can be searched by topic (https://decisionaid.ohri.ca/AZinvent.php). In the US, there are two centers for SDM, one through Dartmouth-Hitchcock Health (https://med.dartmouth-hitchcock.org/csdm_toolkits.html) and one through the Mayo Clinic (https://shareddecisions.mayoclinic.org/).

Recovery in Shared Decision Making

Within mental health care, two specific examples of SDM in practice are the *illness management and recovery* (IMR) and the *wellness recovery action plan* (WRAP) programs (Copeland, 2002; Mueser et al., 2006).

IMR is an approach that was developed for people who experience severe MHCs such as schizophrenia, and it incorporates psychoeducation, cognitive behavioral approaches, relapse prevention, social skills training, and coping skills (Mueser et al., 2006). IMR aligns with PCC as it begins by asking what the service user sees as their meaning of recovery. It consists of structured modules delivered weekly over a year or so for those in the community (a shortened version for people in hospital has also been developed). Table 4.3 includes a few questions on prompting service users to begin to think about what recovery may look like for them (Appendix 25).

Table 4.3   Shared Decision Making: The Meaning of Recovery – Creating a Picture Toward Service User Recovery

To focus on recovery, it is important to understand the service user's goals and what they mean by recovery. Some questions for the service provider to ask the service user that can help facilitate this are:	
What does the word *recovery* mean to you?	John views recovery as the ability to go on with his day-to-day activities without the recurrence of symptoms, and with minimally disruptive or no side effects from medication.
When you think of your life six months into the future, what do you envision? One year from now? Two years from now?	John envisions himself completing the triathlon, challenging himself to reach new personal milestones, and striving not only to reach his fitness goals, but also to redefine what is possible for himself.

WRAP is a systematic approach to developing a personalized recovery plan. It was developed with service user involvement and is to be utilized by service users to manage symptoms and promote recovery (Copeland, 2002). The plan is written down, encompassing a five-part system, is personally developed by the individual, and involves a response plan should the person face unexpected stressors and/or relapse. The commitment to WRAP is about 15–20 minutes per day to review the plan. Copeland (2002) details how to develop a WRAP in her 2002 article. The topic of WRAP is also covered in the Clinical Care chapter (see the section "Clinical Communication" in Chapter 2). Box 4.4 provides an example of questions that may be used to inform a WRAP (Appendix 26).

Box 4.4   Shared Decision Making: Questions to Inform an (Adapted) Wellness Recovery Action Plan

Some questions to consider when developing a wellness recovery action plan (WRAP) may include:

- What are you like when you are well?
- What strategies help you stay well?
- What are signs of the mental health challenge you face?
- What can we do about those signs indicating a crisis or challenge?
- How can we use a crisis plan?
- How do I engage in a WRAP?

For John, when he is well, he is active, determined, and ambitious and acts as an external source of motivation for others. He maintains a busy schedule, which he enjoys. Strategies that help him to stay well are physical exercise, which also helps with mental centering; staying connected with friends and family; and satiating his sense of curiosity by going to new places, trying new activities, events, and cuisines. A sign that he is unwell is that, just like when he is well, he has many ideas. When he is unwell, he acts on these ideas without forming a plan. He shows impulsivity and disregards other people's opinions, which is out of character for him. If these signs occur, they are indicators to himself and to his family that something needs to be done – such as to discuss any life stressors, reevaluate medication or otherwise. Attending the hospital is warranted as a safety measure if needed.

Family Education

John, who is discussed in the previous section, lives at home with his mother and 19-year-old brother. His mother works as an office manager and his brother is in college. John has been attending university but deferred his semester when he experienced his first manic episode.

John's family is worried, as he was very ill when he went into hospital. John had not slept and was speaking about starting three new businesses and had spent about $2,000 worth of his savings, allocated for schooling, in order to purchase supplies to pursue these endeavors. His mother heard him singing and talking to himself in his room, mostly about these business ideas, none of which really made sense to her. She does not really know how to explain John's MHC to the rest of the family and does not know how to approach the topic with John's dad, who lives in another state. She is not sure what bipolar disorder is. She knows John is now on medication, but she was not present for many of the discussions about what the medications do or how long John may be prescribed these medications. She is quite worried about John and wonders if he will experience challenges with his mental health again.

Approaches

John's mother wants to learn more about what he is experiencing and asks John where she can get more information. He gives her some pamphlets that he had been given at the hospital. There she finds general information on bipolar disorder as well as advertisements for information nights for families. In an attempt to alleviate some of her own stress that stems from the uncertainty and the lack of information about what her son is going through, John's mother begins to attend these sessions regularly. She becomes familiar with what bipolar is and with MHCs in general, along with the medications John is taking and how they affect the body. She is also eager to learn about additional services that are offered should they ever require them.

She learns that in gathering information to help John, she is also able to learn and develop coping strategies for herself as well. She finds emotion regulation skills quite helpful, particularly tuning into body sensations to separate her conscious self from the thoughts and feelings within her. By doing so, she is able to take pause, watch those thoughts, and separate herself from the feelings of worry that may lead to stressful situations. Crisis planning, though slightly distressing, helps her feel more prepared in case something is to occur with John in the future. She knows how to most effectively respond to him if he is to ever exhibit symptoms, what phone numbers to call, and where to go if he is in need.

John's mother feels less alone by attending these sessions as she is surrounded by others who are sharing similar experiences. She feels more comfortable with explaining what happened with John to his father as well as to the rest of the family. After seeing how many other people are dealing with similar challenges, the stigma of MHCs does not bother her as much anymore. She also feels a sense of relief after having learned that it is not due to anything she had or had not done as a parent. She realizes that the idea of not knowing what is going on is the most stressful element. After learning about John's MHC and recognizing how to support him, she feels that they will both be able to manage challenges more effectively.

Family involvement in adult mental health care can be difficult as there is a balance to be reached between education, family involvement, and confidentiality of personal health information, as well as the individual's autonomy. Often, this can be difficult for family members. However, there are ways in which education can be provided without necessarily breeching an individual's right to confidentiality. Programs such as family information nights or psychoeducational community events are often offered (Dixon et al., 2001). In addition, family educators are often embedded within first-episode psychosis clinics, and there is a growing body of virtual support communities for family members of service users.

One evidence-based approach to family education is *family psychoeducation* (FPE). This comprises a predetermined set of psychoeducational components, and allows for variability in the size of the group, service user involvement, setting, and the length of the program (Dixon et al., 2001; Lucksted, McFarlane, Downing, & Dixon, 2012). Generally, the components include education about the MHCs, medications, ongoing management, information about available services and service coordination, emotion regulation and stress management, problem solving, and crisis planning. Traditionally, this occurs in diagnosis-specific groups (e.g., with a focus on psychotic disorders or mood disorders). Further, evidence has shown that FPE can decrease relapse and rehospitalization as well as provide overall benefits in areas such as quality of life (Dixon et al., 2001; Lucksted et al., 2012). It has been utilized across diagnoses, such as for adults with schizophrenia and bipolar disorder, as well as more recently for children with mood disorders (Lucksted et al., 2012). The US Substance Abuse and Mental Health Services Administration (SAMSHA) offers a toolkit to assist with implementing FPE (http://store.samhsa.gov/product/Family-Psychoeducation-Evidence-Based-Practices-EBP-KIT/SMA09-4423).

Two examples of FPEs are the Support and Family Education (SAFE) program (Sherman, 2003) and the Family-to-Family Education Program (FFEP) (Dixon et al., 2004). The SAFE program was developed in a Veterans Affairs hospital in Oklahoma City and encompasses 14 psychoeducational sessions (Sherman, 2003). The program is not diagnostic specific and is open to anyone with a family member who experiences MHCs. There is an opportunity at the end of each session to ask questions. A representative from the local National Alliance for the Mentally Ill (NAMI) often attends.

The FFEP is a structured 12-week program taught by family members to family members of those who experience MHCs. As outlined by Dixon et al. (2004), the program provides psychoeducation about MHCs in general, treatments (both pharmacological and non-pharmacological) as well as rehabilitation. It is broadly utilized across North America and Mexico. Research has shown that those who participate in an FFEP report increased knowledge about MHCs and feelings of empowerment (Dixon et al., 2004).

You are working in a family education program and with John's family. As a service provider, you may be asked questions by the family or loved ones of the service user with whom you are working. You may be able to anticipate some of the questions that John's family may have, while also being open to answering other questions that may arise. Box 4.5 lists questions that family members may ask (Appendix 27).

Box 4.5   Family Education: Identifying Family Needs – Questions From John's Family Members

Some potential questions that John's family may ask are:

- What is bipolar disorder?
- How do we explain bipolar disorder to other people, such as John's brother?
- How will we know if John needs to be in the hospital?
- Are there side effects to John's medication?
- Does John need to do anything, such as blood work, on a regular basis?
- How do we help support John in moving forward with his goals for his life?

As a family educator, you are limited by confidentiality. It may be helpful to start your session or meeting with a discussion about these limits. You may say or discuss something such as:

Our sessions are meant to provide information and support for families. As in all health care settings, personal health information is confidential. John has consented to our speaking about his experiences with MHCs today, so we can discuss some of the questions you have asked.

If John had not consented, it might be phrased as something such as:

Our sessions are meant to provide information and support for families. As in all health care settings, personal health information is confidential. So today, we can discuss some general topics and answer some questions. We can also discuss some tools for communicating your questions to your loved one directly.

What you say will depend on the environment in which you are engaged in providing family education. If it is a one-on-one meeting with a single family about one service user, then the conversation may be more specific to that person. This is in comparison with a larger group psychoeducation session where it may be inappropriate to discuss details pertaining to specific individuals, due to confidentiality.

John's mother notices that the group facilitator does an excellent job of providing relevant information to the group. He effectively deals with some very difficult and emotional situations for various family members, including hers. She feels heard and understood by him and those around her. He answers some of the questions that are on people's minds – like, is this my fault? Is it going to be like this from now on? And will my loved one go back to the way they were before? He assures the group that these situations with their loved ones are dynamic (rather than static) and that recovery is possible.

Family members may experience emotions such as sadness, fear, or anger, and they may feel overwhelmed. Some questions to consider are:
- What are some ways that I could validate family members' feelings when they seem to feel this way?
- What sorts of suggestions or new perspectives could I provide the family?

Undergraduate, Postgraduate, and Continuing Health Care Education

Emily is a 23-year-old woman who recently graduated from university and is having difficulty finding employment. She is finding it difficult to "get motivated," finds little interest or enjoyment in activities, and is losing weight because she is too anxious and worried to eat much, essentially losing her appetite. She goes to see her doctor, Amir, a recent graduate, who diagnoses her with major depressive disorder, single episode.

Adult Education Principles

Malcolm Knowles introduced core principles of adult education in the late 1960s. These core principles were based on five tenets: (1) adults are self-directed learners, (2) adults learn from life experiences, (3) adults' learning needs will change with their changing life roles, (4) adults' learning needs are often focused on the problems they encounter in their various roles, and (5) adult learners are driven internally or are self-motivated (Merriam, 2001). Within adult education, there tends to be a spectrum of educational activities ranging from teacher directed to learner directed (Beavers, 2009).

Arising from this early theory of adult education, the focus on self-directed learning was transformed. Self-directed learning includes various approaches and models. Some models are more process focused and others more context focused (Beavers, 2009; Merriam, 2001). The concepts of *process* and *context* and the associated learning content are discussed throughout the adult education literature. Within adult education, the focus often shifts from content-based learning to that of context- and process-based learning (Garrison, 1992; Hansman, 2001). Context-based learning focuses on what can be learned embedded within the contexts where one may be working, and what can be learned from service users of these systems (Hansman, 2001). An example of this may be during medical school, where students can learn clinical examination skills at the bedside, from patients experiencing the illness and from hearing about first-hand experiences, versus learning using an inanimate learning model (i.e., a mannequin). The process focus of adult learning refers to the internal processes of self-reflection and critical thinking, and the interaction these have with the external sources in one's environment(s) (Garrison, 1992). In these models of education, the focus tends to shift from content retention toward the processes of critical appraisal and deeper understanding. Box 4.6 lists questions that prompt Amir to find out more about the effective identification, assessment, and treatment of depression (Appendix 28).

While working with Emily, Amir was told that she did not want to take medication. She also did not want to continue with her current state; instead, she wanted to address her depression in other ways. In practicing person-centered approaches to treatment, this led Amir to further explore the question of other treatment interventions for depression. He was familiar with psychotherapy, exercise, and a few other modalities. Since this was a common diagnosis for service users, he thought it would be worthwhile to build on his current knowledge. From a societal perspective, the move away from medications and toward spiritual, naturopathic, somatic experiencing, body-based approaches, mindfulness, and other forms of therapy was important to investigate so that he was fully informed. He knew that senior staff were very helpful resources of information, and could refer him to further sources of information. In addition, he had access to his classmates' shared online group where they posted general inquiries to seek guidance or post information so that everyone benefited in their own practice.

Box 4.6   Identifying Service Provider Learning Goals: Questions for Amir to Effectively Manage Emily's Diagnosis of Depression

Considering Emily's example, some specific learning goals have been identified below. It may be helpful to think of learning goals in terms of topic areas such as biological factors, psychological factors, and social or environmental factors. Learning goals may include the following:

- How is depression diagnosed? What tools are utilized?
- What are the *Diagnostic and Statistical Manual of Mental Disorders*, 5th edition (DSM-5) criteria for depression?
- What is the neurophysiology of depression?
- What stressors may be affecting her depression?
- What is the prevalence of depression?
- Is there a process to diagnose depression?
- What are the treatments for depression? Are there medications as well as other treatments such as body-based approaches, psychotherapy, or exercise?

Also, think more broadly about what factors are motivating you to learn more. Some questions to help understand these motivations include:

- What are some goals or factors driving me toward further education?
- Are there clinical implications for this learning?
- How will my learning objectives and related questions further my continuing education?
- Are there areas I tend to struggle with when learning new things? What potential struggles may this cause for me? How can I overcome these?

There are also important process steps to achieving educational goals which need to be considered. A few suggestions for consideration include:

- How will I know that I have obtained the above educational goals?
- Where will I engage in this learning?
- Are there other resources that could assist me with engaging in this process?
- Are there other people who may have similar educational goals? Would it be helpful to engage with them?
- Should I join a community of practice or group to assist in achieving my educational goals?

Health Professional Education

For health professional education, each designation has specific requirements set out by the respective governing body, which must be met to obtain and then maintain professional credentials (e.g., social work, occupational therapy, physiotherapy, nursing, psychology, medicine). Within each area, there are also different levels of formal education that each person may be working from, such as undergraduate, graduate, and postgraduate. Further, once someone is licensed within a specific regulated profession, there are requirements for ongoing continuing education. In addition, many individuals seek out extra educational opportunities based on their personal learning goals and/or aspirations.

The mechanism through which PCC is taught across health professions is variable (Lévesque, Hovey, & Bedos, 2013). In a review of the literature, Lévesque and colleagues describe how across multiple health professions, PCC is often taught in the context of clinical rotations. Generally, undergraduate programs such as nursing, social work, and medicine focus on exposure to PCC. As education shifts toward graduate program training, programs such as nursing, occupational therapy, social work, psychology, and medicine often incorporate more advanced skill training in PCC into clinical rotations and may have workshops or specialized seminars focused on this. Continuing education initiatives vary from brief, time-limited sessions, to ongoing, integrated training (Lévesque et al., 2013). There are postdoctoral research opportunities in the area of psychiatric or psychosocial rehabilitation, which take a PCC approach.

It is challenging to look at the diverse health professions together, because there is no uniform curriculum for teaching PCC within this broad group. Many specialized centers which focus on PCC in mental health care are multidisciplinary, such as the Center for Psychiatric Rehabilitation at Boston University (see https://cpr.bu.edu/) or the Department for Psychiatric Rehabilitation and Counseling Professions at Rutgers University (see https://shp.rutgers.edu/psychiatric-rehabilitation/). The latter does offer graduate and doctoral programs within the area of psychiatric rehabilitation; however, one can enter from various academic backgrounds. In comparison to programs which focus on health professional training in a specific designation (e.g., social work, psychology, occupational therapy), psychiatric rehabilitation programs bring together individuals from various academic backgrounds, in a learning environment focused on psychiatric rehabilitation. In designation-specific programs (e.g., social work, psychology, occupational therapy), PCC may be incorporated as part of a broader training program. Thus in the former, the learning focus is different and more intensive and detailed, and in the latter, it tends to be an exposure(s) to the idea and topic area, unless one takes a particular interest and makes it a focus of one's research.

As an example, if we were to take a closer look at the curriculum of the Center for Psychiatric Rehabilitation and compare it with, for example, the curriculum of a master's of science program in occupational therapy, the focus and time allotted to PCC are different. This is not to say that one is superior over the other, but that there are different approaches depending on the focus of the program. For example, the Center for Psychiatric Rehabilitation curriculum discusses "training" more broadly and outlines three types of training at different levels: exposure, experience, and expertise. An outline of this can be found online (https://cpr.bu.edu/develop/training). This broad approach is likely to be taken because it accepts learners from various training backgrounds. In contrast, a master's program in occupational therapy offers education and training in a spectrum of rehabilitation practices, beyond mental health, within their curriculum. Often the curriculum will discuss broader topics such as disability or wellness and within it encompass aspects of mental health. The contrast between these two programs is also likely due to their different training goals and the regulatory requirements that exist for a regulated health profession such as occupational therapy.

Delivery of PCC Education

Recently, there has been a movement within health professionals' education toward problem-based and competency-based education. *Problem-based learning* (PBL) takes place in small groups, with a facilitator or tutor, while aiming to be learner centered, with the core focus on using a problem scenario to develop problem-solving skills and knowledge acquisition through self-directed learning (Dochy, Segers, Van den Bossche, & Gijbels, 2003). There are some aspects of PBL that may still be protected. In medicine, PBL has been shown to lengthen retention of acquired knowledge, when compared with conventional teaching, and increase clinical skills development (Dochy et al., 2003). In occupational therapy, PBL has been seen to assist with improved clinical reasoning skills (Scaffa & Wooster, 2004). In nursing, it has also been seen to increase critical thinking skills over time (Tiwari, Lai, So, & Yuen, 2006).

During Amir's medical training, he experienced problem-based learning where he and his classmates were assigned to small groups with a tutor who was trained as a physician. They met twice a week, and during this time, they were assigned brief, open-ended scenarios of medical challenges that were explored by each group member independently before gathering together to share their findings of how to approach the scenario. Usually, the concrete elements of a diagnosis or ailment were first discussed. There was also a contextual piece to the scenarios that prompted students to think about existing resources that could be accessed or utilized. Furthermore, the varied findings that members brought to the table prompted discussion and debate for choosing one route of assessment and treatment over another. This is where a deeper understanding of the challenge emerged – where a person's context and circumstances led to potentially different approaches to care as compared with another individual with the same medical diagnosis. In this learning format, not only did students learn about the content that they were to research, but this was also an excellent forum to practice the ability to work as a team, anticipate the needs of others, use critical thinking, conduct analysis, obtain and provide feedback, hone clinical reasoning, and exercise professionalism.

Within the health care professions, there have been core competencies identified that guide professional expectations (Verma, Paterson, & Medves, 2006). These core competencies encompass knowledge, practical skills, and problem solving within specific work-related areas making up the health care professional role (e.g., exhibiting professional behavior toward service users and colleagues). Verma et al. (2006) outline how professional competencies within physical therapy, occupational therapy, nursing, and medicine often align. Still, there is no one universal set of competencies for health professionals more generally.

The American Board of Medical Specialties (ABMS) collaborates with specialty Member Boards to uphold standards for the certification of physicians to provide excellence in health care (ABMS, 2019). Ongoing professional development of physician specialists is made in an effort to achieve optimal health care for service users. The Accreditation Council for Graduate Medical Education (ACGME) assesses and monitors the standards of medical education to ensure that resident physicians are competent to provide quality health care (ACGME, 2019). Similarly, core competencies have become a focus of the Royal College of Physician and Surgeons of Canada. This has led to the redevelopment of the CanMEDS framework (Frank, Snell, & Sherbino, 2015) shifting toward competency-based education (CBE). This framework guides educational goals within medicine in Canada. CBE has been described by Frank et al. (2010a):

> Competency-based education (CBE) is an approach to preparing physicians for practice that is fundamentally oriented to graduate outcome abilities and organized around competencies derived from an analysis of social and patient needs. It deemphasizes time-based training and promises greater accountability, flexibility, and learner-centeredness. (p. 636)

CBE is postulated to promote self-directed learning (Frank et al., 2010b).

Public Education

A residential area in a moderately sized city has been identified as a possible location for a methadone clinic. There is a small university located near the proposed city as well. There have been multiple community meetings held about the proposed clinic, and there has been discussion amongst residents about what a potential methadone clinic would mean for their neighborhood concerning their property values and safety. This is in contrast to the public health agency's perspective and philosophy of promoting harm reduction and community integration.

Approaches

Public education can occur in different venues and in different forms. It is complicated by the multiple stakeholder views that need to be incorporated. There is very little research on public education within mental health. However, in practice there are various types of public educational events such as public forums, information in media print, charitable events, and speaker forums.

Although research on public education principles in mental health is sparse, general principles from other areas of health education, such as public health and prevention, can be applied more generally here. One concept employed within public health is that of *health literacy*. This can be applied at an individual or larger community level, and generally refers to the understanding of health-related information to allow for increased control over health decisions and social determinants of health (Nutbeam, 2008). This idea applied to public education entails increasing the general public's knowledge to improve individual and community health. It is based on the idea that when individuals and communities are more aware, they can make more informed choices about their health. It has been suggested that approaches to increase health literacy need to actively engage and involve participants, as well as be interactive (Nutbeam, 2008). Table 4.4 includes points to consider when planning a public education event (Appendix 29).

Table 4.4   Planning Public Education Events: Considerations for Planning

Considering the example of establishing a new methadone clinic in a neighborhood, there are opportunities to potentially increase the health literacy of the community where the clinic has been proposed. Assuming we are engaging the community from the public health perspective, there are some aspects of planning such an event that need to be reviewed. These include considering what such education would encompass from conception to implementation. Guiding questions can include:

What elements would need to be considered when planning a public educational event?	• Location, physical space/capacity, fire codes, etc. • Who is hosting the event (i.e., public health vs. concerned community group) • Are there any financial disclosures or conflicts of interest? Is there any financial support? If so, from whom? Does this bias the event in any way?
What is the primary or core purpose for the event?	• To educate the community and engage them around the importance of harm reduction and safe strategies for opioid replacement
How do you advertise the event?	• Are there resources available to engage a marketing strategy? • Who should hear about the event? • Who is the target audience for the event?
Who would be involved in planning the event?	• Who those individuals are will largely flow from what you determine the core purpose of the event to be
What key piece(s) of information do you want to convey during your educational event?	• Who should convey this information? How? • What medium will be used?
What potential challenges do you need to consider when planning the event for the above community?	• In this example, emotions may be strong, and care must be taken to carefully address community member concerns

Another concept often utilized in public health education is that of prevention. In a review of the literature, Nation et al. (2003) identified core elements of effective prevention programs. These include having information conveyed in different ways over varied methods of dissemination (i.e., more interactive approaches), with this being done by trained individuals, in a manner that is contextually relevant. They also suggest that effective prevention programs often include members of the intervention community being involved with planning and implementation.

Prevention may mean implementing education early to minimize the stigma or negative attitudes about such a clinic within the community. This may mean having town hall discussions or advertisements including first-hand experiences of what the methadone clinic will mean to service users. More broadly, another preventative measure would be to educate about and discuss the potential for addiction with opioids and alternative treatment methods. Box 4.7 lists questions that may be considered for a preventative health campaign (Appendix 30).

Box 4.7   Public Education: Applying Prevention Principles – Preventative Health Campaign Considerations

When thinking about planning a preventative health campaign for educational purposes, you may want to consider the following:

What is the area that requires further education?

What educational campaigns have already been tried in this area?

When you think about campaigns that have already been tried, what was effective or ineffective about them? (It may be helpful to draw a table to compare and contrast campaigns and outcomes.)

What can be improved in future educational campaigns?

Who needs to be involved to make these improvements – i.e., who is the target audience, and how can they become involved, or who is impacted by the problem?

How can we increase participation and action?

What, if any, barriers are there to implementation? How can these be overcome?

Chapter Conclusion

This chapter has looked at person-centered care in relation to education. It took a broad perspective involving service users, family members, health professionals, and the public. It outlined some key principles in each of these areas and challenged the reader to utilize these in order to develop new ways of thinking about education from a person-centered care perspective.

References

Accreditation Council for Graduate Medical Education. (2019). *About us*. Retrieved from https://www.acgme.org/About-Us/Overview

Adams, J. R., & Drake, R. E. (2006). Shared decision-making and evidence-based practice. *Community Mental Health Journal, 42*(1), 87–105. https://doi.org/10.1007/s10597-005-9005-8

American Board of Medical Specialties. (2019). *About AMBS*. Retrieved from https://www.abms.org/about-abms/

Bachelor, A. (2013). Clients' and therapists' views of the therapeutic alliance: Similarities, differences and relationship to therapy outcome. *Clinical Psychology & Psychotherapy, 20*(2), 118–135. https://doi.org/10.1002/cpp.792

Beavers, A. (2009). Teachers as learners: Implications of adult education for professional development. *Journal of College Teaching & Learning, 6*(7), 25–30. https://doi.org/10.19030/tlc.v6i7.1122

Copeland, M. E. (2002). Wellness Recovery Action Plan: A system for monitoring, reducing and eliminating uncomfortable or dangerous physical symptoms and emotional feelings. *Occupational Therapy in Mental Health, 17*(3-4), 127–150. https://doi.org/10.1300/J004v17n03_09

Deegan, P. E., & Drake, R. E. (2006). Shared decision making and medication management in the recovery process. *Psychiatric Services, 57*(11), 1636–1639. https://doi.org/10.1176/ps.2006.57.11.1636

Dixon, L., Lucksted, A., Stewart, B., Burland, J., Brown, C. H., Postrado, L., . . . Hoffman, M. (2004). Outcomes of the peer-taught 12-week family-to-family education program for severe mental illness. *Acta Psychiatrica Scandinavica, 109*(3), 207–215. https://doi.org/10.1046/j.0001-690X.2003.00242.x

Dixon, L., McFarlane, W. R., Lefley, H., Lucksted, A., Cohen, M., Falloon, I., . . . Sondheimer, D. (2001). Evidence-based practices for services to families of people with psychiatric disabilities. *Psychiatric Services, 52*, 903–910. https://doi.org/10.1176/appi.ps.52.7.903

Dochy, F., Segers, M., Van den Bossche, P., & Gijbels, D. (2003). Effects of problem-based learning: A meta-analysis. *Learning and Instruction, 13*, 533–568. https://doi.org/10.1016/S0959-4752(02)00025-7

Drake, R. E., Deegan, P. E., & Rapp, C. (2010). The promise of shared decision making in mental health. *Psychiatric Rehabilitation Journal, 34*(1), 7–13. https://doi.org/10.2975/34.1.2010.7.13

Frank, J. R., Mungroo, R., Ahmad, Y., Wang, M., De Rossi, S., & Horsley, T. (2010a). Toward a definition of competency-based education in medicine: A systematic review of published definitions. *Medical Teacher, 32*, 631–637. https://doi.org/10.3109/0142159X.2010.500898

Frank, J. R., Snell, L. S., Cate, O. T., Holmboe, E. S., Carraccio, C., Swing, S. R., . . . Harden, R. M. (2010b). Competency-based medical education: Theory to practice. *Medical Teacher, 32*, 638–645. https://doi.org/10.3109/0142159X.2010.501190

Frank, J. R., Snell, L., & Sherbino, J. (Eds.). (2015). *CanMEDS 2015 Physician Competency Framework*. Ottawa, ON: Royal College of Physicians and Surgeons of Canada.

Garrison, D. R. (1992). Critical thinking and self-directed learning in adult education: An analysis of responsibility and control issues. *Adult Education Quarterly, 42*(3), 136–148. https://doi.org/10.1177/074171369204200302

Hansman, C. A. (2001). Context-based adult learning. *New Directions for Adult and Continuing Education, 2001*(89), 43–52. https://doi.org/10.1002/ace.7

Heinonen, E., Lindfors, O., Härkänen, T., Virtala, E., Jääskeläinen, T., & Knekt, P. (2014). Therapists' professional and personal characteristics as predictors of working alliance in short-term and long-term psychotherapies. *Clinical Psychology & Psychotherapy, 21*, 475–494. https://doi.org/10.1002/cpp.1852

Légaré, F., & Witteman, H. O. (2013). Shared decision making: Examining key elements and barriers to adoption into routine clinical practice. *Health Affairs, 32*, 276–284. https://doi.org/10.1377/hlthaff.2012.1078

Lévesque, M., Hovey, R., & Bedos, C. (2013). Advancing patient-centered care through transformative educational leadership: A critical review of health care professional preparation for patient-centered care. *Journal of Healthcare Leadership, 5*, 35–46. https://doi.org/10.2147/JHL.S30889

Lucksted, A., McFarlane, W., Downing, D., & Dixon, L. (2012). Recent developments in family psychoeducation as an evidence-based practice. *Journal of Marital and Family Therapy, 38*(1), 101–121. https://doi.org/10.1111/j.1752-0606.2011.00256.x

Merriam, S. B. (2001). Andragogy and self-directed learning: Pillars of adult learning theory. *New Directions for Adult and Continuing Education, 2001*(89), 3–14. https://doi.org/10.1002/ace.3

Mueser, K. T., Meyer, P. S., Penn, D. L., Clancy, R., Clancy, D. M., & Salyers, M. P. (2006). The illness management and recovery program: Rationale, development, and preliminary findings. *Schizophrenia Bulletin, 32*(Suppl 1), S32–S43. https://doi.org/10.1093/schbul/sbl022

Nation, M., Crusto, C., Wandersman, A., Kumpfer, K. L., Seybolt, D., Morrissey-Kane, E., & Davino, K. (2003). What works in prevention: Principles of effective prevention programs. *American Psychologist, 58*(6-7), 449–456. https://doi.org/10.1037/0003-066X.58.6-7.449

Nutbeam, D. (2008). The evolving concept of health literacy. *Social Science & Medicine, 67*(12), 2072–2078. https://doi.org/10.1016/j.socscimed.2008.09.050

Scaffa, M. E., & Wooster, D. M. (2004). Effects of problem-based learning on clinical reasoning in occupational therapy. *American Journal of Occupational Therapy, 58*, 333–336. https://doi.org/10.5014/ajot.58.3.333

Sherman, M. D. (2003). The Support and Family Education (SAFE) program: Mental health facts for families. *Psychiatric Services, 54*(1), 35–37. https://doi.org/10.1176/appi.ps.54.1.35

Tiwari, A., Lai, P., So, M., & Yuen, K. (2006). A comparison of the effects of problem-based learning and lecturing on the development of students' critical thinking. *Medical Education, 40*(6), 547–554. https://doi.org/10.1111/j.1365-2929.2006.02481.x

Verma, S., Paterson, M., & Medves, J. (2006). Core competencies for health care professionals: What medicine, nursing, occupational therapy, and physiotherapy share. *Journal of Allied Health, 35*(2), 109–115.

5 A Person-Centered Approach to Mental Health Care Leadership

A vision without a plan is just a dream.
A plan without a vision is just drudgery.
But a vision with a plan can change the world.

Old Proverb

Introduction

Defining Shared Health Care Leadership

There are enormous challenges to health care delivery at the present time. These challenges are evident at almost every transition point in our existing continuum of care. Difficulties in access to primary care, and for mental health, the availability of a platform of early intervention and community crisis services, have resulted in defaulting to inappropriate use of hospital emergency services. There is a consequent overcrowding and long waits in emergency rooms, lengthy waits for medical and surgical beds and procedures, and especially relevant to this chapter, a lack of timely access to mental health care. Often referred to as "hallway care," this has reached crisis proportions for health care funders, hospital administrators, health care providers, and our patients and families, as health care service users. Access challenges are compounded by obstacles to the flow from acute care and specialized care beds into step-down community services and long-term care facilities when needed. These challenges are further compounded by escalating health care costs coupled with necessary budgetary restraints and an aging demographic, which has increasing physical and mental health needs.

Physicians, other health care providers, and their administrative partners, as well as service users and their informal caregivers, are assets to a vision of a high-quality health care system more generally, and specifically in the delivery of excellent person-centered mental health care. In particular, they are responsible for administratively contributing to this vision as they combine their leader role with their other activities as clinicians, scholars, and teachers. Given the trust that is implicit in their provision of care, they have a responsibility to society to fulfill a social contract that enables the development and continuous improvement of the health care system and the obligation to work with others in working toward this goal (Frank, Snell, & Sherbino, 2015). While nonclinical and clinical administrative leaders bring unique and specific skills to the partnership, there is great strength in the complementary partnership. In a strength-based system, their individual strengths can lead to the development of a strong and effective health care team. The team is further strengthened where the leaders utilize the strengths of individual team members in a complementary model of interprofessional care and particularly when the team shares values of compassionate caring and places service users and their families, as well as other caregivers, at the center of their care in a service user–service provider partnership. It is particularly important to involve service users in their own care (Tondora, Miller, Slade, & Davidson, 2014), as well as in services and systems development, governance, and transformation (Anthony & Huckshorn, 2008).

Sally is in her mid-40s. She is a physician leader in a tertiary care psychiatric hospital. She values a recovery-oriented, person-centered approach to care but worries that while this is the formal strategic direction for her hospital, it is not always apparent in her day-to-day administrative interactions and practices. She is firmly convinced that person-centered clinical care must develop in tandem with person-centered administrative practices if her organizational culture is to have a sustained shift to one that embraces rehabilitation and recovery-oriented care. Sally worries about shrinking health care dollars and, in particular, how this may disadvantage the delivery of mental health services and especially the quality and access to these services. Sally believes that in placing the person and their family at the center of their care, the connection and collaboration between hospital and community services will be the key to an effective person-centered system.

John is Sally's administrative partner. His background is in nursing, and he has a master's degree in business administration. John is the director for the program that Sally leads, but he also has administrative responsibilities for two other tertiary care programs in the hospital. John shares Sally's vision for a person- and family-informed mental health care service but frequently finds himself sandwiched between the budgetary pressures of his senior leaders to whom he reports and the needs of the service users that his programs serve. He worries about a likely gap between what he believes to be high-quality care and some of the realities of delivering this care in a resource-constrained system. Much like Sally, John firmly ascribes to a rehabilitative and recovery-oriented model of care. John would like to be able to develop the leadership skills that would promote effective and efficient care and respects the voices and choices of service users and families.

John and Sally have very different intrinsic leadership, conflict resolution, and learning styles. John is more apt to set a direction and initiate a plan or change without seeking significant input from those who are to implement the directive, but he is open to course-correcting along the way. Sally prefers to seek input from staff at all levels and likes to brainstorm and seek multiple inputs, being open to modifying the plan or changing it before it is initiated. Sally is always invested in doing it right from the outset.

Using Sally's and John's experiences, this chapter will serve as a guide to aspiring health care leaders as they embark on a developmental journey to become successful person-centered leaders. We describe a plausible learning trajectory with established strategies that enable each of these aspiring leaders to reach their career goals while developing their personal strengths and their unique contributions to a successful mental health care team. We show that their developmental pathways can have relevance for other health care leaders and for the shift of an organizational culture to one of rehabilitation and recovery, with continued input from service users and their families at all levels of planning. Although we focus primarily on leadership, other aspects of administration such as operational tactics are addressed too. We have intentionally elected to not include the vast literature on the science of leadership; the separation, and at times conflation, of leader versus manager roles; and the separation and overlap of strategy versus implementation. Rather we have chosen to focus on a practical toolkit approach as we describe a developmental model that could be applied equally to the professional development of leaders and managers.

Chapter Outline

This chapter proceeds with a definition of person-centered leadership. A framework for a reflective learning process follows with a practical approach to becoming a reflective leader. Using John's and Sally's experiences, we learn about the Reflected Best Self Exercise™, which enables Sally and John to develop performance profiles of themselves at their best. We take this a step further as we add the dimension of strength-based leadership to illustrate how this may enable John and Sally to develop themselves, and extend this to creating an effective service user and family partnership to ensure a provider–user relationship-centered team. This leads us to an understanding of the construct of emotional intelligence and its value in ensuring that team members operate with a value base of empathy and an awareness of the importance of care for both the service user and the service provider. We then move to understanding leadership and learning styles and how we can work collaboratively with health care provider partners. We then take the pathway of Sally and John into the realm of collaboration and the development of generative relationships to further the culture of working in unison (while encouraging authentic mutual constructive criticism) to promote the choices and best interests of service users and their families. John and Sally demonstrate collaboration using collaborative working models, and they learn how to have difficult conversations. Finally, we examine the "big picture" and system transformation, understanding those complexities that we can use to have a positive impact on the system, while recognizing other factors that we cannot control, in spite of their effect on our everyday practice. The importance of full partnership with service users and their caregivers is addressed as key to person-centered health care leadership throughout the chapter.

What Is Person-Centered Leadership?

As professional health care leaders, we are committed to the health and well-being of service users and their families, and to society (Frank et al., 2015). CanMEDS 2015 provided a framework for leader role development in Canada that has been adopted internationally. While this framework is geared to resident training, it has applications in continued practice and articulates the leadership practices that can enable leading change in a health care environment.

The key leadership competencies include:

1. Demonstrating "a commitment to patients (service users) by applying best practices and adhering to high ethical standards"
2. Demonstrating "a commitment to society by recognizing and responding to societal expectations in health care"
3. Demonstrating a commitment to professional body regulation. This is *physician-led* in the case of the CanMEDS 2015 Physician Competency Framework but is certainly applicable to the scope of practice of other health care professionals
4. Demonstrating "a commitment" to leader/provider "health and well-being to foster optimal patient care;" again geared to physicians in the case of the CanMEDS 2015 Physician Competency Framework, but with similar widespread applicability to all leader/providers.

Sally and John are identified as committed and capable future leaders by the senior leadership of their organization. Their different leadership styles are evident, as are their individual strengths. An organizational decision is made to invest in a leadership development program. Here, they will develop and enhance their leadership capacity and, particularly, coordinate this with the recently developed strategic plan at their organization. This plan has a person and family-centered strategic direction that optimizes the relationship between the health care provider team and the person with lived experience (service user) and their family. This is in the interest of recovery and rehabilitation, and a requirement if organizations are to optimize success and satisfaction of service users and their caregivers.

Sally and John's Leadership Development Plan

John and Sally meet with their coach, who is both a leadership expert and a publicly disclosed service user of mental health care services; the latter aspect may be particularly helpful to facilitate person-centered leadership. Together they agree on a leadership development trajectory. Recognizing how different John and Sally are in their leadership styles, their coach suggests that they each begin with a process of identifying their individual strengths and learning styles to enable them to find the common ground of situating their leadership through increased self-awareness and reflective practice.

The Reflected Best Self Exercise™

The Reflected Best Self Exercise™ (RBSE; Roberts et al., 2005) is a multistep process that facilitates an understanding of oneself at one's best, based on a reflective analysis of feedback derived from a diverse group of people who know the individual well. The authors of this tool espouse the idea that it is a myth that people need to be well-rounded; few truly high performing people are completely well-rounded. We do best by combining our skills with our deeper, unique talents by grooming ourselves to work within strength-based leadership teams. Further, they indicate that we are a composite of our naturally endowed abilities (talents), skills and strengths (core competencies), deeply held values (principles), and our unique personal experiences that shape us (culture).

The first step in the RBSE process is to identify respondents and ask for feedback. Sally reaches out to her spouse, siblings, friends, a mentor, and senior members of the clinical team as well as colleagues from previous positions with whom she remained in contact.

She requests that they provide her examples of when she was able to demonstrate her strengths in a way that was significant to them in their lives, whether it was within the family, between friends, or in the work environment. Sally has a tendency to downplay her strengths and focus more on areas of improvement. To ask those close to her for positive feedback causes her some dis-ease. This is an approach to personal development that she is not experienced in using. Although she is a bit hesitant in making the request, she asks her contacts if they would be willing to send her their responses in an e-mail. It is not only the fastest and easiest way to gather the information that will be input in an analysis table, but she also wants the feedback to be directly from them, instead of writing an interpretation of what she hears.

One of the responses that she receives is from a former colleague. She had worked as a recently graduated psychiatrist in an outpatient program along with a team of other health care professionals. She receives an e-mail from a psychiatric nurse who was on that team:

The former colleague wrote, "Sally, when I look back on the time that we had worked together, I remember your dedication to working together as a team. Your predecessor had maintained a relatively isolated (and isolating) approach to the various health care trainings and approaches and we tended to have to rely on ourselves. When you came along, I remember your eagerness to collaborate, particularly communicate, and discuss ideas about what would be most effective for our service users and ways that we could improve the program and its service delivery. You being the psychiatrist on the team, I know that others, alongside myself, were appreciative of your willingness to work as a team. Thank you for that – it made for a wonderful workplace."

Another e-mail that Sally receives is from a close friend. They have known each other since their undergraduate education:

The close friend wrote, "As you know, we have shared some deeply personal experiences together and we have kept in touch throughout all of these years. I would say that one of the most meaningful things that you have done was support me during the loss of my child. As you know, it was an unbearable experience for me. You were there to listen, to give me perspective when I was spiraling to places that would not benefit me or my family. I remember when you would call me in the morning to make sure that I was out of bed to start my day, and when you would pull me out of the house to get some fresh air and talk about whatever I wanted. You helped me process my feelings and emotions in a way that helped me get through that experience with new understanding and a new appreciation for everything I had in my life. You were very patient with me. I am so grateful that you are in my life."

Upon reading these e-mails, Sally feels so fortunate to have these individuals in her life and to hear that she was able to support them as she felt they have supported her. The next step in the RBSE process is to recognize patterns. She soon realizes that both individuals, as well as others, speak to the idea that she sees areas of promising growth in others and helps to facilitate that growth, whether it is in a person or a team. A summary of what she discovered is given in Table 5.1.

Table 5.1   Self-Reflection Based on Feedback Using the Reflected Best Self Exercise™ (RBSE): Themes Based on Sally's RBSE

Common theme	Examples given	Possible interpretation
Seeing potential and supporting growth	Fostering collaboration among a clinical team to function more effectively and better serve service users. Listening, validating others in times of hardship, and helping them through these experiences toward new understanding.	*I see things not for what they are, but for what they could be. I have a vision and take the steps to make it happen.*
Inclusive and accommodating of the needs of others	Flexible when team resources are limited, taking on some nonclinical tasks to maintain efficiency of the team. Facilitated introductions of new members in the lunch room when it was not required of her.	*I am adaptable to the needs of a given situation. I value others for who they are as people. I am always willing to learn and develop the skills I require toward successful outcomes.*

For Sally, this exercise highlights some qualities that she is aware of in herself, and other qualities of which she is less aware. She makes a conscious effort to ensure that people are working together, and adapts herself to the needs of the situation so that others feel comfortable and to support them in the development of their skills and abilities. She does not see herself as a visionary, but there are a number of examples that those close to her provide that suggest otherwise. This gives her more insight into being more vocal about where she could see a program or organization heading and anticipating what would be needed for the program to be successful in reaching greater heights and improved outcomes. These insights hint at the notion that she may have the ability to take on senior leadership positions to see her visions come to fruition.

Another area that stands out is that Sally enjoys challenges and has an innate ability to recognize what a situation calls for, and cultivates those abilities that are required to be successful. She also tends to hesitate regarding mentoring others as she sometimes feels as if she is not doing justice to the mentee, but these results suggest that she has the skills necessary to help another individual through a process toward increased competency and confidence at work.

The third step is to compose your self-portrait. This is a summary of the information that is gathered and interpreted to form a clearer picture of your best self. It may be written in a few paragraphs and by filling in the phrase, "When I am at my best, I . . ." This narrative will also help bring together different areas of one's life and help connect various areas that would otherwise appear separate. Sally develops her self-portrait to read as follows:

"When I am at my best, I am able to assess or see the needs of a situation or a person. I am able to use my qualities of adaptability, compassion, and an inherent duty to serve toward a greater good in order to meet those needs. I am able to get a sense of how a person is feeling and anticipate what needs to be done to make that individual feel at ease. I value individuals who cross my path, and I see their strengths, potential, and their contributions to the environment around them. I see the best in people, situations, and events, and I get others to see those possibilities as well.

I value harmony and working collectively toward a common goal. I believe that hearing different perspectives and gathering all of this information is more effective than if one person were to work independently. This collaborative process generates a thorough picture of what we would like to work toward, ensuring that it resonates with all of those involved. I am able to foster authentic relationships with others that persist long after circumstances have brought the individuals together. I have a passion for making a difference in the lives of others, be it in small- or large-scale.

I am a tenacious, hard worker who strives to learn and develop myself and apply these new learnings to the work that I do, and to the people with whom I cross paths. I am an effective planner and goal-setter, and I am able to execute the smaller steps needed in order to accomplish a larger goal. I am a visionary, and I can vividly picture the possibilities and outcomes of a person or organization when direction and focus are taken to achieve such outcomes. I am excited by new challenges as it provides the opportunity to learn, apply myself in new ways, consult and collaborate with others, and achieve something new and meaningful."

Upon writing this self-portrait, Sally realizes that she sometimes becomes so consumed with the technical or procedural aspects of the current role, or putting out fires, that she does not take the time to use her skills to envision the long-term direction of her team. Her time is also divided between clinical practice and leading administrative aspects of the team, which makes it challenging to contribute much to the program vision and decision making. She also has a new appreciation and confidence in her ability to encourage and foster growth in others so that they can leave their distinct mark on their environment. Sally finds this exercise to be very encouraging and a very helpful reminder so that she can be a more workable version of herself and have a greater impact than before.

The next step is to redesign how to go about how she does her job. With this renewed understanding of what she is able to offer, Sally wants to use these strengths so that she can maximize her effectiveness in the current role in terms of the way she completes her work, team functioning, and time management.

In terms of how she does her work, Sally strengthens her collaboration with John and participates more vocally in strategic meetings where she requests to be present. She makes an intentional effort to cultivate the abilities of her clinical team. She provides them with opportunities to learn from one another and to provide input for the direction of the program. She improves her time management by making suggestions to streamline the staff performance review process, which is currently rather cumbersome.

Sally alerts her clinical team to the importance of the existing, but dwindling, service user and family council. By increasing membership and gathering their opinions, needs, and perspectives regarding what the program is to offer service users, this feedback will be leveraged to promote the administrative and clinical practices that will have to occur to have a recovery-oriented and person-centered approach, which is in alignment with the strategic direction of the hospital. This will also need to be a cost-effective solution given the budgetary constraints.

Service user and family council feedback included the discharge experience of the sudden change from receiving hospital treatment to accessing community services. Service users thought that increased communication between the clinical staff and those who worked in community agencies would help service users to better transition, live successfully in the community, and reduce their chances of returning to hospital.

These actions play on Sally's strengths of seeking input from others, gathering information, and applying the skills in such a way that aligns with the hospital's vision of person-centered care practices. Her clinical team is also able to develop themselves further in their roles by liaising with different community service agencies earlier in the treatment process so that service users have the space to discuss what programs and services are working effectively for them, or if another organization is more suited to their current needs. Sally shares the feedback with John and senior-level management, which is very well received. These actions are a step closer toward improved, recovery-oriented, and person-centered outcomes.

Roberts et al. (2005) of the RBSE indicate that one "has more to gain by developing one's ... gifts and leveraging one's ... natural skills than by trying to repair ... weaknesses" (p. 1). Further, they point out that it is necessary to be aware of one's strengths. In terms of weaknesses, they point out that while correctional feedback is important through traditional performance evaluations, this should not be at the cost of neglecting to utilize one's strengths. RBSE is a copyrighted term and is available as a PDF download at the website of the Center for Positive Organizations at the University of Michigan (http://positiveorgs.bus.umich.edu/tools/).

The RBSE provided a starting point for a successful *physician leadership development program* (PLDP), with 25 physicians each participating in a yearlong certificate program. This program ran as a collaboration between the Ontario Medical Association and the Schulich School of Business, Health Administration at York University in Toronto, with 125 physicians completing the program over the course of 5 years.

We have published a quantitative and qualitative review of the program in the *Canadian Journal of Physician Leadership* (Dickens, Fisman, & Grossman, 2016). Qualitative individual observations regarding the value of the RBSE in the PLDP have included such comments as "early in the course, this set the stage for using one's self and self-strengths to build collaborative relationships" and "the RBSE was unexpectedly powerful – it provided a lot of rich free-text data." And the RBSE was linked with another main theme: the enhancement of self-confidence. According to one person, "the RBSE assessment gave me a lot of confidence; a sense of self and how others see me."

Another perspective was the insight into some areas for improvement: "I appreciated the Reflected Best Self Exercise™, for helping me see my strengths [through others' eyes] but also because it pointed to some of my gaps, which created a framework for learning." Continuing beyond the course, the application of self-reflection and utilization of personal strengths continued to influence the personal and professional lives of many of those interviewed. "As a person, I have become much more reflective; I am much more intentional about listening and sensing other people's emotions, then adjusting my stance so I can best communicate with them." Another noted, "I pause to write what I did and what I notice; take a breath." Additionally, "I spend less time worrying about my own weaknesses" and "I am more in touch with my own feelings; I can now label them and thus deal with them more effectively." Another participant commented that "as a person, self-reflection was very helpful; I learned what makes me tick aside from my professional development." Professionally, "the power of reflective practice" enabled "movement from a diagnosis and treatment mindset. I learned to get out from behind my own assumptions and to live a more balanced life." The prescriptive use of the RBSE as a foundation to the course design had an engaging effect: "It was clever how the program got very bright, but often stubborn people to engage in self-reflection. Part of that was creating a safe environment for dialogue."

The RBSE laid the groundwork for another major theme, the value of collaborative relationships and particularly in team building and system change. An interviewee recalled the RBSE and the fact that as the lead in his family health team, "it carried onwards to help me recognize my strengths and the strengths of others." Several participants noted variations on the following comment: "I have learned to lead from my strengths and to offset my weaknesses by collaborating with others in order to effect change" and that "I no longer stress about my weaknesses; there are others out there who can do what needs to be done." One noted that they used to be the "sort of person who would take on more and more stuff, but the program taught me to think in terms of my strengths. That has helped me to let go of the doing that is my instinctive response." As well, "I am better able to identify others' strengths and then encourage/support them in taking on projects that suit their strengths." Finally, one early participant noted, "I am more observant of my colleagues' patterns and I have learned to be more intentional about celebrating successes: both my own and others."

Becoming a Reflective Leader

The coach introduces Sally and John to the principles of reflective practice as a component of their professional leadership and simultaneously introduces them to the concepts of strength-based leadership (Rath & Conchie, 2008).

Reflective practice has received increasing attention in occupational and educational environments in the past few decades (Francis & Cowan, 2008; Schön, 1987; Schutz, 2007). Schön (1987) described reflective practice as "essential to competence in the indeterminate zones of practice" (p. 18). This would be the rule rather than the exception as Sally and John took on their transformative leadership roles.

Their coach regards the development of skill in reflective practice as a necessary part of John's and Sally's learning journey.

While their coach recognizes some utility in having Sally and John complete a literature search in this growing area of study, she also realizes the day-to-day demands on their time: for John, day-to-day operational demands, and for Sally, clinical practice demands. Instead, she provides Sally and John with a framework for a reflective learning process and opportunities to do reflective writing when they face uncertain and complex situations, which, by virtue of their complexity, do not lend themselves to simpler, linear solutions.

Box 5.1 outlines questions to ask oneself after a memorable or challenging experience has occurred (Appendix 31).

Box 5.1   Framework for a Reflective Learning Process: Learning From Your Experiences

1. Describe the experience.
2. Reflection (sometimes called reflection-in-action): How did you behave? What thoughts did you have? How did it make you feel? Were there other factors that influenced the situation? What have you learned from the experience?
3. Theorizing (sometimes called reflection-on-action): How did the experience match (or not) your preconceived ideas – i.e., was the outcome expected or unexpected? What behaviors do you think may have changed the outcome? Is there anything you could say or do now to change the outcome? What action(s) can you take to change similar reactions in the future?

As the director for the program, John faces many challenging situations that prompt reflection toward improved leadership in future situations. There is one instance in particular which remains in his mind even though some time has passed since the occurrence.

Clinicians on the team had full schedules, and the waiting time to enter one of the programs he runs was approximately 6 months. Because of this, there was a need to hire additional clinical staff. Another need was for some of the staff that had come more recently to receive psychotherapy training. Yet another need was to hire more administrative personnel to offset the workload of other administrative staff, who were struggling to manage after hospital-wide policy changes had increased records management processes.

The funding for this tertiary care program had been reduced, resulting in cutbacks. With the numerous priorities that John had to manage, he had to find the most effective way to increase the program's efficiencies while not giving up the quality of care provided to service users and their families.

John thought that it was important to reduce the waiting time – and hence the number of service users waiting to access the program – to improve the quality of care and the overall experience of service users. With a recovery-oriented, person-centered approach in mind, he decided that hiring additional administrative personnel would be the most cost-effective solution for the team. His rationale was that the addition of administrative personnel was less costly than hiring another clinician, and that this individual would help to manage some of the administrative duties that the clinicians were taking on, so that they had more time to provide care to more service users. Hiring a new clinician was also eliminated as a possibility due to the learning curve a new clinician would require – John did not think that dedicating the time required for this would be feasible given their current situation. Psychotherapy training for some of the clinicians was also considered a lesser priority because of the cost and time commitments that it would require.

To convey this information to the team, John held meetings with staff to inform them of the budgetary changes and the potential implications. Staff were alarmed when they heard that there would be cutbacks, but John assured them of job security – but that some of the anticipated plans for the program would change. John was no stranger to having difficult conversations with his team and knew that regular, transparent communication was most effective to keep everyone informed, dispel any rumors, and allow individuals to voice any concerns they may have.

When the final decision was made, he anticipated that there would be some tension among the clinical staff in relation to the cuts to training. He did not want his staff to feel undervalued, as they were all assets to the program. The regular meetings that provided the team with updates, he thought, would help to resolve these issues. He believed he was thorough in justifying his decision when he informed the team. When told, the team was quiet at first, and in the coming days, he noticed that what he had anticipated came to fruition – some of the clinical staff who would not receive psychotherapy training were less participatory in team meetings, and not as keen as usual in their work. Instead of these individuals being able to lead group sessions, they were required to do so with a trained colleague. At this point, he realized that the changes might have been much better received if he had taken a different approach, but he was unsure of what else he could have done in the situation.

Upon working more closely with Sally and their coach on their individual leadership styles, he realized that he tends to plan and go ahead with his ideas without sufficiently engaging those who are impacted by the choice. In this case, it may have been useful to include the team in the decision-making process, or alternatively, delegate team discussions to, and seek input from, Sally who is strong in this area.

Now that John is going through this process of building upon his leadership abilities, he is more aware of his directive leadership style and the implications that it can have for the team. He is aware of a more effective approach to leading, and moving forward, he exercises these insights with his current staff. He shares his long-term vision with the team, which includes addressing the issue of training and many other program components, which gives the team a sense of security in knowing that the program has a clear direction. John looks forward to further developing his competencies.

Developing and Leading Service User-Centered Teams

As Sally and John develop their RBSE profiles, they are surprised at how valuable this has been. They each feel energized and more confident about tackling issues that are impairing the service user experience.

The RBSE prepares individual leaders to utilize their personal *leadership strengths*. However, they are aware that to create a recovery-oriented system that will truly make a difference in the quality of life for the people they serve who experience mental health challenges (MHCs), they need to learn how to bring out the best in their treatment teams. In preparation for the crucial step of team development, they are each provided with a book by Tom Rath and Barry Conchie (Rath & Conchie, 2008). These authors posit that the most effective leaders always invest in their own strengths, surround themselves with people whose individual strengths maximize the team, and they understand the needs of their "followers" (in our case, service users and families). They identify four domains of leadership strength, which include:

1. Executing
2. Influencing
3. Relationship building
4. Strategic thinking

Instead of one dominant leader who tries to do everything, or individuals who all have similar strengths, contributions from individuals who excel in at least one of the four domains lead to a strong and cohesive team. The authors conclude: "Although individuals need not be well-rounded, teams should be" (Rath & Conchie, 2008, p. 23). They further identify multiple themes that cluster into these four domains of leadership. John and Sally are able to do the StrengthsFinder exercise (Buckingham & Clifton, 2001) and understand where each of them excels, as a starting point to building their treatment team.

In summary, those with executing as a dominant strength will make things happen; they are the implementers. Those with a dominant strength of influencing are able to widely spread the team's ideas, increase comfort with the ideas, and facilitate their uptake. Those whose strength is relationship building are the glue that binds the team together, and they can make the whole much greater than the sum of the team's parts. Those with strategic thinking as a strength are able to absorb and integrate information and benefit the team's decision making and thinking for a better future. Table 5.2 lists the domains of leadership along with associated strengths.

Sally's StrengthsFinder identifies her predominant strength in the domain of relationship building with themes of adaptability, empathy, connectedness, and positivity. John's StrengthsFinder identifies his predominant strength in the domain of executing with themes of achiever, deliberative, focus, and responsibility. They are aware that they will need to balance their team and be mindful of including those with strength in the influencing domain and in the strategic thinking domain.

Table 5.2   Identifying Individual Strengths: Four Domains of Leadership and Thirty-Four Strengths

1. Strategic thinking	2. Executing	3. Influencing	4. Relationship building
"Knowing where to go"	"Getting some-where"	"Getting there with others"	"Keeping others on your team"
Analytical	Achieving	Activation	Adaptability
Context	Arranging	Command	Developer
Futuristic	Belief	Communication	Connectedness
Ideation	Consistency	Competition	Empathy
Input	Deliberation	Maximization	Harmony
Intellection	Discipline	Self-assurance	Includer
Learner	Focus	Significance	Individualization
Strategic	Responsibility	Wooing	Positivity
	Restoration		Relator

Note. Adapted from Rath & Conchie, 2008.

Emotional Intelligence

Emotional intelligence or emotional quotient (EQ) is the ability to monitor one's own and others' emotions, to discriminate among them, and to use the information to guide one's thinking and actions (Salovey & Mayer, 1990). EQ is a way of recognizing, understanding, and choosing how we think and act. It shapes our interactions and our personal insights and provides a context for us to set priorities and conduct our daily business, both professionally and personally. It has been estimated to be responsible for as much as 80% of our success in life.

High levels of EQ are embedded within strong and empathic person-centered leadership. Leaders with high EQ will have a calm, assuring demeanor no matter what the situation. They will instill trust in those around them, listen with compassion, and speak kindly. They will be perceived by their team as approachable, and they will make informed choices.

Fariselli, Freedman, Ghini, and Valentini (2008), in a white paper titled "Stress, Emotional Intelligence, & Performance in Healthcare," found that EQ is strongly predictive of performance. While this applied across all levels of leadership, the highest prediction was at the senior leadership level. They also found that high EQ mitigated stress – that is, high EQ is predictive of low stress levels. On the other hand, perceived stress reduces performance.

John and Sally embrace the concept of EQ and readily make the connection between this construct and the ways of feeling and behaving within the construct of person-centered leadership. They develop an awareness of how their performance could be impacted by high levels of work and life stress.

John reflects on his own past experiences as a clinician. He is trained as a registered nurse. From his years of work in an inpatient psychiatric unit, he has carried some clinical experiences with him to the present. When he was working with a service user who had severe depression, he was liaising with the service user's family on how they could be of support to their loved one, the resources that were available, and the most effective approach to care for her. As a newer team member and clinician, he felt himself getting affected emotionally by the situation and was particularly focused on the family's hardships. He had difficulty separating the family's emotions from his own. He felt that this hindered his ability to maintain his professionalism and affected him for a number of days afterward including when dealing with other service users and their families. He did not want this experience to reoccur, as there were many challenging situations in his line of work. To be effective in his role, he had to learn techniques and have better insight into himself to maintain a sense of calm and composure, not only for himself, but for the service users and their families as well.

Since that time, John has made a conscious effort to be more aware of his emotions, body sensations, and the emotions of others. He makes sure to separate others' emotions from his own to provide care in a compassionate, professional manner. Rather than completely identifying with his emotions, he is able to experience an emotion, watch it as something within but separate from him, observe the accompanying sensations he feels in his body, and finally move through the emotion. Giving the time and attention his emotions require allows him to then make the choice to set them aside so that he is able to provide high-quality service user care.

He also listens more and has ceased to immediately provide advice, which he was quick to do as a new graduate. He now realizes that many people want to be heard more than anything else, and that sometimes an attentive person is all that someone needs rather than any advice or guidance itself. He also recognizes the importance of validating others' feelings. In doing so, he is able to develop a greater level of trust with service users and their families, along with his colleagues. With the actions he has taken since his early career, he has also noticed changes to his personal relationships. Furthermore, he has carried these skills forward into his graduate training toward a master's degree in business administration and in his current role as director of the program. He continuously cultivates these skill sets because of the profound difference it makes in his own ability to manage situations and in how people respond to him as an employee, a leader and in his personal life. He recognizes that he has come a long way from that memorable experience and embraces the notion of being a lifelong learner to continuously improve his attitudes and skills.

Generative Relationships

With the understanding of strength-based leadership and well-rounded teams, John and Sally's coach considers the value of taking John and Sally through some exercises in building collaborative relationships as a fundamental basis for strength-based and person-centered administrative problem solving. She determines that this will be a very necessary prerequisite to tackling a major challenge to their hospital that has resulted from service pressures on their acute care partner hospitals. These pressures are in turn impacting service user care and service providers in their tertiary hospital environment. As a start, she introduces them to the concept of generative relationships.

A *generative relationship* (Lane & Maxfield, 1996) produces new sources of value between individuals, which cannot be foreseen. It is created by the interaction between the parties. The relationship produces something which one of the members of the relationship could not have produced alone. In contrast, partnerships or joint ventures may or may not be generative; each partner may know a priori what needs to be done: each has a gap or deficiency which cannot be addressed by the other joint venture partner.

Fostering generative relationships is a key responsibility of successful leaders; generative relationships allow new strategies, new directions, and innovative ideas to emerge. They are in sharp contrast to the use of a central authority to set directions.

Generative relationships become valuable in complex contexts when the future is uncertain and especially when the industry, sector, and/or society is undergoing transformational change. This is very relevant to current health care transformation. Generative relationships allow the parties to learn as they cocreate a new product.

Essence of Collaboration

Collaboration is a complicated relationship process that takes ongoing maintenance to sustain itself. It is not enough that collaboration occurs episodically in facilitated gatherings; it needs to be part of the day-to-day experiences of people, for it to be part of the culture. The need for trust is essential in maintaining effective working relationships.

Zimmerman and Hayday (1999) posed an effective model for developing collaborations in the context of generative relationships, which they have referred to as the *generative relationships star*. Looking at it as a four-pointed star, each point represents one of the letters in the word *star*, with each representing one key aspect of generative relationships, and each is on a continuum from very low to very high levels of the particular attribute.

Zimmerman and Hayday (1999) describe each letter of the STAR acronym as follows:

Separateness: differences in perspectives in background, training, skills, and perspectives. If all of the parties are similar, they may have heated discussions, but be unable to challenge assumptions and see things from a different perspective.

Tuning: talking, listening, and taking the time to work through challenges. This creates opportunities to challenge the status quo and explore creative solutions. Time together also allows the parties to reflect so that they can grow and learn together.

Action: opportunities for acting together to cocreate something new. Talking can be developed into action.

Reason to work together: the parties have a reason to work together and share ideas and resources, even if only for a limited time. To see one another as attaining mutual benefit from their alignment as allies, rather than adversaries, will make it more likely that they emerge with solutions of substantial value. They can talk to and learn from one another rather than each creating something alone.

The S-T (separateness and tuning) relationship is conceptual, and necessary to generate unanticipated insights and value propositions, while the A-R (action and reason to work together) relationship is structural and allows new products and services to emerge.

The evenly pointed S-T-A-R will grow a climate of trust, allowing the generative relationship to flourish. Relationships with more generative potential are seen to have longer points on the Generative Relationship STAR. A visualization of the S-T-A-R can be found in Figure 5.1.

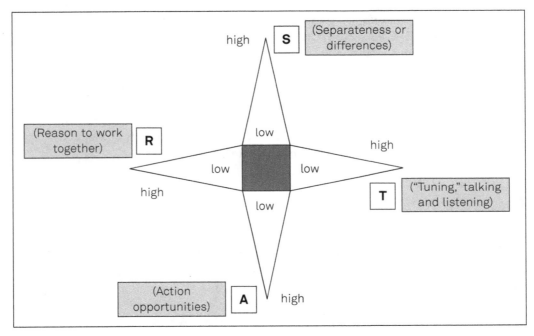

Figure 5.1   The generative relationships as symbolized by STAR. Reprinted from "A Board's Journey Into Complexity Science: Lessons From (and for) Staff and Board members," by B. Zimmerman, and B. Hayday, 1999, *Group Decision and Negotiation, 8*(4), 281–303. © 1999 by Springer. Reprinted with permission.

Leading Person-Centered Change

With this new set of tools in their toolbox, Sally and John are asked to lead a service user experience project. Their tertiary care center is challenged by a combination of an increased demand for admissions from their acute care hospital partners, coupled with delays in admission to intensive case management and safe housing in the community. This has created several pressure points for service users and families in the treatment journey and a sense of frustration and fatigue among mental health care teams wanting to provide compassionate person-centered care.

Recognizing that this will be very time-intensive and time-consuming, senior leadership at the hospital determine that John and Sally will have a contracted project facilitator to assist them. Wisely, a person with lived experience of MHCs, as well as expertise in strength-based project methodology, is hired for the position. Additionally, based on the input from the coach, and taking John's and Sally's strengths into consideration, they hire an individual who has shown strengths in the strategic thinking leadership domain to complement the existing team. It is also agreed that any project-related decision making will be conducted collaboratively with the organization's service user and family councils.

Person-Centered Project Methodology

Typically, leaders and managers will have been exposed to the process of *SWOT* analysis:
- Strengths
- Weaknesses
- Opportunities
- Threats

SWOT analysis (Team FME, 2013) follows the traditional approach to change where we look for the problem, complete a diagnosis, and find a solution in order to match the internal position of an organization to the external environment. Specifically the notion is to explore the internal strengths and weaknesses of an organization's business with the external opportunities and threats. In this methodology, strengths enable an organization to develop an effective strategic direction, while weaknesses inform the organization of ways that it can protect itself against external threats.

When Sally was managing her current team, they had used a SWOT analysis for the psychiatric outpatient program with the clinical team to identify any areas that could be improved, as seen in Table 5.3 (Appendix 32).

Table 5.3 SWOT Analysis: Strengths, Weaknesses, Opportunities, Threats for a Psychiatric Outpatient Program

Strengths	Weaknesses
• Fully staffed, qualified clinical team • Established hospital program • Clarified scope to ensure appropriate referrals of service users • Interdisciplinary team offering different medical and rehabilitative treatment approaches • Positive work culture and effective collaboration within team	• High level of referrals to program, leading to wait lists • Revolving-door phenomenon, where service users repeatedly return to the program • Coverage lacking when staff take unscheduled leaves • Program evaluation measures are lacking in the program
Opportunities	**Threats**
• Development of program performance metrics to justify continued funding, including feedback from service users and families • Ability to train students and receive increased funds • Exploring latest research evidence for increasingly effective treatment options to reduce revolving door phenomenon • Engage in research projects to further elevate the awareness of the program and to further explore the most effective treatment options • Further enhance team member competencies and abilities	• Funding dollars are uncertain year-to-year • Some staff are on contract until further notice, which can affect staffing levels • Mental health fads, which can dictate the direction of funding dollars • High stress clinical and nonclinical roles may impact individual and team functioning • Risk of vicarious trauma for staff

The biggest concern and priority for Sally and John's team is to eliminate, or at least considerably reduce, the waiting time for services. Without secure funding for the following years, and no reasonable chance of receiving additional dollars, hiring another staff member is unlikely. Clinicians are working with full caseloads, and they cannot see themselves providing care to additional service users without risk of burnout. A possibility to address the waitlist could be to provide online information or modules to those on the waitlist so that they receive some form of support while they await entry into the program. This seems like a plausible option; however, it does not eliminate or change the waiting time in a significant way, and that will only increase the amount of work for the team.

Another area of concern is to reduce the "revolving door phenomenon," whereupon service users enter, exit, and reenter the hospital system, repeatedly. This may be seen as a challenge to address because, at first glance, it is unclear what factors are contributing to these occurrences. As highlighted in the SWOT analysis, the treatment interventions may be explored further to see if there is evidence for new, more effective interventions. However, even if different treatment approaches are determined to be more effective, there is no funding allocated for additional training of clinicians to practice these novel techniques. A team member suggests that perhaps the community services are not meeting the needs of service users, hence they return to the program. This is a possibility; however, little can be done beyond adding more community services to the referral list and liaising with community partners which would also add to the current workload. The team thinks that perhaps developing stronger family programs for service users would be an effective way to cultivate a support system for those receiving services so that the support will continue after the service user completes the program. The discussion continues in this manner.

Other areas of concern are the contract positions and the lack of security in receiving funding dollars from year to year to sustain the program, even though it is an established program that is well-received by other units and by management.

In addition to all of these concerns, there are a number of factors that are outside of the team's direct control, including a change in government which will likely alter the extent of funding that the program receives, new health care policies, and an increase in need for their services from a societal perspective, which will heighten waitlist challenges.

While a SWOT analysis may have utility, reliance on this may hamper project implementation. Many organizations follow the process of articulating a vision, creating a mission statement, using a SWOT analysis, creating strategic imperatives, and then developing

Table 5.4   Characterizing the External Environment: PESTLE Analysis of the External Environment

Factor	Example
Political	Government policy affects wait time strategies, drives health care developments such as early psychosis programs
Economic	Financial shifts in currency, interest rates affect hospital funding, social assistance
Social	An aging population demands increased mental and physical health end-of-life funding, generational differences determine that millennials focus on work/life balance
Technological	New technologies and new products such as electronic patient records and telehealth foster innovation
Legal	Legislation influences age discrimination, elimination of mandatory retirement age, minimum wage, disability
Environmental	Weather and climate change affect farming and food production, carbon footprint, changes in disease patterns

Additional elements, captured by L(o)NG PESTLE are
- Local factors
- National factors
- Global factors

Note. PESTLE = political, economic, social, technological, legal, and environmental. Based on Law, 2009.

tactics to determine the direction of the business and where they are to be investing time and resources. The outcome is a plan for the year that functions as a road map for the organization. However, one issue with a typical SWOT analysis is that the process encourages at least half of the planning time to be focused on the negatives and gaps within an organization, with the intent of fixing issues and problems – a draining and often exhausting experience that leaves employees feeling defeated. A number of potential roadblocks may challenge implementation. An internal focus can create blind spots where the group may only be seeing their own perspective, which flies in the face of all that Sally and John have learned about working in the context of collaborative relationships. Other roadblocks may arise in staff resistance to implementation; or the external landscape can change, which may make the strategy a challenge to implement as seen in Table 5.4 (Law, 2009) (Appendix 33).

Sally is very proud of her team – they are effective workers with strong skill sets. And yet, their discussions are not highlighting any of those things. Instead, the team is feeling drained from the lack of control they have to improve the most pressing issues of the program. Sally notices that some of the team members are becoming skeptical of any potential solutions that may have an impact in addressing the challenges at hand. A low mood in the office continues into the rest of the week. As hard as everyone is working, it feels like it is not meeting the needs of the organization. Sally herself feels this way and wonders why a meeting that is meant to be productive and inspiring turns out to be one that lowers team morale. They listed several strengths of the team, but it appears to be overshadowed by the challenges of the program and the inability to clearly address these challenges in an effective manner. She wants to take another approach to have more productive, morale-boosting planning meetings with the team.

Shifting to Strength-Based Models for Change

While we need to understand challenges to change, when we emphasize and amplify those, we risk missing the solutions because we lose sight of our potential strengths. A strength-based methodology that is congruent with the person-centered and strength-focused theme of this chapter is that of *appreciative inquiry* (Cooperrider & Whitney, 2005). Appreciative inquiry methodologies have been applied to organizations, with outstanding results (Sprangel, Stavros, & Cole, 2011). Appreciative inquiry traditionally uses the *4-D* approach (Stavros, Cooperrider, & Kelley, 2003) to a change project:

Discovery: Identify existing moments of excellence, core values, and best practices – "what are we doing well?"

Dream: Envision positive possibilities – "given our strengths, where can we reach higher?"

Design: Create structures, processes, and relationships to support the dream – "can we draw on other existing models to create our ideal?"

Delivery/Destiny: Develop an effective, inspirational plan for implementation – "are we ready to set up our implementation plan?"

The addition of an initial definition step can help to frame the project (Mohr, 2001). Appreciative inquiry is then an ongoing iterative cycle consisting of those five phases.

A specific application of this positive approach to change is a *SOAR* analysis, based on *strengths*, *opportunities*, *aspirations*, and *results*. SOAR is a positive approach to thinking and planning, through conversations that promote collaboration, shared understanding, and commitment to action (Stavros & Hinrichs, 2011). SOAR integrates appreciative inquiry to create a transformational process.

SOAR contrasts with SWOT in its focus on strengths and opportunities, aligning and expanding them until they lessen or manage our weaknesses and threats. Weaknesses and threats are not ignored but are given the appropriate focus within the opportunities and results conversation. As a counterpoint to SWOT analysis, SOAR can be "a profoundly positive approach to strategic thinking and planning that allows an organization to construct its future through collaboration, shared understanding and a commitment to action" (Stavros & Hinrichs, 2011, p. 3). It resonates with the appreciative inquiry framework for the strategic planning process, from creation to implementation. SOAR leverages appreciative inquiry to focus on the positives while still addressing areas of need, as seen in Table 5.5.

Table 5.5   Strength-Based Models for Change: Comparing the 5 *Ds* of Appreciative Inquiry With the 5 *Is* of SOAR

5 *Is* of SOAR	5 *Ds* of Appreciative Inquiry
Choosing to SOAR INITIATE	Decide what to learn about DEFINITION
Asking the SOAR questions INQUIRE	Conduct an inquiry into the topic and assemble learnings DISCOVERY
Creating a shared vision IMAGINE	Generalize these learnings into an image of how the organization would function if they were fully alive DREAM
Designing the initiative INNOVATE	Develop hypotheses about how to translate these learnings into the organization's social architecture DESIGN
Going from possibilities to inspired action IMPLEMENT	Create the appropriate innovations based on the hypothesis of the previous phase DELIVERY/DESTINY

Note. SOAR = strengths, opportunities, aspirations, and results. Adapted from Stavros, Cooperrider, & Kelley, 2003, and Stavros & Hinrichs, 2011.

John and Sally's Project

The strategic plan for Sally and John's organization identifies the service user experience as a high priority for change. In exploratory focus groups, they hear repeated narratives of the dehumanizing experiences for individuals with MHCs and their families as they attempt to navigate the labyrinth of services, especially at times of personal high need. When symptoms peak and safety concerns escalate, patients and families default to the use of the acute care hospital emergency room where they encounter lengthy waits, a sense of being a lesser priority than those presenting with physical symptoms, and a lack of privacy coupled with high security, even when they present no risk to the safety of others. The words demeaning and humiliating come up repeatedly in the focus group narratives.

While this appears at face value as an acute care delivery problem, it is far more complex, with many moving parts. It is clear to Sally and John that to build a strategy that will enable a positive, person-centered experience from acute care through to tertiary hospital care and into the community, with streamlined access back again when needed, they will have to engage stakeholders within and outside of the hospital system and include service users and families in the process. This will especially be the case in the course of persistent MHCs.

Planning the Project

John and Sally are enthused with the SOAR and appreciative inquiry methodology. Understanding the value that a collaborative focus (Stavros & Hinrichs, 2011) will bring to the overall outcome, they set out to involve a diverse group of stakeholders representing each part of the organization, as well as others outside the organization, to maximize diverse viewpoints. They recognize that their stakeholders must at a minimum include service users and family members, direct care staff across the hospital continuum of care, and related community players. Using this methodology supports systems thinking; decisions will be made that consider the far-reaching implications of ensuing actions. They determine that they must have a senior leader from each hospital as corporate sponsors and a representative from their political bureaucracy so that their plan will be supported and enabled at the highest levels.

They are very much aware of the critical importance of engaging staff and other stakeholders – including clients and partners – to discover the conditions that created the organization's greatest successes. They will have to ask powerful and positive questions to generate images of possibility and potential. They accept that threats, weaknesses, or problems will not be ignored, and instead will be reframed. Discussion will focus on "what we want" rather than "what we don't want." From their training and with the encouragement of their project facilitator, they know that the key success factor will be the identification of aspirations and desired results by the group. It is these aspirations which will create a compelling vision of the future using the best of the past while challenging the status quo.

In pursuing this service user experience project, Sally and John are well-equipped and excited to take on this new challenge with everything they have learned. John will use his skills of focus and responsibility to ensure that the project is executed as planned, in a timely matter, and in such a way that it achieves its goals. Sally is keen to use her skills of positivity, adaptability, and connectedness to effectively collaborate with different stakeholders and keep genuine relations toward achieving a common goal. She knows that these skills are necessary to forge partnerships now and into the future in order for service users to receive seamless, person-centered care.

Before this new training, although Sally and John worked well together, there were times when they were at odds, with different approaches that each wanted to take. Examples of that include when deliberating with the clinical team, making administrative decisions, and in their communications. Now, however, they both have a new appreciation for each other's strengths, and they both understand that their success in the project is greatly dependent on the different skills they bring to the table. These unique qualities they each have enhance the development of the project which will lead to more effective outcomes than either of them could produce alone.

Sally uses her skills to manage many of the stakeholder engagement sessions. With a compassionate ear, she listens to each of the stakeholder's concerns, openly discusses each of their strengths, and creates what is possible when they develop deeper collaborations with one another. The project facilitator is also present at these meetings to add a strategic lens to the conversation, develop a picture of what their future collaborations could look like, and identify the steps that will be needed. John identifies the actionable goals and the specific tasks, such as delegating responsibilities to the respective parties, with timelines to ensure that everyone is on track to meet their objectives.

Sally, John, and the project facilitator also recognize the need to leverage the power of influence. They invite a senior executive of the hospital. John clearly communicates the findings of the family councils and inspires a sense of urgency with the stakeholders; they feel the need to do their part to make this project a success. In terms of developing generative relationships, a number of aspects are considered. All of the different stakeholders lead to a high level of separateness, where several individuals from different educational, experiential, and training backgrounds with different perspectives highlight what is important to each of them. This leads to a rich discussion on the issue of the psychiatric hospital system and how they may make improvements.

Service users and their families voice the fact that the waiting times are detrimental to the recovery process – it is sometimes difficult to get a person experiencing MHCs to willingly agree to seek help until it is a crisis situation, which may be extremely stressful for the individual and for the family.

Many different forums, councils, and discussions are conducted with various parties. One of the challenges identified is the high number of admissions. Many parties wonder why staffing cannot simply be increased to meet the demand. Senior management of the hospital describe funding allocations and that there is simply no room in the budget to accommodate more staff, along with many other challenges in other areas of the hospital. They have to make do with what they already have. At the same time, staff cannot add more service users to their current caseloads without compromising the quality of person-centered care.

This is when engagement with the representative from their political system proves to be advantageous. Her involvement can support change – the argument is made for the funding of a psychiatric program that will accept those in the acute care hospital setting with MHCs. This will be a more effective service for some of the service users.

Those who work in community agencies have another suggestion to mitigate hospital admissions. Creating a greater awareness of community programs and promoting regular use of the services to mitigate the need for hospital admission may prove to be helpful. Community organizations generate awareness and promotion campaigns in postsecondary institutions, public areas, and meeting areas. Agencies also establish relationships among one another so that they each have a better sense of the services that are offered. These relationships will direct service users to more effective services as needed. Agencies promote the services to service users as well as to their families to encourage and strengthen the support network. Further collaboration will occur when service users take on the opportunity to design the posters and distribute them in the community. These sorts of opportunities to take action are mutually beneficial while each party works toward shared goals.

Upon the closing of the meetings, the participants thank Sally, John, and the team for holding these sessions. They appreciate the work that they are doing, along with the opportunity to collaborate with others from so many different stakeholder groups who are all an important part of the conversation. This format allows for everyone to learn about each other and gain insights to effectively meet service user needs. Service users and their families who are present show an appreciation for all of the considerations that are made in order to provide effective service delivery.

Sally and John's 5D Cycle of Appreciative Inquiry

Definition:
- The purpose of this project is to improve the quality of person-centered administrative and clinical practices, in alignment with the hospital's vision. Specifically, increases in admissions to the tertiary care unit and delays in intensive case management and safe housing, due to several wide-spread system factors, are leaving service users and their families to feel devalued and frustrated by the mental health system.
- This project will achieve streamlined, efficient access to mental health services at all levels of care, where service users receive the support that is effective for them in a timely manner and extends beyond their hospital experience into the community as well.

Discovery:
In terms of the existing strengths:
- We have dedicated, highly skilled staff who work tirelessly to provide the most effective care possible, within administrative and program constraints
- The overall collaboration and sense of unity between hospital staff to support one another to optimize the service user experience is excellent
- We currently have a number of connections with community organizations who provide services from which service users benefit and who are willing to collaborate further
- Dialogue and regular communications with other hospitals is ongoing to discuss the impacts and application of policy changes and regional challenges

- Family councils are currently held to seek service user and family input into planning of programs and services
- A variety of programs, therapeutic approaches, and modalities are used to treat service users depending on their unique needs

Dream:

In terms of what can be:

- Prevent service users from being service users in the first place
- When required, families are comfortable and confident navigating the mental health system, or even better, do not have to navigate the system at all, because it is transparent, clear, and straightforward to access
- Clarity and transparency in the mental health system requires strong communication between staff, management, senior leadership and the organization as a whole before this can be carried forward to clear communication with outside organizations, service users, and their families
- Service users are referred to the services that fit their needs the first time on intake so that they are not shuttled between different services that they then have to navigate
- Eliminate delays in referral services

Design:

In terms of creation:

- Clarify the vision of the person-centered approaches that the hospital strives for, and paint a clear picture of what this looks like along with how this is achieved; this will aid those in implementation roles to carry out their responsibilities in a person-centered manner
- Conduct increasingly thorough intakes of service user history upon initial admission to the hospital
- Increase the number of referral organizations that provide safe housing services or intensive case management; perhaps extend geographic boundaries
- Offer an early years program to new parents wishing to learn effective parenting strategies, coping skills for life stressors – connected to community agencies
- Awareness campaigns to eradicate the stigma of MHCs and the importance of seeking help early as needed
- Reach the general public through half-hour broadcasts to educate on staying well, signs of MHCs, what to do, and where to seek help
- Permeate the school system so that students learn strategies for mental wellness early
- Empower service users with the skills to stay well and have a fulfilled life through a focus on person-centered approaches through doing
- Demonstrate research abilities through evidence-based research and collaborations with the university

Destiny:

In terms of delivery and implementation:

- The hospital communications department, in consultation with senior leaders and person-centered care practitioners and administrative leaders, communicates examples, stories, and bulletins of person-centered practices that staff can apply in their own roles

- Feature staff examples to maintain strong, positive culture and provide recognition to staff
- Demonstrate research abilities through evidence-based research and collaborations with the university
- Use a more thorough assessment tool on intake to gather poignant information that will lead to increased accuracy for the most effective services that are needed
- Initiate social assistance, income support, and job-seeking processes earlier so as to address challenges in safe housing due to financial constraints
- Emphasize early goal setting with service users so that referrals for services following tertiary care are put into place to avoid delays in discharge

Value of Strength-Based Methodology in Person-Centered Health Care System Change

As an important starting point to wider-scale system change, strength-based approaches such as SOAR and appreciative inquiry serve to create momentum by helping to engage those with a vested interest in successfully building a plan together. The energy created in the course of the process enables people to focus on and maximize what the collective group does well, and creates enthusiasm and excitement, pushing individuals and organizations toward optimal performance. The SOAR process also creates and aligns purpose and values as they relate to service delivery.

With the assistance of their facilitator and the support of their senior leadership team, Sally and John plan their project methodology in the context of what they have learned. Recognizing the difficult conversations that this complex project will likely generate and with a determination to keep the service user and family experience central to the final destiny of the project, the project facilitator introduces a further concept: the influencer diagnostic framework.

Patterson, Grenny, and McMillan (2013) add to the concepts of strength-based strategies by building on those in a step-by-step approach to finding common ground in conversations that are emotionally charged, where opinions differ, and stakes are high (Vital-Smarts, 2017).

The *six source influencer model* is particularly valuable in creating a template to lead change and bring a group together who must be engaged if they are to develop a compelling vision. The six sources of influence concept provides different perspectives on how change may occur. These six sources can highlight the reason for a change, or a lack thereof, and can be used as a tool to address and bring about long-lasting change. Also included in Table 5.6 are suggestions to address each of the influences that are conducive to desired outcomes (Patterson, Grenny, & Maxfield, 2008).

Table 5.6   Program Project Planning Using the Six Source Influencer Model: Considerations Toward Leading Change

	Motivation	Ability
Individual	*Personal motivation*	*Personal ability*
	Make it motivating	Surpass the limits
	Creating new experiences and new motives	Setting incremental mini-goals that are clear and achievable
	Clear, frequent feedback about progress	
Social	*Social motivation*	*Social ability*
	Harness peer pressure	Find strength in numbers
	Find strength in opinion leaders, formal leaders, peers	Use the enabling power of an essential network of relationships
	Create positive deviance	
Structural (environment)	*Structural motivation*	*Structural ability*
	Reinforce personal and social motivators, particularly individual and community satisfaction	New practices emerge from the physical environment: people working in proximity to one another

Note. Adapted from Patterson, Grenny, & Maxfield, 2008.

John and Sally ensure that they take all of the necessary steps to ensure that the initiative is a success. They look at various levels of influence for both staff and service users to ensure that they are engaged in the process changes. They emphasize to staff that there will be opportunities for new learning, which includes learning what works and what does not work. These learning experiences will lead to improved process changes and to more effective care for service users.

Additionally, service users and their families are informed that there may be hiccups in service delivery for a time in order to provide an improved user experience in the near future.

Sally and John set small targets that are achievable, which includes the use of a more thorough intake assessment and the development of new-found relationships with other community organizations. This removes the notion of a daunting overhaul of processes and changes it into a series of more manageable changes. The team is also open to feedback after the "completion" of each goal, to ensure that it has the desired outcomes, with course corrections as needed. For instance, service providers in the emergency ward are involved during and after the development of the new intake assessment form. Time is given for service providers to use the new tool and provide further feedback to ensure its utility.

John and Sally also engage champions – at least one or more in every hospital wing, among both service providers and management. This allows those who have questions to ask a peer or manager with whom they are familiar. It also builds momentum among hospital staff so that most service providers see the changes as effective, and even necessary. Further, suggestion boxes are in place to collect anonymous feedback. Service users are also encouraged to voice any proposed solutions to challenges they experience to their service provider or using an anonymous suggestion box. John and Sally make themselves available to answer any questions in person, by telephone or via e-mail.

During the change process, new wellness carts circulate around the hospital every month for staff. These carts consist of wellness items such as aromatic soaps, lotions, beverage mugs, teas, and other items that staff can use in or outside of work. Free massages by a registered massage therapist are also offered to staff by appointment, on-site. This is also an opportunity to ensure that the physical environment is optimal for both hospital staff and service users. Ergonomic challenges – for example, with desks, seating, and computer monitors – are addressed, and televisions are added to a number of the waiting rooms for service users. These changes are well-received by those involved and support the transition amid the larger changes in the hospital.

Optimizing Engagement in the Project

Isaacs (1999) proposed a four-player model which broadly assigns group membership. The innovators are the early adopters of change, who are referred to as the *movers*. The second group are the *followers*. They are the opinion leaders (they readily follow the innovators in the change process and thus become the opinion leaders) who will be valuable in implementation. Then there are the *bystanders* who bring an invaluable reflective perspective and act as a sounding board that is very influential. Finally, there are the *opposers* who resist change and are challengers to the process. The last is the most difficult group to engage and can be the naysayers and saboteurs of the project. This model is visually represented in Figure 5.2.

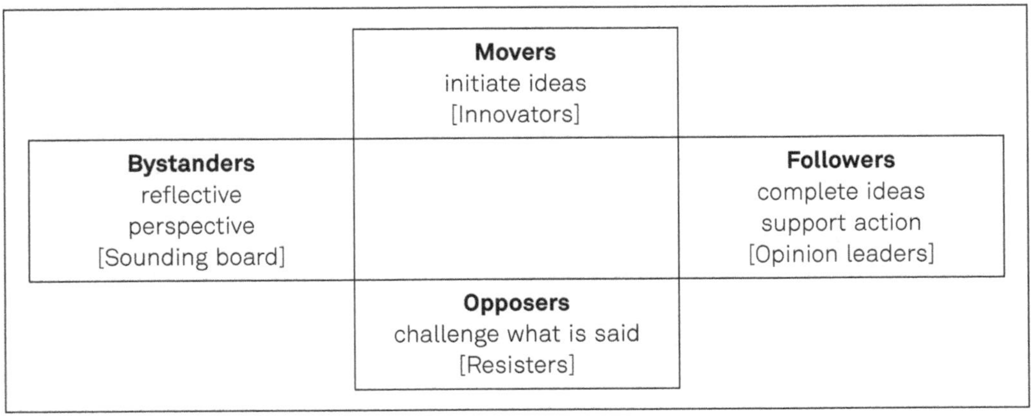

	Movers initiate ideas [Innovators]	
Bystanders reflective perspective [Sounding board]		**Followers** complete ideas support action [Opinion leaders]
	Opposers challenge what is said [Resisters]	

Figure 5.2 Four-player model. Adapted from Isaacs, 1999.

Knowing the many attempts that have been made to problem solve the challenges at hand, and being aware of the central importance of engagement if there is to be a successful outcome, Sally and John spend time with both their coach and with the project facilitator to understand the engagement process and potential pitfalls that may occur in spite of their careful planning and inclusiveness. They know that the core cultures of the project partners have become ones of mistrust rather than trust, and the engagement will not be possible without rebuilding that trust. This would necessitate real opportunities for measurable change and an assurance that feedback can be safely expressed and heard. Most importantly, they commit to ensuring that they are not planning for person-centered care without the active presence and meaningful input of those who will be care recipients. They are confident that the powerfully motivational aspects of SOAR and appreciative inquiry methodology that they will be using, and their emphasis on developing generative relationships, will mitigate any potential for some participants to be unengaged and for low stakeholder morale.

Nevertheless, they are informed about the engagement continuum. Approximately a third of the group will probably work with passion and feel a profound connection to their organization. They will drive innovation and move their organization forward. About half of the group will put in time but not passion into their work. About 15% will be unhappy regardless, and will undermine or even sabotage the accomplishments of those who are engaged.

With the coaching, training, and support of their coach and their project facilitator, John and Sally are acutely aware of their need to attend to the process of the project and the achievement of their strategic intentions to implement participatory person- and family-centered care. They are invested in the facilitated experience, will draw out diverse viewpoints, and will encourage positive conversations about past, current, and potential future successes. They are committed to the process and determined to be patient. They know that the time required can vary in length and that working through the 5Ds and the 5Is can take several sessions to allow an opportunity for participants to clearly articulate the ideas formulated through this process, and for dialogue to occur. A compressed process could be potentially costly for service users, with a high risk of failure.

Successful Outcomes

In the course of a six-month process, Sally and John enable key themes to emerge. Having a facilitator is important as it allows them to be actively involved in the process. Their careful selection of stakeholders, and the input of those with experience of a system that has not always worked well, enables solutions to emerge. The group becomes increasingly engaged in the construction of the strategic person-centered movement for the organization. They are also aware of how their success is enabled by the unwavering support of the leadership of all affiliated organizations, as well as their full partnership with their organizations' service user and family councils. They are supported in their intention to continue with follow-up and ongoing evaluation to ensure that there is continued implementation. This must include metrics and data, including that for satisfaction (service user, family, and service provider), along with a shift in culture that values compassionate care and incorporates the service user and family experience in its design.

The Challenge of Large-Scale System Change

Successful innovations and culture shifts very often remain local. Large-scale system changes generally require disruption and a degree of rigor that can be uncomfortable and feel unsafe. We value the ideal of a universal health care system (including our mental health care system), which is available to all, built around the needs and experiences as well as the active input of service users, who best understand the journey of MHCs, and in which services are readily accessible when needed.

The reality of rising health care costs outstripping the growth in our collective incomes threatens to create a gap that is challenging to bridge unless we understand the importance of an adaptive capacity in our health care and our mental health care system(s). Some answers may lie in the principles of *complexity science* and *disruptive innovations*.

Complexity science (Plsek & Wilson, 2001) describes the loosely organized academic field that has grown up around the study of complex biological and social systems. Complexity science is not a single theory – it encompasses more than one theoretical framework, and it is highly interdisciplinary, seeking to answer some fundamental questions about living, adaptable, changing systems.

How is this relevant to sustainable large-scale system change? The answer lies in characteristics of complex adaptive systems that include a high degree of adaptive capacity, giving them resilience in the face of perturbation. They are nonlinear so that small changes in inputs can cause large effects or very significant changes in outputs, allowing innovations to develop organically. Innovations emerge at the *porous* edge because of the loosely regulated nature of the system.

When translating the principles of complex adaptive systems to a sustainable and integrated mental health care system, the management approach is to emphasize transformational leadership which operates with influence rather than power, even at the highest levels. Command and control is replaced with positive and negative attractors rather than stakeholder compliance with organizational dictates.

Plsek and Wilson (2001) espouse the idea that the learning and adaptive characteristics of a complex adaptive system are to be leveraged to encourage agility rather than throttled by optimization focused on out-of-date requirements, directed by multiple and inflexible specifications: *min specs* as opposed to *max specs*.

Complementing the principle of complex adaptive systems and also very applicable to large-scale, sustainable, and cost-effective system change is the principle of disruptive innovations, first described by Christensen, Grossman, and Hwang (2008). Initially applied to disruptive technology in business models, there has been a more recent application to health system development, with proponents arguing that the answer for more affordable health care will come not from an injection of more funding, but rather from innovations that aim to make more and more areas of care cheaper, simpler, and more in the hands of service users (Christensen et al., 2008).

Applying these principles to an integrated and sustainable delivery system that enhances quality of care, the application of complexity science and disruptive innovation optimizes accessibility and utilizes the active input of service users and families. This transformation validates the importance of expanding the scope of practices of various clinicians, includes peer support to ensure access to a pyramid of services, and endorses interprofessional care. There needs to be ease of movement for service users within this pyramid, with the most cost-efficient, easily delivered services in generous supply at the base of the pyramid, and the scarcest, high-cost resources at the apex. Accountability to ensure fluidity and accessibility at all levels of the system and seamless continuity remains essential for successful wide-scale system change.

Chapter Conclusion

This chapter has taken an instructional approach to guide a process that can be utilized in implementing a strategic focus, in this case related to overrun hospital-based mental health services. It is essential that the person traversing a MHC and their family are placed at the center of their care, in partnership with their service providers and surrounded by an integrated system of care. Most important is the added emphasis on the elements of a collaborative culture. Collaboration is a complicated relationship process that takes ongoing maintenance to sustain itself. It is not enough that collaboration occurs episodically in facilitated gatherings; it needs to be part of the day-to-day experiences of people for it to be part of the culture. The need for trust and authenticity is essential in maintaining effective working relationships.

The processes that have been outlined in this chapter can be generalized to other multisystem health care challenges. Ultimately, it will be the development of health care networks and communities of person- and family-centered practices that will allow both large-scale service system change and a health care culture shift. Moreover, the focus on rehabilitative and recovery-oriented clinical services, as espoused in the other chapters of this handbook, is an imperative for an optimum mental health care system.

In the sage words of Rabbi Hillel (in the *Ethics of the Fathers*, 1:14, written between 40 BC and AD 10), an elder from many centuries ago whose words have great present relevance: "If I am not for myself, who will be for me?" In contemporary terms this sage wisdom (also the following quotes) can translate to:
- Maintain healthy habits – look after myself, practice self-compassion
- Stay connected with my core values and beliefs
- Identify stressors within my control – learn to set limits and say no
- Savor the times when I make a difference, embrace positive feedback
  "But if I am only for myself, what am I?"

- Help create a sense of community and connectedness at work
- Share our stories, support and debrief with one another
- Nurture relationships with family and friends
"If not now, when?"

References

Anthony, W. A., & Huckshorn, K. A. (2008). *Principled leadership in mental health systems and programs.* Boston, MA: Boston University Press.

Buckingham, M., & Clifton, D. O. (2001). *Now, discover your strengths.* New York, NY: The Free Press.

Christensen, C. M., Grossman, J. H., & Hwang, J. (2008). *The innovator's prescription: A disruptive solution for health care.* New York, NY: McGraw-Hill.

Cooperrider, D., & Whitney, D. D. (2005). *Appreciative inquiry: A positive revolution in change.* San Francisco, CA: Berrett-Koehler.

Dickens, P., Fisman, S., & Grossman, K. (2016). Strategic leadership development for physicians. *Canadian Journal of Physician Leadership, 2*(3), 80–86.

Fariselli, L., Freedman, J., Ghini, M., & Valentini, F. (2008). *Stress, emotional intelligence, & performance in healthcare* [White paper]. Retrieved from Six Seconds – The Emotional Intelligence Network website http://prodimages.6seconds.org/media/WP_Stress_EQ.pdf

Francis, H., & Cowan, J. (2008). Fostering an action-reflection dynamic amongst student practitioners. *Journal of European Industrial Training, 32*(5), 336–346. https://doi.org/10.1108/03090590810877067

Frank, J. R., Snell, L., & Sherbino, J. (Eds.). (2015). *CanMEDS 2015 Physician Competency Framework.* Ottawa, ON: Royal College of Physicians and Surgeons of Canada.

Isaacs, W. N. (1999). Dialogic leadership. *Systems Thinker, 10*(1), 1–5.

Lane, D., & Maxfield, R. (1996). Strategy under complexity: Fostering generative relationships. *Long Range Planning, 29*(2), 215–231. https://doi.org/10.1016/0024-6301(96)00011-8

Law, J. (2009). *A dictionary of business and management* (5th ed.). Oxford, UK: Oxford University Press.

Mohr, B. J. (2001). Appreciative inquiry: Igniting transformative action. *Systems Thinker, 12,* 1–5.

Patterson, K., Grenny, J., & Maxfield, D. (2008). *Influencer: The power to change anything.* New York, NY: McGraw-Hill.

Patterson, K., Grenny, J., & McMillan, R. (2013). *Crucial conversations: Tools for talking when stakes are high* (2nd ed.). New York, NY: McGraw-Hill.

Plsek, P. E., & Wilson, T. (2001). Complexity, leadership, and management in healthcare organisations. *British Medical Journal, 323*(7315), 746–749.

Rath, T., & Conchie, B. (2008). *Strengths based leadership: Great leaders, teams, and why people follow.* New York, NY: Gallup Press.

Roberts, L. M., Spreitzer, G., Dutton, J., Quinn, R., Heaphy, E., & Barker, B. (2005). How to play to your strengths. *Harvard Business Review, 83*(1), 74–80.

Salovey, P., & Mayer, J. D. (1990). Emotional intelligence. *Imagination, Cognition and Personality, 9*(3), 185–211. https://doi.org/10.2190/DUGG-P24E-52WK-6CDG

Schön, D. A. (1987). *Educating the reflective practitioner: Toward a new design for teaching and learning in the professions.* San Francisco, CA: Jossey-Bass.

Schutz, S. (2007). Reflection and reflective practice. *Community Practitioner, 80*(9), 26–29.

Sprangel, J., Stavros, J., & Cole, M. (2011). Creating sustainable relationships using the strengths, opportunities, aspirations and results framework, trust, and environmentalism: A research-based case study. *International Journal of Training and Development, 15*(1), 39–57. https://doi.org/10.1111/j.1468-2419.2010.00367.x

Stavros, J. M., Cooperrider, D., & Kelley, D. L. (2003, November). Strategic inquiry appreciative intent: Inspiration to SOAR, a new framework for strategic planning. *AI Practitioner,* 10–17.

Stavros, J. M., & Hinrichs, G. (2011). *The thin book of ® SOAR: Building strengths-based strategy.* Bend, OR: Thin Book.

Team FME. (2013). *SWOT analysis: Strategy skills.* Retrieved from http://www.free-management-ebooks.com

Tondora, J. M., Miller, R., Slade, M., & Davidson, L. (2014). *Partnering for recovery in mental health: A practical guide to person-centered planning.* Oxford, UK: Wiley-Blackwell.

VitalSmarts. (2017). *More than 2 million people trained* [Home page]. Retrieved from http://www.vitalsmarts.com/

Zimmerman, B., & Hayday, B. (1999). A board's journey into complexity science: Lessons from (and for) staff and board members. *Group Decision and Negotiation, 8*(4), 281–303. https://doi.org/10.1023/A:1008709903070

6 Conclusion

This handbook has explored person-centered approaches for those who experience mental health challenges (MHCs) in the realms of clinical care, research, education, and health care leadership. MHCs may include disorders which affect mental, behavioral, and emotional states, as well as one's ability to fully participate in day-to-day activities (Substance Abuse and Mental Health Services Administration, 2015). The person-centered approach is an effective means through which services and care may be provided. It is a multidimensional construct and is person-focused, person-driven, person-sensitive, and person-contextualized (Rudnick & Roe, 2011).

For each of these realms, there are a few key points that may be applied:

Clinical Care

- Service provider attitudes that are in line with person-centered approaches include compassion, genuineness, the ability to empower the service user, and unconditional positive regard
- Person-centered care in clinical care may involve, but is not limited to:
  - rapport building with the service user
  - assessment of the service user's MHCs, barriers, and goals
  - educating the service user, along with their informal supports as applicable
  - considering the service user's values, preferences, and experiences
  - supporting service users in their goals toward recovery
  - collaborating to select and implement care to meet service users' needs

Research

- Research is an important foundation for providing effective person-centered care that can elucidate the strategies that are more likely to be helpful and those less likely to be helpful, and for whom
- Research can aid in understanding the processes and experiences related to MHCs and effective care delivery

- Contrary to traditional research involving "expert opinion," participatory approaches to research emphasize collaboration and equal distribution of power between researchers and service users, which is known as participatory action research
- Such a person-centered approach recognizes that each research partner brings their own expertise and experience to a collaborative research process

Education

- Education is integral to every aspect of mental health care provision and plays a role for many parties including service users and their family members, peer supports, front-line staff, physicians, students, and administrators
- Shared decision making is key for person-centered care in education, whereby service users and service providers work in collaboration to access information and/or resources that allow for service users to select and/or be actively involved in decisions impacting their care
- Decision aids are formal tools that can assist in making informed choices as well as to understand which way one is leaning (either toward or away from) with regard to any decision
- Self-directed learning, based on adult education theories, includes various approaches which are a medium through which health care professionals may gain person-centered care knowledge and skills

Health Care Leadership

- Challenges to health care delivery highlight the need for reform, for which person-centered approaches, if implemented, may be useful
- Collaboration among physicians, other health care providers, and their administrative partners, as well as service users and their informal caregivers, are all needed toward a vision of high-quality person-centered mental health care
- Collaboration is a process that takes ongoing maintenance to sustain itself, requiring that it be part of the day-to-day experiences of a team for it to be part of the culture
- Such collaboration can be seen as a strength-based system, where a strong and effective interprofessional health care team places service users and their caregivers at the center of their care, where they are also involved in services and systems development as well as governance and transformation

With these ideas in mind, implementation of person-centered care across mental health services and other health care settings can be beneficial in a number of ways. Adopting person-centered approaches may reduce the "revolving door syndrome," where service users return to access acute care. Service users may be more satisfied with service providers who use person-centered approaches for care planning. Future work will focus on continuing to incorporate the service user perspective on care to elucidate this perspective to inform clinical practice. In terms of research, a participatory action approach, though established and in line with person-centered approaches, may not have been implemented to its full potential to date. When it is used, it can provide evidence to support unmet needs of service users along with the effectiveness of different approaches to care and services. The variability in person-centered approaches within the health care profession curriculum lends itself to opportunities whereby educators have the opportunity to provide students with person-centered approaches, attitudes, skills and practices, which they may subsequently take into clinical, research, and administrative realms. This may involve the shared decision-making approach, which may minimize service users feeling as though they do not have a say in their own care.

Finally, health care leadership ought to work toward the development and continuous improvement of the health care system, which may be accomplished through strengthening health care networks and communities of person- and family-centered practices that will allow both large-scale service system change and shifts in health care culture.

References

Rudnick, A. & Roe, D. (Eds.) (2011). *Serious mental illness: Person-centered approaches*. London, UK: Radcliffe.

Substance Abuse and Mental Health Services Administration. (2015). *National Survey on Drug Use and Health*. Retrieved from https://www.nimh.nih.gov/health/statistics/prevalence/serious-mental-illness-smi-among-us-adults.shtml

Appendix: Tools and Resources

To complement the handouts presented in the book printable pdf files of the appendices are available for download at: https://us.hogrefe.com/downloads/hpcmhc

Your login password is:

568Ncksa33

Appendix 1: Catching Our Own Assumptions

Appendix 2: Points for Discussion to Build a Therapeutic Clinical Relationship

Appendix 3: Resource Sheet for Wellness Self-Management

Appendix 4: Soliciting Service User Input

Appendix 5: Treatment Options Template

Appendix 6: Environmental Scan of the Influence of Culture

Appendix 7: Step-by-Step Goal Setting

Appendix 8: Scheduling: Using a Structure to Manage One's Daily Activities

Appendix 9: Decisional Balance

Appendix 10: Journaling What Is Important to You

Appendix 11: Social Network Roles

Appendix 12: Taking a Closer Look at Behaviors

Appendix 13: Multifactor Assessment of a Service User's Current Situation

Appendix 14: Understanding Another Person's Perspective

Appendix 15: Working Toward Your Goals

Catching Our Own Assumptions

Ask yourself – what preconceived ideas do I have about this person? This can be based on or in relation to:	
Name	
Age	
History	
Race/ethnicity	
Mental health challenge and diagnosis	
Family	
Cognitive ability	
Gender	
Religion	
Culture	
Lifestyle	
Vocation	
My previous relationships (personal or professional)	
Other	

From: Akhtar et al.: *Handbook of Person-Centered Mental Health Care* © 2021 Hogrefe Publishing

Points for Discussion to Build a Therapeutic Clinical Relationship

The following are points for discussion that the service provider can ask to further the initial conversation and build trust:	
What brings you to seek support?	
What would you like to get out of counseling or therapy?	
What do you want me, as your service provider, to know about you?	
What would you like me to do while working with you?	
What would you like me to avoid doing while working with you?	

From: Akhtar et al.: *Handbook of Person-Centered Mental Health Care* © 2021 Hogrefe Publishing

Resource Sheet for Wellness Self-Management

Routines or things that I can do to take care of myself	
Symptoms or signs telling me that challenges with mental health are returning	
Community resources that I can access if I am in need	

From: Akhtar et al.: *Handbook of Person-Centered Mental Health Care* © 2021 Hogrefe Publishing

Soliciting Service User Input

When it comes to discussing and working through my care plan:	
I am concerned about	
I want/need/value	
I would appreciate it if the service provider would	
I would appreciate it if the service provider would not	

Treatment Options Template

Treatment option	
Risks	
Benefits	
Questions or concerns	
Why this option may work for me	
Why this option may not work for me	

Environmental Scan of the Influence of Culture

Cultural context	Native culture:
	Views of challenges with mental health in culture:
	Service user views of mental health challenges:
Historical context	Major occurrences or events in the culture:
	War (past or present):
Worldview	Sociocentric (collectivist) or egocentric (individualist):
	Hierarchical (rankings) or egalitarian (equality):

Values and traditions	Religion/spirituality: Family: Gender roles:
Acculturation and identity	Length of time in current location: Similarities vs. differences of native and mainstream cultures: Level of acculturation:
Verbal and nonverbal communication	Service user statements on the impact of culture on life:

Note. Adapted from Desjardins, Gritke, & Hill, 2011.

Step-by-Step Goal Setting

Main goal	
First action-based objective	
Steps to be taken	• • •
Second action-based objective	
Steps to be taken	• • •

Note. Adapted from Townsend & Polatajko, 2007.

From: Akhtar et al.: *Handbook of Person-Centered Mental Health Care* © 2021 Hogrefe Publishing

Scheduling: Using a Structure to Manage One's Daily Activities

	Sunday	Monday	Tuesday	Wednesday	Thursday	Friday	Saturday
7 a.m.							
8 a.m.							
9 a.m.							
10 a.m.							
11 a.m.							
12 noon							
1 p.m.							
2 p.m.							
3 p.m.							
4 p.m.							
5 p.m.							
6 p.m.							
7 p.m.							
8 p.m.							
9 p.m.							
10 p.m.							
11 p.m.							
12 mid-night							

From: Akhtar et al.: *Handbook of Person-Centered Mental Health Care* © 2021 Hogrefe Publishing

Decisional Balance

Pros of not engaging in the behavior/ activity:	Cons of not engaging in the behavior/ activity:
•	•
•	•
•	•
Pros of engaging in the behavior/activity:	Cons of engaging in the behavior/activity:
•	•
•	•
•	•

From: Akhtar et al.: *Handbook of Person-Centered Mental Health Care* © 2021 Hogrefe Publishing

Journaling What Is Important to You

Rate, out of 10, how I am feeling and why.	
What do I want?	
Who do I want to be?	
Whom do I look up to? Why?	
What do I value?	
What do I believe?	

From: Akhtar et al.: *Handbook of Person-Centered Mental Health Care* © 2021 Hogrefe Publishing

Social Network Roles

What my family provides or does for me that is unique	
What my friends provide or do for me that is unique	
What only I can provide or do for myself	

From: Akhtar et al.: *Handbook of Person-Centered Mental Health Care* © 2021 Hogrefe Publishing

Taking a Closer Look at Behaviors

Observation of service user behaviors may help to identify aspects of cognition in which the service user may be having challenges. Identifying such aspects may guide care planning.

If there are signs of	They may be experiencing challenges with
Difficulty perceiving or integrating experiences	Attention
	Sensations
	Problem-solving abilities
	Generalizing abilities
Disorganized behavior and perseverating on ideas	Flexibility of thought
	Sequencing
	Logic
Executive dysfunction or metacognition (inability to execute goal-directed, purposeful behavior by regulating behavior) resulting in maladaptive behaviors – for example, aggression, perseveration, anxiety, and self-injury	Impulse control
	Managing frustration
	Judgment
	Memory
	Emotional dysregulation

From: Akhtar et al.: *Handbook of Person-Centered Mental Health Care* © 2021 Hogrefe Publishing

Multifactor Assessment of a Service User's Current Situation

A multifactor assessment addresses the following, accounting for both strengths and challenges (fill out the entries for the person being considered):	
Person	• Physical or biomedical: • Cognitive: • Psychiatric: • Developmental: • Affective:
Environmental	• Social: • Institutional: • Cultural: • Physical:
Occupational	• Self-care: • Productivity: • Leisure:
Motivation	• •
Risks	• •

Note. Adapted from Law et al., 1996.

From: Akhtar et al.: *Handbook of Person-Centered Mental Health Care* © 2021 Hogrefe Publishing

Understanding Another Person's Perspective

The questions below can help to better understand an event, along with the person(s) involved.	
What was said?	
Who said it?	
Where was it said?	
When was it said?	
Why was it said?	
What might the other person be thinking?	
What might the other person be feeling?	
What is important to the other person?	
How might the other person behave?	

Working Toward Your Goals

What have you learned and discovered from your current situation?	
Where would you like to see yourself in the future (related to goals)?	
What strategies can help to keep you on track toward your goals?	

From: Akhtar et al.: *Handbook of Person-Centered Mental Health Care* © 2021 Hogrefe Publishing

Life Review

Service users in older adulthood may be asked these and other questions to glean their life experiences and promote reflection. Keep the individual situation of the service user in mind to ensure this exercise is beneficial, rather than unproductive or even triggering. The following are a sample of questions that could be asked:

Tell me about a pleasant memory that you hold close to you.	
Describe how you met your life partner or close friend.	
What is your most treasured childhood memory?	
If you could pass along advice to your children, grandchildren, and/or younger self, what would it be?	

From: Akhtar et al.: *Handbook of Person-Centered Mental Health Care* © 2021 Hogrefe Publishing

Catching Our Own Assumptions as Researchers

Ask yourself, what are my assumptions? Is the topic of discussion among people who experience mental health challenges related to:	
Individual issues, such as poor budgeting, low financial literacy, interrupted education, absence of job skills, or limited problem-solving skills?	
Challenges related to mental health, such as age of onset, specific symptoms, or response to treatment and/or medication?	
Community-level factors, such as employment rates, housing vacancy rates, and available supports?	
Policy-level issues, such as levels of social income supports, availability of social housing, and supports for transitioning to employment?	
How would solutions look different based on assumptions?	
How would you determine which assumptions have evidence?	

From: Akhtar et al.: *Handbook of Person-Centered Mental Health Care* © 2021 Hogrefe Publishing

Points for Research Team Discussion

These are points to consider when building trust among researchers, service users, and service providers.

- What brings you to this research?
- What do you want to get out of this research?
- What do you want us to know about you?
- Is there anything that you would like, to make your participation more meaningful?
- Is there anything that you would like the research team to avoid doing while working together?

Research Team: Who Is Missing?

- What perspectives do we have represented already on the team?
- What spheres of life are touched upon by the research topic?
- Who knows about the topic that is not here?
- Who cares about the topic?
- Who needs to care about the topic?
- Who is missing?

How Will We Conduct This Research?

- What do we want to accomplish by the end of the research?
- What kind of evidence is needed?
- Who do we want to know about the research? What would they find to be important?
- How will we find the research participants?
- How will we maintain the cohort of research participants?
- How will we acknowledge the participation of research participants?
- Who will collect the data? Who will analyze the data?
- Who will review the literature?
- Who will identify study implications?
- What other analyses could be done from this data?
- How will we share the results?

Shared Decision Making: Eliciting Shared Understanding Between Service Users and Service Providers

When engaging in shared decision making, the process may occur in a series of steps. The following questions are examples of what may be asked when working with a service user:	
1. What are the choices to be made?	• •
2. Do you, the service provider, feel you have the ability to understand the information that needs to be sought?	*Yes or No* If you answer *no*, what are the reasons (e.g. pharmacology out of scope of your practice)? And what resources could assist in helping you to understand?
3. Does the service user have the ability to understand the information that needs to be sought?	*Yes or No*

If *yes* is the answer to all of the above questions, then you need to elicit the service user's values and preferences.

From: Akhtar et al.: *Handbook of Person-Centered Mental Health Care* © 2021 Hogrefe Publishing

Questions to Identify Service User Values and Preferences

- What do you enjoy doing?

- What activities have you done in the past?

- What goals would you like to achieve?

- What prevents you from achieving these goals?

- What has frustrated you when working toward your goals in the past?

With the information that has been gathered, what is the evidence for and against the decision and how does that influence the outcome of the decision to be made?

From: Akhtar et al.: *Handbook of Person-Centered Mental Health Care* © 2021 Hogrefe Publishing

Therapeutic Alliance Check-In

These are some examples of questions that can be helpful for service provider reflection when working with service users:

- Is the therapeutic alliance progressing? If not, why not?

- How much effort are you contributing to the clinical relationship? The service user?

Another, often helpful, and very important approach is to check in with the service user. Some questions you may ask in that case are:

- What is positive about our time together?

- What would you change about our interactions?

- Is there anything you would like me to do to ensure that you are getting the most out of our time together?

From: Akhtar et al.: *Handbook of Person-Centered Mental Health Care* © 2021 Hogrefe Publishing

Shared Decision Making: Enhancing Service User Communication

A few suggested questions for the service user to ask themselves and/or the service provider are:

- What are the choices I have to consider? Are there other options that have not been considered?
- What is my role in the decision-making process?
- What if we disagree with each other?
- How do I find information about the decisions I need to make?
- Are there other things I would like my service provider to know? (If yes, then it may be helpful to make a list so that you can be sure to remember these points when you next speak to the service provider.)

From: Akhtar et al.: *Handbook of Person-Centered Mental Health Care* © 2021 Hogrefe Publishing

Shared Decision Making: The Meaning of Recovery

To focus on recovery, it is important to understand the service user's goals and what they mean by recovery. Some questions for the service provider to ask the service user that can help facilitate this are:

What does the word recovery mean to you?	
When you think of your life six months into the future, what do you envision? One year from now? Two years from now?	

From: Akhtar et al.: *Handbook of Person-Centered Mental Health Care* © 2021 Hogrefe Publishing

Shared Decision Making: (Adapted) Wellness Recovery Action Plan

Some questions to consider when developing a wellness recovery action plan (WRAP) may include:

- What are you like when you are well?
- What strategies help you stay well?
- What are signs of the mental health challenge you face?
- What can we do about those signs indicating a crisis or challenge?
- How can we use a crisis plan?
- How do I engage in a WRAP?

Family Education: Identifying Family Needs

Some potential questions that family may ask are:

- What is the specific mental health challenge?
- How do we explain the specific mental health challenge to other people?
- How will we know if our loved one needs to be in the hospital?
- Are there side effects to the medication they will be taking?
- Does our loved one need to do anything, such as blood work, on a regular basis?
- How do we support our loved one in moving forward with life goals?

From: Akhtar et al.: *Handbook of Person-Centered Mental Health Care* © 2021 Hogrefe Publishing

Identifying Service Provider Learning Goals

It may be helpful to think of learning goals in terms of topic areas such as biological factors, psychological factors, and social or environmental factors. Learning goals may include the following:

- How is the condition diagnosed? What tools are utilized?
- What are the Diagnostic and Statistical Manual of Mental Disorders, 5th edition (DSM-5) criteria for the condition?
- What is the neurophysiology of the condition?
- What stressors may be affecting the condition?
- What is the prevalence of the condition?
- Is there a process to diagnose the condition?
- What are the treatments for the condition? Are there medications as well as other treatments such as body-based approaches, psychotherapy, or exercise?

Also, think more broadly about what factors are motivating you to learn more. Some questions to help understand these motivations include:

- What are some goals or factors driving me toward further education?
- Are there clinical implications for this learning?
- How will my learning objectives and related questions further my continuing education?
- Are there areas I tend to struggle with when learning new things? What potential struggles may this cause for me? How can I overcome these?

There are also important process steps to achieving educational goals that need to be considered. A few suggestions for consideration include:

- How will I know that I have obtained the above educational goals?
- Where will I engage in this learning?
- Are there other resources that could assist me with engaging in this process?
- Are there other people who may have similar educational goals? Would it be helpful to engage with them?
- Should I join a community of practice or group to assist in achieving my educational goals?

From: Akhtar et al.: *Handbook of Person-Centered Mental Health Care* © 2021 Hogrefe Publishing

Planning Public Education Events

There are opportunities to potentially increase the health literacy of a community regarding issues of importance. Assuming we are engaging the community from the public health perspective, there are some aspects of planning such an event that need to be reviewed. These include considering what such education would encompass from conception to implementation. Guiding questions can include:

What elements would need to be considered when planning a public educational event?	
What is the primary or core purpose for the event?	
How do you advertise the event?	
Who would be involved in planning the event?	
What key piece(s) of information do you want to convey during your educational event?	
What potential challenges do you need to consider when planning the event for the above community?	

From: Akhtar et al.: *Handbook of Person-Centered Mental Health Care* © 2021 Hogrefe Publishing

Public Education: Applying Prevention Principles

When thinking about planning a preventative health campaign for educational purposes, you may want to consider the following:	
What is the area that requires further education?	
What educational campaigns have already been tried in this area?	
When you think about campaigns that have already been tried, what was effective or ineffective about them? (It may be helpful to draw a table to compare and contrast campaigns and outcomes.)	
What can be improved in future educational campaigns?	
Who needs to be involved to make these improvements – i.e., who is the target audience, and how can they become involved, or who is impacted by the problem?	
How can we increase participation and action?	
What, if any, barriers are there to implementation? How can these be overcome?	

From: Akhtar et al.: *Handbook of Person-Centered Mental Health Care* © 2021 Hogrefe Publishing

Framework for a Reflective Learning Process

1. Describe the experience.
2. Reflection (sometimes called reflection-in-action): How did you behave? What thoughts did you have? How did it make you feel? Were there other factors that influenced the situation? What have you learned from the experience?
3. Theorizing (sometimes called reflection-on-action): How did the experience match (or not) your preconceived ideas – i.e., was the outcome expected or unexpected? What behaviors do you think may have changed the outcome? Is there anything you could say or do now to change the outcome? What action(s) can you take to change similar reactions in the future?

From: Akhtar et al.: *Handbook of Person-Centered Mental Health Care* © 2021 Hogrefe Publishing

Strengths, Weaknesses, Opportunities, and Threats (SWOT) Analysis

Strengths	Weaknesses
•	•
•	•
•	•
•	•
•	•
Opportunities	**Threats**
•	•
•	•
•	•
•	•
•	•

PESTLE Analysis Characterizing the External Environment

Factor	Example	
Political	Government policy affects wait time strategies, drives health care developments such as early psychosis programs	
Economic	Financial shifts in currency, interest rates affects hospital funding, social assistance	
Social	An aging population demands increased mental and physical health end of life funding, generational differences determine that millennials focus on work/life balance	
Technological	New technologies and new products such as electronic patient records and telehealth foster innovation	
Legal	Legislation influences age discrimination, elimination of mandatory retirement age, minimum wage, disability	
Environmental	Weather and climate change affect farming and food production, carbon footprint, changes in disease patterns	
Additional elements, captured by L(o)NG PESTLE are • Local factors • National factors • Global factors		

Note. PESTLE = political, economic, social, technological, legal, and environmental. Based on *A Dictionary of Business and Management* (5th ed.), by J. Law, 2009, Oxford, UK: Oxford University Press. Copyright 2009 by Oxford University Press.

Subject Index